Leibniz

'Jolley has done a fabulous job, and the result is perfectly suited for its intended purpose and audience. The work is very clearly written; the organization is excellent; and the coverage comprehensive. The needs of students and beginners are indeed well-served here, but the result is not bland.'

Vere Chappell, University of Massachusetts, USA

'The best introduction available.'

Glenn Hartz, Ohio State University, USA

'Reading this gave me great pleasure . . . it is interesting, illuminating, systematic, thorough and above all pleasantly, smoothly and accessibly written. A splendid book.'

Roger Woolhouse, University of York, UK

'An excellent work. It will clearly establish itself as the best introduction to the thought of Leibniz, and I would recommend it to students wrestling with this difficult philosopher for the first time.'

Brandon C. Look, University of Kentucky, USA

Routledge Philosophers

Edited by Brian Leiter
University of Texas, Austin

Routledge Philosophers is a major series of introductions to the great Western philosophers. Each book places a major philosopher or thinker in historical context, explains and assesses their key arguments, and considers their legacy. Additional features include a chronology of major dates and events, chapter summaries, annotated suggestions for further reading and a glossary of technical terms.

An ideal starting point for those new to philosophy, they are also essential reading for those interested in the subject at any level.

Hobbes	A. P. Martinich
Locke	E. J. Lowe
Hegel	Frederick Beiser
Rousseau	Nicholas Dent
Schopenhauer	Julian Young
Freud	Jonathan Lear

Forthcoming:

Spinoza	Michael Della Rocca
Hume	Don Garrett
Kant	Paul Guyer
Fichte and Schelling	Sebastian Gardner
Husserl	David Woodruff Smith
Rawls	Samuel Freeman

Nicholas Jolley

Leibniz

Routledge
Taylor & Francis Group

LONDON AND NEW YORK

First published 2005
by Routledge
2 Park Square, Milton Park, Abingdon, Oxon OX14 4RN

Simultaneously published in the USA and Canada
by Routledge
270 Madison Ave, New York, NY 10016

Routledge is an imprint of the Taylor & Francis Group

Typeset in Joanna MT and Din by
RefineCatch Ltd, Bungay, Suffolk
Printed and bound in Great Britain by
TJ International Ltd, Padstow, Cornwall

British Library Cataloguing in Publication Data
A catalogue record for this book is available from the British Library

Library of Congress Cataloging in Publication Data
  Leibniz / Nicholas Jolley.
    p. cm.—(Routledge philosophers)
  Includes bibliographical references and index.
    1. Leibniz, Gottfried Wilhelm, Freiherr von, 1646–1716.   I. Title.
II. Series.
B2598.J57 2005
193—dc22   2004022912

ISBN 0-415-28337-X (hbk)
ISBN 0-415-28338-8 (pbk)

Acknowledgements

I am very grateful to Brian Leiter, the series editor, for inviting me to write this book, and to Tony Bruce, the Philosophy editor for Routledge, for his constant advice and encouragement. During the course of writing the book I have had a number of stimulating conversations about Leibniz with Jeffrey McDonough, Alan Nelson, Lawrence Nolan, John Whipple and June Yang; I have also benefited from correspondence with Paul Hoffman, Paul Lodge, and Donald Rutherford. I am deeply indebted to three referees for Routledge for their careful and constructive comments on the penultimate draft. Finally, I should like to thank Kristina Wischenkämper for her skilful copy-editing.

Quotes from Richard Francks and R. S. Woolhouse (eds), *G. W. Leibniz: Philosophical Texts*, 1998, are used by permission of Oxford University Press.

Quotes from Nicholas Jolley, 'Leibniz: Truth, Knowledge and Metaphysics', in Parkinson (ed.), *The Renaissance and Seventeenth Century Rationalism* (2003) are used by permission of Taylor & Francis.

Nicholas Jolley

A German Academy of Sciences (ed.), *G.W. Leibniz: Sämtliche Schriften und Briefe* (Darmstadt and Berlin: Berlin Academy, 1923–). References are to series and volume.

AG R. Ariew and D. Garber (eds and trans.), *G.W. Leibniz: Philosophical Essays* (Indianapolis and Cambridge, Mass.: Hackett, 1989)

AT C. Adam and P. Tannery (eds), *Oeuvres de Descartes*, 12 vols (Paris, 1897–1913; repr. Paris: Vrin/CNRS, 1964–76)

CSM J. Cottingham, R. Stoothoff and D. Murdoch (trans.), *The Philosophical Writings of Descartes*, 3 vols (Cambridge: Cambridge University Press, 1985). Volume III (*The Correspondence*) incorporates a revised version of Anthony Kenny's translation of Descartes's letters and is abbreviated as 'CSMK'

D L. Dutens (ed.), *G.G. Leibnitii Opera Omnia* (Geneva, 1768)

DM *Discourse on Metaphysics*

G C.I. Gerhardt (ed.), *Die Philosophischen Schriften von G.W. Leibniz*, 7 vols (Berlin: Weidmann, 1875–90)

Gr G. Grua (ed.), *G.W. Leibniz: Textes Inédits*, 2 vols (Paris: Presses Universitaires de France, 1948)

H E.M. Huggard (trans.), *G.W. Leibniz: Theodicy* (London: Routledge and Kegan Paul, 1952)

JS N. Jolley (ed.) and D. Scott (trans.), *Nicolas Malebranche: Dialogues on Metaphysics and on Religion* (Cambridge: Cambridge University Press, 1997)

L L.E. Loemker (trans. and ed.), *G.W. Leibniz: Philosophical Papers and Letters* (2nd edn: Reidel, Dordrecht, 1969)

LO T. Lennon and P.J. Olscamp, *Nicolas Malebranche: The Search After Truth* (2nd edn, Cambridge: Cambridge University Press, 1997)

M G. Mollat (ed.), *Rechtsphilosophisches aus Leibnizens ungedrückten Schriften* (Leipzig: Haessel, 1885)

NE *New Essays on Human Understanding*

P G.H.R. Parkinson (ed.), *G.W. Leibniz: Philosophical Writings* (London: Dent, 1973)

R P. Riley (ed.), *Leibniz: Political Writings* (2nd edn, Cambridge: Cambridge University Press, 1988)

RB P. Remnant and J. Bennett (trans. and eds), *G.W. Leibniz: New Essays on Human Understanding* (2nd edn, Cambridge: Cambridge University Press, 1996)

WF R. Woolhouse and R. Francks (trans. and eds), *G.W. Leibniz: Philosophical Texts* (Oxford: Oxford University Press, 1998)

1646	born in Leipzig on 1 July
1648	Peace of Westphalia concludes Thirty Years War
1653	enters the Nicolaischule in Leipzig
1661	enters the University of Leipzig
1662	awarded the degree of Bachelor of Philosophy
1663	matriculates at the University of Jena
1664	awarded degree of Master of Philosophy
1666	matriculates in the Faculty of Law at the University of Altdorf near Nuremberg
1667	awarded the degree of Doctor of Law at the University of Altdorf; declines the offer of a professorship
1668	appointed as assistant to the legal adviser to the Elector of Mainz through the patronage of Baron Johann Christian von Boineburg
1672	arrives in Paris on a diplomatic mission
1673	visits London and attends sessions of the Royal Society; elected as an external member of the Society
1675	discovers the differential calculus
1676	visits London again and is shown some of Newton's mathematical papers; visits The Hague where he discusses philosophy with Spinoza; appointed to the post of Court Councillor to the Duke of Hanover
1679	death of Leibniz's employer, Duke Johann Friedrich of Brunswick

1680	Ernst August succeeds his brother Johann Friedrich as Duke of Brunswick (later Elector of Hanover)
1684	publishes his discovery of the differential calculus
1686	composes the *Discourse on Metaphysics*
1687	leaves Hanover for a tour of southern Germany, Austria and Italy in search of archival material for his projected history of the House of Brunswick
1690	returns to Hanover
1695	publishes 'New System of the Nature and Communication of Substances'
1698	death of Elector Ernst August of Hanover; succeeded by his son, Georg Ludwig
1700	elected external member of the French Academy of Sciences; appointed first President of the newly founded Berlin Academy of Sciences
1703–5	composes *New Essays on Human Understanding*
1705	death of Queen Sophie Charlotte of Prussia
1710	publishes *Essays in Theodicy*
1711	accused of plagiarism by John Keill in the *Philosophical Transactions*, the journal of the Royal Society; writes to Hans Sloane, the secretary of the Society, demanding justice
1712	begins two-year stay in Vienna; appointed Imperial Court Councillor
1714	composes 'Principles of Nature and Grace' and *Monadology*; on death of Queen Anne, Elector Georg Ludwig of Hanover succeeds to British throne as George I
1715	begins correspondence with Samuel Clarke, disciple of Newton
1716	dies in Hanover on 14 November

Gottfried Wilhelm Leibniz is undoubtedly one of the major philosophers of the Western tradition, but he is also an unusually difficult philosopher. His two most famous doctrines are apt to appear bizarre and implausible: many readers find it hard to overcome their initial resistance to the theory of monads and the thesis that the actual world is the best of all possible worlds. Indeed, the latter thesis made Leibniz an easy target at the hands of Voltaire in *Candide* (1759). A further source of difficulty is of a wholly different nature. Although he published one philosophical book, Leibniz never produced a definitive statement of his philosophical theories and arguments; there is no Leibnizian masterpiece which can be set beside Benedict de Spinoza's *Ethics* (1677) or John Locke's *Essay Concerning Human Understanding* (1690). Instead the reader is forced to turn to a countless array of essays and letters in order to gain a coherent picture of his philosophical achievements. Most of Leibniz's works, both long and short, were unpublished during his lifetime, and have only gradually been exposed to the light of day in the three hundred years or so since his death; indeed many of his writings remain unpublished to this date. Leibniz himself was well aware of how difficult it was for his contemporaries to appreciate his contributions to philosophy, for he wrote: 'He who knows me only from my published writings does not know me' (D VI 1 65).

Despite the fragmentary character of many of his writings, Leibniz is a systematic philosopher; his ideas in logic, metaphysics, theology, and the foundations of physics form a largely coherent whole. In this respect Leibniz is characteristic of his age and opposed in spirit to our own. Today, although there are a few prominent exceptions, analytic philosophers tend to approach philosophical problems in a piecemeal fashion; they tackle questions about the nature of knowledge and belief or the relationship between mind and body in isolation from other areas of philosophy. The greatest philosophical minds of the seventeenth century tended to adopt a different tack; they sought to construct grand philosophical systems in which particular problems of moment to their contemporaries would find a solution. The system itself would then gain credit from its ability to solve particular problems. Such philosophers were often encouraged in their systematic ambitions by the belief that our native faculty of reason is a reliable instrument whose power had been effectively hidden by slavish dependence on the authority of Aristotle and his medieval disciples. Moreover, the collapse of Aristotle's system in the era of the Scientific Revolution left a void which early modern philosophers often aspired to fill.

MIRRORS OF GOD

In his ambition to construct a system Leibniz is, thus, far from being alone among seventeenth-century philosophers. But Leibniz is unusual in where he finds the deepest inspiration of his system. As we shall see, Leibniz was highly responsive to the conceptual problems posed by the new science of his time; he was also fascinated by the legacy of medieval philosophy. Arguably, however, it is the philosophy of the Renaissance on which he draws for the main theme of his system. Despite the complexity of many of his theories and arguments, the underlying theme of his philosophy is a remarkably simple one deriving from the Neoplatonic philosophers of the age preceding Leibniz's own: it is the idea that the universe is a harmonious collection of substances which reflect the qualities of God, its creator. The idea is perhaps best expressed in the *Discourse on Metaphysics* (1686), the first work of his philosophical maturity:

Each substance is like a whole world, and like a mirror of God,
or indeed of the whole universe, which each one expresses in its
own fashion – rather as the same city is differently represented
according to the different situations of the person who looks at it.
In a way, then, the universe is multiplied as many times as there
are substances, and in the same way the glory of God is redoubled
by so many quite different representations of his work. In fact
we can say that each substance carries the imprint of the infinite
wisdom and omnipotence of God, and imitates them as far as it
is capable of it.

(DM 9 WF 61)

In this book we shall see that the 'mirror of God' theme is a powerful
tool for understanding the major areas of Leibniz's philosophy.

One major area of his philosophy in which the 'mirror of God'
thesis plays a prominent role is his metaphysics. But before we can
see how, we need to say something about the nature of metaphysics
itself. Ever since Aristotle metaphysics has been understood to be
that part of philosophy which is concerned with the question:
'What is being?' or, less dauntingly perhaps, 'What really is there?'[1]
We might be tempted to take a first stab at answering this question
by saying: 'There are tables, chairs, computers, and so on'. But of
course philosophers will not be satisfied with any mere inventory
of objects in the world: they seek to answer this question at a higher
level of abstraction. We might then try to answer the question by
noting what these items have in common: they are physical objects.
If we were then to hold that all the items in the world are fundamentally physical in nature, we would be led to a distinctively
metaphysical thesis, namely materialism. A form of this doctrine
had been advanced in Leibniz's time by his older contemporary,
Thomas Hobbes, who claims uncompromisingly: 'The world . . . is
corporeal, that is to say, body . . . and every part of the universe
is body, and that which is not body is no part of the universe'
(*Leviathan*, IV.46). On the other hand, reflection on the existence of

minds might give us pause, for minds do not seem to have physical properties such as size and shape. We might, then, be tempted to amend our answer by saying that there are two very different basic kinds of things: minds and bodies. (Such an account of what there is can of course accommodate God as a supermind.) A sophisticated version of this doctrine – namely, dualism – had been advanced in Leibniz's time by Descartes and his disciples, and had achieved wide currency. As we shall see in Chapters 2 and 3, Leibniz is satisfied with neither of these answers to the question: 'What really is there?'. Especially in his later philosophy Leibniz argues that the fundamental building-blocks of the universe are all simple, imma-terial entities which he terms 'monads'. Like Plato before him, Leibniz thus holds that the physical world of tables and chairs is less than fully real; in this sense they are both idealists. But Leibniz's version of idealism differs from the older Platonic version in its insistence that reality is ultimately mental, or at least quasi-mental, in nature. The basic entities in Plato's metaphysics, the Forms, may be immaterial, but they are not for that reason mind-like.

In the passage from the *Discourse on Metaphysics* Leibniz speaks of the nature of substances, and in doing so he places himself within a long tradition. Since Aristotle the question: 'What is being?' had been understood as equivalent to the question: 'What is substance?' or 'What exists in a primary way?'. Part of the Aristotelian legacy is the idea that substance is that which has a genuinely independent existence. The nature of the independence in question had been conceived in different ways, and it is no easy matter to sort out the relations between the different conceptions of independence. But by Leibniz's time one kind of independence which was attributed to substance was causal: a substance was supposed to be the source of its states or properties. Leibniz's great contemporary Spinoza had indeed interpreted the notion of causal independence or self-sufficiency so strictly that he had been led to argue, following a hint in Descartes, that there is only one substance, namely God, which he also identified with Nature. Leibniz strongly rejects

Spinoza's conclusion, but he agrees with Spinoza in regarding causal independence as integral to the nature of substance. As we shall see, Leibniz argues that monads, the basic building-blocks of the universe, though created by God, are all in a sense causally independent or self-sufficient.

We can now see how the 'mirrors of God' theme illuminates some of the most striking features of Leibniz's metaphysics. By virtue of being simple, immaterial and causally self-sufficient, monads resemble God their creator. It must be admitted, however, that Leibniz sometimes soft-pedals the thesis that all substances are mirrors of God in favour of something more familiar and more orthodox: this is the thesis, deriving from the Book of Genesis as seen through philosophical lenses, that the human mind is made in the image of God (S. Brown 1999: 274).[2] In the *Monadology* (1714), for instance, Leibniz writes that whereas all souls mirror the universe, human minds themselves are mirrors of God (WF 283). Certainly throughout his philosophical career the 'mirrors of God' thesis is highly visible in those areas of his thought where he narrows his focus to human minds. In his theory of knowledge Leibniz argues that human minds resemble God not only in their causal self-sufficiency, but also in their cognitive self-sufficiency: minds are endowed with innate ideas, and can thus draw knowledge out of their own depths. In his philosophy of action the 'mirror of God' theme is even more straightforward; for Leibniz offers an analysis of freedom which shows how human and divine actions are free in the same sense; the decisions of human minds mirror God's choice among possible worlds in the act of creation. In his ethics Leibniz argues not merely that the structure of human choice resembles the structure of divine choice, but that human beings should seek to imitate divine goodness as far as they can. And finally, in a rather complex way, the thesis that human minds are mirrors of God is even present in Leibniz's theodicy – that is, his attempt to defend God's character against the charge of injustice. Here Leibniz argues not merely that God chooses the best of all possible worlds, but also that the best possible world is the one in which the happiness of minds is as great as can be. The maximal happiness of minds is grounded in their possession of God-like perfections, such as knowledge and virtue, which make them pre-eminent among substances.

These are remarkable doctrines, and one may wonder why Leibniz was attracted to them. To cite precedents in Neoplatonic philosophy or the Book of Genesis is not adequate by way of explanation; it is only to push the problem one stage further back. It is true that Neoplatonic philosophy enjoyed a great revival during the Renaissance, but one may still ask why a philosopher of Leibniz's stature should have been attracted to it. And it is equally true that, as a Christian, Leibniz could not afford to discount the Book of Genesis, but one may still ask why he should have given such philosophical weight to a theme that could be extracted from this biblical text.

There is no doubt that part of the appeal of the 'mirror of God' theme for Leibniz is theological. According to Leibniz, any adequate conception of God implies that he seeks to maximize his own glory, and he can accomplish this goal best by creating a universe which expresses his perfections as fully as possible. But there can also be little doubt that the 'mirror of God' theme provided a framework in which particular philosophical problems could be solved. To say that all substances are in a sense causally self-sufficient is to say that they are in a way God-like; it is also to solve a problem about the nature of causality which came to the fore as a result of the Scientific Revolution. To say that the ultimate building-blocks of the universe are souls or soul-like entities is again to say that they resemble God; it is also to solve a problem about the nature of matter which occupied Leibniz throughout his philosophical career.

THE PROJECT OF SYNTHESIS

Leibniz's thesis that human minds in particular are mirrors of God underwrites another leading characteristic of his philosophy which links him with the Renaissance: this is what we may call his project of synthesis. Since all human minds reflect the divine perfections, including of course omniscience, they all have insight into truths about the universe; Leibniz concedes, however, that the perception of these truths is in varying degrees obscure and confused. Thus Leibniz has a theoretical basis for his conviction that every philosopher has some apprehension of the truth, even if in many cases this apprehension is one-sided. Leibniz expresses this conviction by saying that most philosophical sects are right in what they assert, but not in what they deny (L 655). In this spirit Leibniz seeks to synthesize the views of opposing philosophical schools. If this is eclecticism, it is eclecticism of a principled kind.

Leibniz's project of synthesis or reconciliation sets him apart from the rival philosophers in the period, but it is important to see how. Other great philosophers, such as René Descartes, were interested in synthesis in one sense; they attempted to reconcile the principles of the new mechanistic science with the tenets of traditional theology. In his Meditations (1641), for instance, Descartes not only lays the foundations for his new physics; he also offers proofs of the existence of God and seeks to place the doctrine of personal immortality on a secure basis by proving the 'real distinction' of mind and body. Nonetheless, Descartes is wholly characteristic of the great philosophers of his age in his insistence on the need for a radical break with the philosophical past; as he writes at the beginning of the Meditations, the edifice of knowledge must be reconstructed on wholly new foundations (CSM II 2). In particular, Descartes and leading contemporaries, such as Hobbes, tend to adopt a contemptuous attitude towards the Scholastics, the medieval philosophers who drew on Aristotle for their inspiration.

Leibniz, no less than Descartes, is committed to showing that the new science can coexist with the claims of traditional theology. But true to his principled eclecticism, Leibniz parts company with Descartes by adopting a far more positive and accommodating attitude towards the philosophical tradition. Whereas Descartes saw only barren subtleties in the writings of the Scholastics, Leibniz insists that there is much of real substance in their teachings; as he is fond of saying, there are nuggets of gold buried in the dross (NE IV.viii RB 431). Wholesale rejection of the Scholastic legacy is thus not a sensible policy to adopt. Moreover, Leibniz does not simply survey the Scholastic tradition as an outsider, able to appraise its merits and defects in a spirit of detachment; it is arguable that he himself remains in some degree inside this tradition. The continuity of Leibniz's thought with Scholasticism is evident in some of the problems which he placed on his philosophical agenda, and in the spirit in which he tried to solve them. It would be an exaggeration to say that Leibniz was the last of the Scholastics, but it is fair to observe that total emancipation from Scholasticism was something he neither sought nor achieved.

On principled grounds Leibniz may have sought to achieve reconciliation, but he could also be sharply critical of other philosophers, especially among his contemporaries and recent predecessors. Indeed, Leibniz often needed the stimulus of disagreement with other philosophers to prompt him to put pen to paper; he actively sought out opportunities for engaging in philosophical debates. Much of Leibniz's best work is to be found in dialogue with other philosophers. Sometimes these debates take the form of correspondence with his contemporaries, such as Antoine Arnauld and Samuel Clarke; at other times they take the form of more or less explicit debate with philosophers who, for one reason or another, either would not or could not enter into an exchange of views with Leibniz. The *Discourse on Metaphysics*, for instance, the first major work of his maturity, is to a large extent a refutation of an unorthodox brand of Cartesianism; his *New Essays on Human Understanding* (1703–5) is a point-by-point critique of Locke's theory of knowledge. Leibniz was nowhere more vehement than in his critique of Spinoza whose pantheistic and necessitarian views he attacked on grounds of impiety and defective logic alike. Yet in the eyes of some of his readers Leibniz 'protests too much' in his opposition to Spinoza. By a strange irony it has been Leibniz's fate to be accused himself of being a 'closet Spinozist'; in particular, ever since Arnauld, Leibniz has appeared to be committed to a version of determinism which leaves no room for human freedom in the sense of the ability to do otherwise.[3] The justice of this accusation will be examined in Chapter 5.

A SYSTEMATIC PHILOSOPHER?

In this book, then, Leibniz will be presented as a systematic philosopher whose thought is dominated by a large theme deriving from the Neoplatonic tradition. The claim that Leibniz is a systematic thinker might seem to be beyond controversy. Certainly Leibniz himself regularly referred to his philosophy as a 'system'; indeed, the word 'system' appears in the very title of the first published exposition of his philosophy.[4] Yet the image of Leibniz as a systematic philosopher has recently been challenged on various grounds (C. Wilson 1999: 372–88). It thus seems appropriate to defend the claim against objections and make concessions where necessary.

One reason why Leibniz's credentials as a systematic thinker have been challenged is the apparent striking contrast between his work and that of Spinoza. In his masterpiece the *Ethics* Spinoza sets out his philosophy 'in the geometrical manner' associated with Euclid; that is, starting with axioms, definitions, and postulates, he seeks to offer rigorous demonstrations of his philosophical theses in metaphysics, theory of knowledge, psychology, and ethics. Whether Spinoza's demonstrations are formally valid has been strongly disputed, but Spinoza at least presents his philosophy to the reader as a deductive system. It is true that none of Leibniz's major philosophical works is systematic in this sense. Some of the most famous brief expositions of his thought, such as the *Monadology* and the *Principles of Nature and Grace* (1714), serve up his metaphysics in a 'take it or leave it' manner; indeed, they even come close to dispensing with deductive argument altogether. Thus if Spinoza's *Ethics* is held up as the standard by which systematicity is measured, Leibniz seems to fall far short.

A further reason for challenging Leibniz's credentials as a systematic philosopher has to do with the development of his thought during the course of his career. Bertrand Russell, for instance, believed that Leibniz's system had stabilized by the time of the *Discourse on Metaphysics* of 1686, and in this opinion he was followed by many readers. More recently, writers have emphasized that even on central issues Leibniz's thought remained fluid at this date. Surely no issue is more central in Leibniz's philosophy than the question of what are the fundamental building-blocks of the universe, yet Leibniz seems to have experimented with various answers to this question before he finally settled on the theory of monads. And even in the last phase of his philosophy Leibniz appears to have left some loose ends dangling on important topics. Although the issue is controversial, Leibniz seems never to have made up his mind completely on how to accommodate bodies within a metaphysics which recognizes only soul-like entities as fully real.

Such recent sceptics about Leibniz's credentials as a systematic philosopher have certainly performed a useful service. But it is a mistake, I think, to suppose that they force us to abandon the view that Leibniz is a systematic philosopher; rather, they simply force us to be more careful about explaining how this claim should be understood. It is true of course that Leibniz never cast his philosophy in geometrical form as Spinoza did, but, as two of his recent editors have pointed out, Leibniz is systematic in the sense that he was constantly aware of the implications of his thought on one topic for other areas of his philosophy (WF 6). The problem of the nature of truth, for instance, may seem like a specialized and technical question insulated from those parts of his philosophy which deal with issues that concern human life. But Leibniz was conscious that his distinctive theory of truth has implications not only for human freedom but for the vindication of God's character against the charge of injustice; indeed, Leibniz ingeniously deploys the theory of truth and its consequences to defend the thesis that the world which God created is the best of all possible worlds. Even where it may be misguided to look for deductively watertight connections, there are at least themes which recur in different areas of his philosophy. Moreover, even if it is true that Leibniz changes his mind on some topics, it is a no less impressive fact about his philosophy that on certain issues he never wavered; the idea that substances are active principles of unity, for instance, is one of the great constants of his philosophy.

According to the famous Greek proverb, 'the fox knows many things but the hedgehog knows one big thing'. Many years ago Isaiah Berlin made use of this proverb in order to draw a distinction between two kinds of philosophers and writers: the hedgehogs are those who subordinate everything to one overarching idea; the foxes are those who have many incidental insights but are either unable or unwilling to integrate them into a comprehensive vision (Berlin 1953). In terms of this distinction Spinoza is the paradigm hedgehog; Locke, at least as he is traditionally presented, is the paradigm fox. Leibniz may be less easy to classify. Some may think that, like Berlin's Tolstoy, he was by temperament a fox who aspired to be a hedgehog. But despite the variety of his ideas and interests, a strong case can be made for saying that he is more of a hedgehog than a fox.

SUMMARY

Leibniz is an unusually difficult philosopher for two main reasons. First, his two most famous doctrines – the theory of monads and the thesis that the actual world is the best of all possible worlds – can seem bizarre and implausible. Second, Leibniz never produced a philosophical masterpiece; instead, his philosophy must be extracted from a countless array of essays and letters. Nonetheless, in spite of the fragmentary character of his writings Leibniz is a systematic philosopher whose philosophy is governed by a simple idea deriving from Neoplatonism: the universe is a collection of entities, which mirror God, their creator. This thesis is conspicuous in Leibniz's metaphysics, that part of his philosophy which seeks to answer the question of what there really is. Leibniz's mature answer to this question is a form of idealism: the basic building-blocks of the universe are monads or soul-like entities, which, in their simplicity, immateriality, and causal self-sufficiency reflect the qualities of God. The 'mirror of God' theme is perhaps even more prominent in those areas of Leibniz's philosophy where he narrows his focus to human minds; it plays a major role in his theory of knowledge, his account of freedom and even his solution to the problem of evil. In the next section it is argued that the 'mirror of God' theme underwrites Leibniz's project of synthesis: since all minds reflect divine omniscience, all philosophers have some perception of the truth. In this spirit Leibniz seeks to synthesize the views of opposing philosophical schools. Whereas older contemporaries such as Descartes sought to reconcile the new science with traditional religious doctrines, Leibniz seeks in addition to reconcile the views of Ancients and Moderns, Platonists and Aristotelians. In the concluding section of the Introduction Leibniz's credentials as a systematic philosopher are defended against recent challenges. It is true that, unlike Spinoza, Leibniz never set out his philosophy in the geometrical manner. Moreover, even on central issues his thought continued to develop and on some topics, such as the status of bodies within his metaphysics, it remained fluid. Nonetheless, it is argued that Leibniz is a systematic philosopher in the sense that he was aware of the implications of his thinking on one topic for other areas of his thought. For example, his theory of truth is not an isolated technical doctrine but one that has important implications for his solution to the problem of evil.

FURTHER READING

S. Brown (1984) *Leibniz*. (An introductory study which emphasizes the intellectual context of Leibniz's philosophy.)

S. Brown (1999) 'The Proto-Monadology of the *De Summa Rerum*,' Brown (ed.), *The Young Leibniz and his Philosophy*. (Emphasizes the Neoplatonic roots of Leibniz's theory of monads.)

C. Mercer (2000) *Leibniz's Metaphysics: Its Origins and Development.* (A magisterial, scholarly study which traces the development of Leibniz's early philosophical views.)

B. Russell (1937) *A Critical Exposition of the Philosophy of Leibniz.* (A classic but controversial study.)

C. Wilson (1989) *Leibniz's Metaphysics: A Historical and Comparative Study.* (An important study of the development of Leibniz's metaphysics.)

C. Wilson (1999) 'The Illusory Nature of Leibniz's System,' Gennaro and Huenemann (eds.), *New Essays on the Rationalists.* (An important recent challenge to the thesis that Leibniz is a systematic philosopher.)

One

Leibniz: Life and Works

Perhaps no event is more important for understanding Leibniz's life than the Thirty Years War (1618–48) which devastated his native Germany, a country divided then (as for years to come) into countless states of unequal size. The Thirty Years War had a number of dimensions; it was perhaps primarily a dynastic quarrel, but it was also a religious conflict between Protestants and Roman Catholics. The fact that there was an ideological dimension to the conflict is of great significance for understanding Leibniz's lifelong preoccupation with what we may call 'peace studies';[1] it helps to explain why Leibniz devoted so much energy to devising plans for reconciliation between groups which were divided at the level of ideas. In the religious sphere Leibniz sought to reconcile not only Catholics and Protestants but also Calvinists and Lutherans within the Protestant fold. And, as we have seen in the Introduction, Leibniz's peace-making activities extended to the philosophical sphere as well. Here he sought to find areas of agreement between such groups as the Platonists and Aristotelians, Cartesians and anti-Cartesians, and above all, Ancients and Moderns.

Leibniz was perhaps the last great Renaissance man who in Bacon's words took all knowledge to be his province. Apart from being a philosopher of the front rank he was a mathematician of genius and a physicist of some distinction; he also made notable contributions in such fields as history, law, politics and diplomacy. Within the space of this chapter it is not possible to do justice to the entire range of his interests and activities. I shall aim to illustrate accordingly some of the main themes of his life while also explaining the circumstances in which his major philosophical works came to be written.

Leibniz was born in Leipzig in July 1646, the son of a university professor. As a boy he was amazingly precocious and, although he attended the local Nicolaischule, he was largely self-taught. At the age of eight he was granted access to his father's library and began a course of reading in the classical authors, Church Fathers, and the Scholastics. As an adolescent he first confronted the problem which was to occupy him in one form or another for much of his career. Towards the end of his life he recalled for a correspondent's benefit how at the age of fifteen he resolved the conflict between the teachings of the Ancients and the Moderns:

> As a child I studied Aristotle, and even the Scholastics did not repel me; and I am not displeased (*faché*) by them even now. But Plato also at that time, along with Plotinus, gave me some satisfaction, not to mention other Ancients whom I consulted later. Being emancipated from the Trivial Schools I fell upon the moderns, and I remember that I went for a walk by myself in a wood near Leipzig called the Rosendal, at the age of fifteen, to decide whether I should retain substantial forms. Finally mechanism prevailed and led me to apply myself to mathematics.
>
> (L 654–5: translation modified)

Later in life, as Leibniz explains, he came to believe that there was in a sense no need to choose between the substantial forms of the Scholastics and the mechanistic theories of the Moderns.

The future direction of Leibniz's philosophical interests is also foreshadowed in his university education. Leibniz entered the local university at Leipzig in April 1661 and later wrote a bachelor's dissertation entitled 'Metaphysical Disputation on the Principle of Individuation' (1663); the dissertation bears early witness to

Leibniz's lifelong interest in problems about the nature of identity and individuation (i.e., what distinguishes different individuals of the same kind). After graduation Leibniz turned to the study of law and wrote a doctoral dissertation entitled 'On Difficult Cases in Law' (1666). Even Leibniz's legal training is not without relevance to his philosophical career, for in his one published philosophical book, the *Essays in Theodicy* (1710), Leibniz acts as a defence counsel for God; he pleads God's cause before the bar of reason, as it were, against the charge of injustice.

Like most great minds of the age Leibniz was not attracted by the prospect of an academic career. The universities in the seventeenth century were generally bastions of intellectual conservatism and offered few opportunities for gaining exposure to the most recent advances in philosophy and the natural sciences. When the University of Altdorf (near Nuremberg) offered Leibniz a professorship, he declined the offer; at this stage Leibniz was set on a legal career. After a year of drifting (in which he flirted with alchemy) Leibniz entered the service of the Elector of Mainz as a legal adviser. Here he enjoyed the patronage of Johann Christian von Boineburg, a convert to Catholicism who encouraged Leibniz to develop his interest in promoting the cause of Church reunion; he persuaded Leibniz to write on the issue of disputed points of doctrine between the Churches. But Leibniz's attention was soon to be engrossed by a more immediate threat to the peace of Europe. In the early 1670s France under Louis XIV was pursuing an expansionist foreign policy, and Germany and Holland were the leading targets of French aggression. Leibniz responded to the situation by devising a characteristically ingenious plan for diverting French expansionism away from the frontiers of Germany; in the 'Consilium Aegyptiacum' (1672) he proposed that instead of attacking Germany France should direct its aggressive energies against non-Christian Egypt. It is apparent that, at this stage, Leibniz's enthusiasm for peace did not extend beyond the boundaries of Europe and Christendom. Leibniz was given permission by the

Court of Mainz to go to Paris to present the plan to the French government.

Leibniz may have been sincerely committed to the Egyptian plan, but once in Paris he let the matter drop: he never found the opportunity to present the plan to the French government. In fact, it is difficult to avoid the suspicion that the Egyptian plan was to some extent a pretext for visiting Paris, which was then not only the cultural but also the intellectual capital of Europe. Leibniz's years in Paris were enormously important for his whole intellectual development; it is during these years, for instance, that Leibniz made the acquaintance of Arnauld and Malebranche, perhaps the two leading French philosophers of the age; for the first time also he studied Descartes's philosophy at first hand. The Paris years are especially important for Leibniz's development as a mathematician; in Paris Leibniz began the serious study of higher mathematics under the tutelage of Christiaan Huygens. The limits of Leibniz's mathematical expertise to this date had been embarrassingly exposed on a visit to the Royal Society in London in 1673; when Leibniz boasted of a mathematical discovery he had made, he was told by John Pell that he had been anticipated by the French mathematician François Regnauld (Müller and Krönert 1969: 32). (However, the Royal Society did express an interest in his calculating machine.) During his years in Paris Leibniz developed as a mathematician to the point where he was indeed capable of making a major breakthrough; in 1675 he discovered the differential calculus. Leibniz's discovery, published in a journal in 1684, sowed the seeds of the later 'priority dispute' with Isaac Newton. As we shall see, this ugly controversy was to cast a cloud over his final years.

If mathematics was the principal focus of Leibniz's attention during his stay in Paris, philosophy was not forgotten either. Leibniz himself dated his philosophical maturity from the *Discourse on Metaphysics* of 1686, but in these years he wrote a number of essays which have only recently begun to attract serious attention from scholars. How far the main doctrines of Leibniz's mature philosophy are anticipated in these papers remains a matter of scholarly dispute, but there is little doubt that the Neoplatonic themes which they display were never recanted. The end of Leibniz's stay in Paris is marked by what is perhaps the most fascinating event in his entire philosophical career. In 1676 Leibniz found a pretext to visit Spinoza in The Hague, having learned that Spinoza was at work on a philosophical treatise of great importance. Spinoza showed Leibniz the manuscript of the *Ethics*, and the two men discussed philosophy together over several days. Although there is no written record of their conversation, it seems likely that these discussions were among the most rewarding in the whole history of philosophy.

HANOVER: POSITION AND DUTIES

By the end of his stay in Paris Leibniz was obliged to establish a proper career for himself; his patrons, von Boineburg and the Elector of Mainz, had died over three years before. In 1676 Leibniz accepted an official position at Hanover, a small provincial town administered by a Duke acting through a Court council of which Leibniz himself was to become a member. Leibniz's official duties were various; he was librarian, historian, and political adviser. In addition to his official duties Leibniz meddled in all sorts of activities; he served as an unofficial technological adviser on projects such as the draining of the silver mines in the Hartz mountains.

Although he occupied this position until his death in 1716, Leibniz was never satisfied with his life in provincial Hanover. Over the next forty years he exercised considerable ingenuity in seeking out pretexts to spend as much time away from Hanover as possible. One such pretext arose from the fact that he had been commissioned by his employer to write a history of the House of Brunswick. The ruling family in Hanover was an ambitious dynasty which was later to succeed to the English throne, and it seems that what Leibniz's employers wanted was a popular work which would puff their reputation. Leibniz, however, persuaded himself that the task of writing the history required extensive original research, and to this end he undertook a two-and-a-half year journey in Southern Germany and Italy in search of archival material. Another such pretext was furnished by Leibniz's interest in the establishment and promotion of scientific academies; the Royal Society in London and the Académie des Sciences in Paris provided the prototypes. Here Leibniz was answering to a serious scholarly need. In the seventeenth century learned journals were few, and communications between scholars and scientists were poor; the establishment of scientific academies helped to improve scholarly communication and to prevent the needless duplication of research. The promotion of projects for founding scientific academies served as an excuse for visits to such cities as Berlin, Dresden, and Vienna; it also gave him the opportunity to make the acquaintance of illustrious figures such as Czar Peter the Great. However, only the Academy at Berlin came to fruition.

DISCOURSE ON METAPHYSICS AND CORRESPONDENCE WITH ARNAULD

As we have seen, Leibniz dated his philosophical maturity from the *Discourse on Metaphysics* which he composed in 1686. Although it was a fairly comprehensive exposition of his system, characteristically for Leibniz the work is a contribution to a debate. The *Discourse* needs to be understood against the background of the controversy between Nicolas Malebranche and Arnauld. To all appearances Malebranche and Arnauld had much in common; they were both members of Catholic religious orders and they were both partisans of the new Cartesian philosophy. Nonetheless, the two philosophers had been locked in controversy since the publication of Malebranche's *Treatise on Nature and Grace* in 1680. This work had deeply offended Arnauld by its theodicy, which holds that even in the distribution of grace God acts through general laws and volitions; in the eyes of Arnauld such a thesis was inconsistent with a proper understanding of God's providential care for particular human beings. Somewhat surprisingly Arnauld widened his attack to include much of Malebranche's unorthodox brand of Cartesian philosophy, especially his distinctive theory of ideas and knowledge.[2]

The *Discourse on Metaphysics* is in many ways a response to a bitter controversy which he had followed with close attention. Unlike Arnauld, Leibniz found much to admire in the *Treatise on Nature and Grace* but he could not share Malebranche's conviction that God could have created a more perfect world if he had not been obliged by concern for his glory to subscribe to general laws of nature. And, like Arnauld, Leibniz found much in Malebranche's metaphysics and theory of knowledge that was not to his taste. Leibniz could not accept Malebranche's occasionalist insistence that God alone is a true cause, and that creatures are devoid of genuine causal powers of their own (see further Chapter 2). Nor could he accept Malebranche's radical Augustinian thesis that we see all things in God – that is, we perceive the world by means of ideas located in God himself. In opposition to Malebranche's occasionalism Leibniz advances what later came to be known as his system of pre-established harmony; in opposition to Malebranche's theory of vision in God Leibniz advances his Platonic–Cartesian thesis that God has endowed our minds with a stock of innate ideas. And in opposition to Malebranche's thesis in theodicy that in a sense God could have done better, Leibniz advances his famous thesis that the actual world is the best of all possible worlds (see further Chapter 6).

The fact that the *Discourse on Metaphysics* is not only an exposition of his own system but a critique of Malebranche helps to explain why Leibniz decided to send the work (or rather a summary thereof) to Arnauld. Leibniz sympathized with Arnauld's own criticisms of Malebranche; they agree, for instance, that in maintaining that the world is a neglected work, in the sense that God has not made it as perfect as he might have done, Malebranche fails to do justice to the essential goodness of divine creation (Nadler 1994). Yet Leibniz may well have had another motive for sending the work to Arnauld; Leibniz's characteristic ecumenism may have come into play. Leibniz seems to have hoped that the *Discourse on Metaphysics* would provide a philosophical framework in which the theological disputes between Protestants and Roman Catholics could be resolved. As one of the leading theologians and philosophers of the time, Arnauld certainly had the stature to serve as a party to such negotiations, but in one way perhaps he was rather a strange choice; because of his unorthodox, Jansenistic brand of Catholicism Arnauld was out of favour with his own Church and had indeed been living in hiding for some years.[3]

Leibniz, then, may have had several motives for seeking out Arnauld's judgement on the *Discourse on Metaphysics*. But if Leibniz hoped for Arnauld's ready approval of the work, he was to be bitterly disappointed, for Arnauld reacted with hostility to Leibniz's teachings. Arnauld was particularly disturbed by Leibniz's thesis that for every person there is a complete concept in the mind of God which contains once and for all everything that will ever happen to him or her. Arnauld informed the intermediary in the correspondence, Count Ernst von Hessen-Rheinfels, that this doctrine introduced 'a more than fatal necessity' (WF 98). Clearly stung by Arnauld's criticisms, Leibniz mounted a vigorous defence of his own position, and his response initiated a correspondence, which continued intermittently for some years, and greatly illuminated the points at issue between the two men. In addition to defending himself against the charge of fatalism, Leibniz seized the opportunity to explain his revival of medieval doctrines, such as the theory of substantial forms, for the benefit of a sceptical Arnauld. Arnauld confronted the doctrine with standard Cartesian objections, and in general he served as an intelligent proxy for Descartes himself.

THE 'NEW SYSTEM'

Leibniz's disappointment over Arnauld's reaction seems to have left its mark on his subsequent choice of strategy for presenting his philosophical views. In 1695 Leibniz was persuaded to publish a brief account of his metaphysics in a highly visible French journal: the 'New System of the Nature and Communication of Substances' was the first work in which he appeared as a philosopher before a wide Continental readership. In the 'New System' Leibniz does not seek to disguise the fact that his philosophical views had encountered a sceptical response from those to whom he had privately communicated them; he even alludes to Arnauld's frosty reaction when he writes that 'one of the greatest theologians and philosophers of our time . . . had found some of my opinions quite paradoxical' (WF 144). But nowhere in the 'New System' does Leibniz give any hint of the grounds for Arnauld's coolness; nowhere does he mention his theory of complete concepts and its apparent implications for the issues of human and divine freedom. Moreover, although in the Discourse on Metaphysics Leibniz had seemed to derive his metaphysics from first principles, there is no suggestion of demonstration in the 'New System'; the doctrine of the pre-established harmony in particular is presented as simply the most intelligible explanation of the data.

Composed in part at the prompting of the distinguished churchman Jacques-Bénigne Bossuet, the 'New System' seems especially designed to appeal to a French readership familiar with the philosophy of Descartes and his disciples. In the opening sections of the work Leibniz is careful to prepare the ground for his rehabilitation of the medieval theory of substantial forms; he appears anxious to dispel the impression that he is a provincial German unacquainted with the new developments in philosophy. Digressing into autobiography, Leibniz explains that after an early study of the Scholastics he had been charmed by the modern mechanical philosophy, until he came to discover its limitations (WF 145). Moreover, Leibniz seeks to gain a hearing for his system by emphasizing its ability to solve the problem of the union of mind and body which had exercised Descartes and his successors; this is the problem of giving an account of the apparent interaction between two such heterogeneous substances. As Leibniz writes, 'as far as we can see from his writings Descartes gave up the game at this point' (WF 149). Leibniz pays his respects to the occasionalist solution to the problem proposed by Malebranche and others, but he goes on to indicate how it is unsatisfactory in his eyes. With the 'New System' Leibniz is seeking to position his doctrine of pre-established harmony as one of the candidates for a solution to the puzzle that no serious philosopher can afford to ignore.

In one way Leibniz's strategy in the 'New System' paid off handsomely. Leibniz may have won few converts to his doctrine of pre-established harmony, but at least he found a hearing. The 'New System' aroused intense interest on its publication in the *Journal des Savants* and sparked a number of replies from leading French philosophers; these in turn prompted responses from Leibniz in the form of explanations or clarifications of the 'New System'. Among the most notable of the responses was Bayle's article 'Rorarius' in his *Critical and Universal Dictionary*. Pierre Bayle summarized his sceptical reaction to Leibniz's 'New System' by remarking that it elevates the power and intelligence of divine art above anything that we can understand (WF 225). The remark was clearly intended in a critical spirit, but Leibniz at least pretended to take it as a compliment. Despite the fact that they may have been to some degree at cross-purposes the exchange between Leibniz and Bayle is a philosophically rewarding one which illuminates the differences between Leibniz's doctrine of pre-established harmony and occasionalism.

LEIBNIZ, LOCKE, AND THE *NEW ESSAYS ON HUMAN UNDERSTANDING*

In France, versions of Cartesian philosophy, of varying degrees of orthodoxy, continued to hold sway until the end of the century. In England, however, a new philosophical star was rising on the horizon: in 1690 John Locke had published his masterpiece, *An Essay Concerning Human Understanding*, which came to be regarded as one of the classic statements of empiricist philosophy. Leibniz first read Locke's *Essay* in 1695, and, as was his habit, he recorded his reactions in writing; he wrote a mildly critical but mainly complimentary paper which he sent to a Scottish acquaintance, Thomas Burnett, in the hope that he would communicate it to Locke himself. During the last years of the century Burnett kept Leibniz abreast of the various controversies in which Locke was involved. Leibniz was informed of the storm of controversy which had greeted Locke's suggestion that matter might think; he also heard that, on the basis of his philosophical and religious works alike, Locke was strongly suspected of leaning towards the heresy of Socinianism. The Socinians were the ancestors of the modern Unitarians, and their characteristic tenets were the denial of the Trinity and of the divinity of Jesus Christ; they also denied the existence of innate ideas and the natural immortality of the soul.

In the years around the turn of the century Leibniz made a number of attempts to enter into a correspondence with Locke. Leibniz was clearly hoping for the kind of wide-ranging discussion of philosophical issues which he had earlier conducted with Arnauld and Bayle. However, his efforts were unavailing. Locke had indeed received Leibniz's first comments on the *Essay* and he responded with merely polite and conventional expressions of gratitude. (In private Locke was scathing about the quality of Leibniz's criticisms.) Locke responded in the same vein to Leibniz's subsequent overtures. Leibniz might have simply given up at this stage, but then in 1700 the French translation of Locke's *Essay* was published. The appearance of the translation was doubly significant: it made it easier for Leibniz to study Locke's philosophy carefully, and it alerted Leibniz to the fact that the *Essay* would be assured of a wide continental readership. Suspecting perhaps (with some distaste) that Locke's philosophy would now become fashionable, Leibniz wrote a point-by-point commentary on the *Essay* which he later turned into a dialogue. He clearly intended to publish the work with the aim of forcing Locke to reply finally to his criticisms. The work was indeed almost ready for publication when Locke found a new way of evading Leibniz's criticisms; he died in the autumn of 1704. Leibniz then suppressed the work – partly on the ground that it would be unfair to publish a critique when its target could no longer defend himself, and partly on the ground that he could not now achieve his aim of engaging Locke in a public debate. As a result the New Essays on Human Understanding lay buried among Leibniz's manuscripts in Hanover until fifty years after his death.

The New Essays on Human Understanding is a deeply puzzling and frustrating work. Rambling and repetitive, it also bears all the marks of having been hastily converted into the form of a dialogue; indeed, the work must rank among the least skilful examples of this venerable genre of philosophical literature. More seriously perhaps, Leibniz makes little or no attempt to come to grips with Locke's assumptions or even with the announced goals of the Essay. Despite its severe shortcomings, the New Essays is an important work because it reveals aspects of Leibniz's philosophy of mind and knowledge which are not fully represented elsewhere in his writings. Predictably the New Essays has been seen as a classic confrontation between rationalist and empiricist theories of knowledge. In fact, however, it is clear from Leibniz's statements about the work that his main aim is not to refute Locke's theory of knowledge at all; it is rather to defend an immaterialist theory of mind against what he regarded as Locke's insidious attacks on the doctrine; Leibniz, like Locke's English critics, was deeply troubled by Locke's 'thinking matter' hypothesis. As we would expect, then, Leibniz's chief preoccupations in the work have more to do with metaphysics than the theory of knowledge (Jolley 1984).

THE *ESSAYS IN THEODICY*

The New Essays was thus one major treatise which remained unpublished during Leibniz's lifetime and for many years after his death. A few years after completing this work, however, Leibniz published a substantial philosophical treatise on another subject; this was the Essays in Theodicy (1710), the one philosophical book which did appear in print during his lifetime. 'Theodicy' (the justice of God) was a term which Leibniz himself had invented, and as the title thus suggests, in this work he returned to a theme which had occupied him since the beginning of his philosophical career. The problem was the old one of reconciling the presence of various kinds of evils in the world with the existence of an omnipotent God who is also just and benevolent.

There is an unusual poignancy in the circumstances surrounding the work's composition, for the book was in a way a posthumous tribute to a royal patron whom he very much admired. Queen Sophie Charlotte of Prussia was the brilliant daughter of Electress Sophia of Hanover, and Leibniz had kept up his acquaintance with the young queen during his frequent visits to the court in Berlin. When she had died prematurely in 1705 (at the age of thirty-six), Leibniz was absolutely devastated; he seems to have suffered something like a nervous collapse, even breaking off his cherished correspondence for months on end (Müller and Krönert 1969: 195). In a letter to Thomas Burnett, Leibniz explained how the work had its origins in conversations with the young queen about the philosophy of religion:

> The greatest part of this work was composed in a piecemeal fashion, when I found myself in the company of the late Queen of Prussia, where these matters were often discussed, on the occasion of the Dictionary and other works of Bayle's which were there much read. In our conversations I was in the habit of replying to the objections of Mr Bayle, and of showing the Queen, that they were not as powerful as certain people, not well disposed towards religion, wanted to make believe. Her Majesty commanded me quite often to put my replies in writing, so that one could examine them carefully. After the death of this great Princess I collected these pieces and augmented them at the urging of friends who were informed about them, and from them I composed the work of which I have just spoken, which is an octavo of considerable size.

As I have thought deeply about this matter since my youth, I claim
to have discussed it in depth.

(G III 321)

The Dictionary in question was of course the work in which Bayle
had raised objections to Leibniz's system of pre-established harmony. Bayle sought to show how the teachings of the Christian
faith were totally opposed to the deliverances of reason; the old
problem of reconciling the justice of God with the facts of human
suffering was one which reason was unable to solve. Bayle's professed objective, however, was not to undermine Christian teachings;
it was rather to show how they must be accepted on faith alone, and
could receive no support from reason. Ever since his own time
readers have questioned the sincerity of Bayle's professed aims, but
whatever may be the truth on that issue, there is no doubt that his
combination of scepticism and fideism represented a stance wholly
at variance with Leibniz's rationalistic approach to the philosophy
of religion.

As Leibniz indicates in correspondence with Burnett, the *Theodicy*,
like the *New Essays* before it, was composed sporadically, and though
it was the one philosophical book that Leibniz did see fit to publish,
it has no greater claims than the *New Essays* to be regarded as
Leibniz's masterpiece. The *Theodicy* may avoid the pitfalls of the
dialogue form, but it has some of the same faults as the *New Essays*; it
shows a tendency to ramble, and is burdened by excessive erudi-
tion. At least when he appeared before the public in print, Leibniz
never succeeded in wearing his learning lightly. Nonetheless, despite its shortcomings, the *Theodicy* is a major work which contains
important material not only about the problem of evil but also on
the subject of human freedom. If it is not a definitive work, it at
least represents the culmination of Leibniz's thought on topics
about which, as he tells Burnett, he had meditated since his
youth.

THE *MONADOLOGY* AND RELATED WRITINGS

The *Theodicy*, difficult as it is, was one of the pillars on which Leibniz's fame rested in the eighteenth century. Another work on which Leibniz's reputation rested in the century ahead was the so-called *Monadology* which was written only a few years later in 1714 and published soon after his death. Like its companion piece, the *Principles of Nature and Grace*, the *Monadology* was composed for the benefit of a highly placed friend with the aim of spreading Leibniz's ideas in aristocratic circles. In style these two essays could hardly be more different from the *Essays in Theodicy*. Whereas the *Theodicy* is lengthy and laborious, the *Monadology* and the *Principles of Nature and Grace* are short and brilliant, if lacking in argument; they have rightly been viewed as masterpieces of condensed exposition.

The *Monadology* and the *Principles of Nature and Grace* are perhaps best regarded as popular presentations of the final idealist metaphysics to which Leibniz had been committed since around 1700. For a number of years Leibniz had been explaining his doctrine of monads and defending it against objections in correspondence with two academics, Burcher de Volder, a Professor of Philosophy at Leiden, and Bartholomew Des Bosses, a Professor of Theology at Hildesheim near Hanover. Taken together these two protracted exchanges of letters constitute perhaps the most important source for an understanding of Leibniz's final metaphysics.

The correspondence with Des Bosses, however, presents problems for the reader from which the earlier exchange is largely free. De Volder was a Cartesian, and for his benefit Leibniz expounds his system with uncompromising explicitness against the objections which a Cartesian could be expected to raise; accordingly, Leibniz concentrated his efforts on showing how the doctrine of monads was required to ground a proper understanding of physical force. Des Bosses, however, was a very different kind of academic, for he was a Jesuit Professor of Theology. To many readers this aspect of Des Bosses is relevant to understanding Leibniz's apparent willingness to compromise the purity of his doctrine of monads by introducing an extraneous element into his metaphysics, the theory of the substantial bond (*vinculum substantiale*). (See Chapter 3.) As a Roman Catholic, Des Bosses was curious to know whether Leibniz could succeed in accommodating the Catholic dogma of transubstantiation in his metaphysics: this is the dogma that in the celebration of the Mass the whole substance of the consecrated bread and wine is replaced by the substance of the body and blood of Christ. As a Lutheran, Leibniz was under no doctrinal pressure to accept this dogma; in correspondence with Des Bosses he constantly refers to it as 'your doctrine'. Nonetheless, as we have seen, Leibniz was an ecumenist who cared deeply about winning allies for his views among Roman Catholics. Leibniz's introduction of the *vinculum substantiale* has thus often been seen more as the concession of a diplomatist than as the creed of a philosopher (Russell 1937: 152).

THE LEIBNIZ–CLARKE CORRESPONDENCE: THE QUARREL WITH THE NEWTONIANS

In the last year of his life (1715–16) Leibniz was involved in controversy with Samuel Clarke, an English rationalist metaphysician and disciple of Newtonian physics. The tone of the controversy was unusually acrimonious, but for all its bitterness the controversy generates at least as much light as heat. Prompted by Leibniz's provocative remark that Locke and Newton had contributed to the decline of natural religion in England, the controversy ranged widely over the philosophical foundations of Newtonian physics. The correspondence remains a leading source for Leibniz's views on the ontological status of space and time. As we shall see in Chapter 3, Leibniz defends a relational theory of space and time in opposition to the Newtonian thesis that they have an absolute existence independently of bodies and events.

To understand the bitter tone of the correspondence it is essential to know about its origins, which are at once complex and fascinating. A year before the correspondence began, Leibniz's employer, the Elector Georg Ludwig of Hanover, had ascended the British throne as King George I, and he and his courtiers had left Hanover for London. Leibniz was characteristically absent from Hanover at the time of George's departure, and on his return he was not encouraged to join him. There were two very different reasons for George's reluctance to invite Leibniz to come over to England. One reason was that Leibniz still had not completed the history of the House of Brunswick, which he had been commissioned to write many years before. Indeed, although he had assembled (and in part published) an important collection of archival material, he had not even started the actual writing of the history itself. (Leibniz's tardiness in this respect prompted his secretary to remark that even in his historical researches Leibniz knew how to draw things out to infinity.) The other reason had wider ramifications. George I was well acquainted with the fact that Leibniz had been involved in a quarrel with Newton for many years; he also knew that Newton had by this time achieved the status of a symbol of national prestige. The King was accordingly reluctant to offer a gratuitous provocation to his new subjects by inviting Newton's arch rival to form part of his court in London.

The origins of the dispute between Leibniz and Newton went far back. As we saw earlier in this chapter, by the end of his stay in Paris Leibniz had advanced as a mathematician to the point where he discovered the differential calculus (1675); Leibniz had published his discovery in a journal article in 1684. The problem was that during a visit to England Leibniz had been given access to some papers of Newton's in which ideas relating to the differential calculus were expressed in code. Newton thus came to believe that Leibniz had plagiarized the differential calculus from him, for although he had published his results after Leibniz's article, he had discovered the calculus a little before his German rival. Newton never entered the fray directly, but he encouraged his disciples such as John Keill to accuse Leibniz of plagiarism. As a foreign member of the Royal Society Leibniz naturally wrote to the Secretary,

Hans Sloane, to demand justice. The result was that a tribunal was established to examine the charges. Sadly, for Leibniz, the tribunal effectively found in favour of Newton. Justice, although long delayed, has finally been done to Leibniz. Today historians of mathematics are generally inclined to exculpate Leibniz on the charge of plagiarism. The scholarly consensus is now that Leibniz and Newton independently discovered the differential calculus; indeed, it is Leibniz's notation, not Newton's, which is still in use today among mathematicians.

CONCLUSION

Leibniz, a lifelong bachelor, died in Hanover in November 1716 at the age of seventy. According to his biographers, he refused the offer of Holy Communion on his deathbed; this action was of a piece with his settled habit of non-attendance at church. His absence from church was presumably one reason why he had acquired a reputation as a non-believer among the local citizenry. The depth of Leibniz's commitment to a form of theism, heavily influenced by Neoplatonic philosophy, is beyond reasonable dispute; the sincerity of his Christian faith is a matter of controversy. It is sometimes tempting to suppose that he viewed the Christian Churches and the doctrinal differences between them simply with the eyes of a politician, intent on promoting schemes for reconciliation. As against this, it should be noted that Leibniz refused to convert to Roman Catholicism when such a conversion was the price demanded for highly attractive offers of employment. Perhaps, however, Leibniz's refusal to convert was more a sign of lingering suspicion of Catholicism than of any positive attachment to the Lutheran faith in which he had been raised.

Leibniz's funeral has been aptly described as a scandal to Germany (Mates 1986: 30). Even if, unlike Mozart, he was not buried in a pauper's grave, he was not accorded the honours which might have been expected in the case of a man of his genius who had achieved a truly international reputation by the time of his death. His employer, George I, had of course removed to England, but even the remnants of the court in Hanover declined an invitation to attend. Presumably they judged that they would not be giving any offence to their master by staying away.

It is not difficult to understand the feelings of exasperation which Leibniz inspired in lesser men such as George I. This is not just a matter of his failure to complete the history of the House of Brunswick that he had been commissioned to write. Leibniz gave other grounds for exasperation as well. With all his prodigious gifts he never wrote a philosophical masterpiece to set beside Spinoza's *Ethics* or Kant's *Critique of Pure Reason* (1781). Indeed he found it difficult to complete projects in general. Instead, he dissipated his enormous energies on a huge array of projects in a staggering variety of fields: philosophy, mathematics, theology, law, politics, and history. Further, many of his schemes — for example, for Church reunion — were wildly impractical. Although he prided himself on being a politician, he never understood that politics is the art of the possible. More fundamentally, although he shared the obsession with technological innovation and improvement that is so characteristic of the modern age, he lacked an intuitive sense of the direction in which history was moving. Here the comparison with Locke, one of his great philosophical contemporaries, is inescapable. Locke firmly understood that the best hope of peace in the religious sphere lay in securing agreement to the principle of toleration; people who had been locked in conflict over religious issues must agree to differ. Leibniz, by contrast, believed that the best hope of peace lay in schemes for reunification of the Churches based on the search for agreement on disputed articles of faith. In fact, the century which lay ahead was to cease to care very much about such issues.

In spite of the maddening aspects of his character and temperament, Leibniz was a philosophical genius of the first order, who in dispute with other philosophers proved to be amazingly resourceful in argument. In our own age the fact that he failed to produce a single masterpiece matters less than it did to his contemporaries, for so much of his best philosophical work is now available to the reader; today we are in a position to see how systematic his thought really was. In any case, his philosophical system, as we shall see, remains supremely worthy of study.

SUMMARY

Perhaps no event is more important for understanding Leibniz's life than the Thirty Years War which devastated his native Germany; it helped to shape his lifelong preoccupation with 'peace studies'. Throughout his career Leibniz devoted himself to attempts to reconcile various groups – political, religious, and philosophical – which were divided on ideological grounds. This chapter explores this theme, among others, in a selective account of Leibniz's extremely active life; it also describes the circumstances in which his major works came to be written. In the account of Leibniz's early years it is shown how some of his mature philosophical interests are foreshadowed in his youthful university studies; his interest in problems of identity and individuation is a case in point. Although Leibniz was offered professorships, like other seventeenth-century intellectuals he turned his back on the academic world in favour of a more public career. A brief period of employment as a diplomat and legal adviser led to an extended stay in Paris, which was extremely formative for his development as a philosopher and mathematician. Leibniz finally settled down in Hanover in his native Germany where, in addition to his official duties as court councillor, librarian, and historian, he acted as an adviser in many fields. Although Hanover remained his base for the last forty years of his life, his varied interests – for example, in historical research and in projects for founding scientific academies – led to many extended periods of absence. After a survey of Leibniz's range of activities, the focus of the chapter turns to the circumstances in which his major works were written. The *Discourse on Metaphysics*, the work from which Leibniz dated his philosophical maturity, was

partly an expression of his ecumenical interest in promoting reconciliation between the Roman Catholic and Protestant Churches. A
summary of the work was sent to the Catholic theologian and
philosopher, Antoine Arnauld, which led to an important correspondence on philosophical issues; Arnauld's generally frosty
reaction to Leibniz's views and, in particular, his complaint that
they introduced 'a more than more fatal necessity' may have led
Leibniz to suppress the *Discourse*. In any case, when Leibniz first
published his philosophy in the 'New System', he made no mention of the doctrines which offended Arnauld; instead he aimed his
work at a French readership familiar with Descartes's philosophy
and emphasized his solution to the problem of mind–body union
which defeated Descartes. In the first decade of the eighteenth century Leibniz wrote two lengthy works which were responses to the
views of leading contemporaries. The *New Essays on Human Understanding*
is a point-by-point refutation of Locke's philosophy in his *Essay*.
Although often regarded as a classic defence of a rationalist theory
of knowledge against empiricism, the work is as much concerned
to defend an immaterialist theory of mind. The other work, the
Essays in Theodicy, which unlike the *New Essays* Leibniz did publish, is a
response to Pierre Bayle's fideistic thesis that Christian doctrines
cannot be rationally justified; in opposition to Bayle, Leibniz
defends divine justice and offers a solution to the problem of evil.
In the last years of his life Leibniz expounded his theory of monads
in brilliant summaries such as the *Monadology* and defended it in
correspondence with other philosophers. The final years of his life
are also remarkable for one of his most important exchanges of
philosophical views. Leibniz's correspondence with Clarke, a disciple of Isaac Newton, is a classic defence of the relational theory of
space and time against the Newtonian absolutist theory.

FURTHER READING

E. Aiton (1985) *Leibniz: A Biography*. (A recent biography which is strong on
Leibniz's mathematical and scientific interests.)

R. Ariew (1995) 'Leibniz, Life and Times,' Jolley (ed.), *The Cambridge Companion to Leibniz*. (A useful survey of Leibniz's life and interests.)

G. Friedmann (1946) *Leibniz et Spinoza*. (An important scholarly study of Leibniz's relations with Spinoza and his philosophy.)

A.R. Hall (1980) *Philosophers at War: The Quarrel Between Newton and Leibniz*. (The most important scholarly study of the relationship between Leibniz and Newton.)

N. Jolley (1984) *Leibniz and Locke: A Study of the New Essays on Human Understanding*, Ch. 2. (Examines the English background to Leibniz's relations with Locke and stresses the importance of theological issues.)

B. Mates (1986) *The Philosophy of Leibniz: Metaphysics and Language*, Ch. 1. (A lively, readable account of Leibniz's life.)

G.M. Ross (1984) *Leibniz*. (A clear account which challenges some received ideas about Leibniz's life.)

R.C. Sleigh (1990) *Leibniz and Arnauld: A Commentary on their Correspondence*, Chs 1 and 2. (Places Leibniz's correspondence with Arnauld in the context of his ecumenical concerns.)

E. Vailati (1997) *Leibniz and Clarke: A Study of their Correspondence*. (A scholarly study which documents the intellectual context of Leibniz's correspondence with Clarke.)

Two

The Metaphysics of Substances: Unity and Activity

I have argued that perhaps the deepest theme in Leibniz's metaphysics is that substances, the fundamental building-blocks of the universe, are all mirrors of God (DM 9, WF 61). The theme may have roots in the Neoplatonic tradition, but Leibniz does not of course confine himself to recycling ancient themes; he presents new arguments for the thesis which address seventeenth-century concerns and problems. In the first half of the chapter we shall see how Leibniz criticizes two leading philosophical systems of his time, those of Descartes and Malebranche, for failing to do justice to the unity and activity of substances, properties which they all share with God. We shall then go on to see how in the *Discourse on Metaphysics* Leibniz presents a positive case for these and other God-like properties of substances. In particular, we shall see why Leibniz thinks that substances are in a sense omniscient and as causally self-sufficient as is consistent with their status as creatures.

One of the primary aims of this chapter will be to introduce the reader to some of the great constants of Leibniz's metaphysics as they appear in the first works of his philosophical maturity; the unity, indivisibility, and activity of substances, for instance, are themes which are fully present in these works and never disappear from subsequent writings. But we shall also find that though these themes are set in stone, on other issues Leibniz's thought remains surprisingly fluid at this stage. We could make the point in logical terminology by saying that although the intension of the term 'substance' is fixed, its extension remains undetermined; in other words, though Leibniz is clear about what is involved in being a substance, he is less clear about what items in the world satisfy the description. It is not until Leibniz's final turn to the theory of monads that his thought stabilizes on this latter issue, and even then (as we shall see in Chapter 3) he leaves some loose ends dangling.

UNITY: THE CRITIQUE OF DESCARTES

Perhaps the most prominent constant theme of Leibniz's metaphysics is that substances, the basic building-blocks of the universe, must be genuine unities. Leibniz defends this thesis most clearly while criticizing Descartes's metaphysics which, in his view, violates this fundamental condition of being a substance. In Descartes's austere metaphysics the universe is composed of two kinds of created substances: mind whose essence is thought, and body or matter whose essence is extension, the property of being spread out in three dimensions. We shall see in Chapter 4 that Leibniz is by no means uncritical of Descartes's doctrine of mind or thinking substance, but it is Descartes's account of extended substance which is the target of his special scorn. In the *Discourse on Metaphysics* and related writings Leibniz may be uncertain whether any body is a substance, but he is quite certain that body, as conceived by Descartes, does not fit the bill. As Leibniz remarks, if bodies are substances, their nature cannot possibly consist only in extension, that is to say, in size, shape, and motion (DM 9, WF 60).

We have seen in the previous chapter that Leibniz was critical of modern philosophers such as Descartes for their neglect and contempt of the Aristotelian tradition; as Leibniz is fond of saying, there is much gold buried in that dross. One of the nuggets of gold which in Leibniz's eyes Descartes had unreasonably rejected was the teaching of Aristotle on the nature of substance. In the *Discourse on Metaphysics* and the subsequent correspondence with Arnauld, Leibniz argues that Descartes goes astray in his metaphysics through his failure to think through the implications of Aristotle's teachings seriously.

Aristotle's central teachings about the nature of substance are composed of two main strands. In the first place, Aristotle devises a linguistic test to analyse our notion of what it is to be a substance or genuine thing; substances are 'ultimate subjects of predication'. Now Alexander the Great, for Aristotle, passes this test since, while many things can be predicated of Alexander – we can say, for example, that he was a Macedonian and a famous general – Alexander himself cannot be predicated of anything else; there is nothing of which we can say that it is an Alexander (except perhaps in a deviant, figurative sense). The same point can be made in slightly different terms by saying that the name 'Alexander' can appear only in the subject position in the sentence and never in the predicate position. Honesty, by contrast, fails to pass Aristotle's test for being a substance, for while honesty is a subject of predication, it is not an ultimate subject, since it can itself be predicated of other things; we can say, as Othello falsely did, that Iago is full of honesty (cf. Bennett 1984: 55–6). Thus Aristotle's linguistic test divides the universe into substances and non-substances in such a way that it does justice to our intuitions about which items are genuine things, and which are not.

The second main strand in Aristotle's thought is that substances are 'substrata of change'; here Aristotle expresses a characteristically Greek preoccupation with the fact that the world in which we live is one of constant flux. As Aristotle says in the Categories: 'The most distinctive mark of substance appears to be that while remaining numerically one and the same, it is capable of admitting contrary qualities' (ch. 5, 4a). Once again Alexander the Great illustrates Aristotle's point well. Although of course he never instantiates both properties simultaneously, Alexander the baby is 2 feet tall and Alexander the general is, say, 6 feet tall, yet it is one and the same individual throughout. Similarly, the oak tree in the park was once a sapling, and further back, an acorn; yet the properties which it has as a full-grown oak are very different from the properties which it had as a sapling or an acorn.

In his philosophy Leibniz seeks to do justice to both strands in Aristotle's teaching about substance. In his critique of Descartes's metaphysics, it is arguably the first strand which is most important. Although, as we shall see, Leibniz believes that it is possible to offer a deeper analysis of the nature of individual substances, he is explicit in his endorsement of the first strand in Aristotle's account: 'It is certainly true that when several predicates are attributed to the same subject, and this subject is not attributed to any other, it is called an individual substance' (DM 8, WF 59). Here Leibniz indicates that he regards being an ultimate subject of predication as a sufficient condition for being a substance. But it is clear that being an ultimate subject of predication is also a necessary condition for being a substance, for this assumption is crucial to Leibniz's attempt to show that matter, as conceived by Descartes, is not a genuine substance. In the correspondence with Arnauld, Leibniz mounts the following powerful argument against Descartes's doctrine of extended substance:

1 No aggregate is an ultimate subject of predication.
2 Any entity whose essence is extension is an aggregate.
3 Therefore, no entity whose essence is extension is an ultimate subject of predication.

Since being an ultimate subject of predication is a necessary condition of being a substance, it follows that no entity whose essence is extension is a substance. Thus Cartesian bodies cannot be genuine substances.

The argument is intriguing, but its premises are in need of clarification and support. When Leibniz speaks of aggregates, it is clear that the paradigm examples are things like armies and navies; armies are composed of soldiers and navies are composed of sailors. We may wonder, then, why an army fails the test of being an ultimate subject of predication. An army of course is as much a subject of predication as honesty; we can say, for example, that the Fifth Army fought bravely. Leibniz's explanation of why an army is not an ultimate subject of predication is found in a letter to Arnauld: 'it would seem . . . that what constitutes the essence of a being by aggregation is only the way of being of the things that make it up; for example, what makes the essence of an army is just the way of being of the men who make it up' (WF 124). Leibniz's point is that statements about armies can be fully analysed at least in principle in terms of other statements about the individual soldiers and their relations (Sleigh 1990: 123).

The second premise of the argument is also in need of clarification and defence. No one could deny that an army or a flock of sheep is an aggregate, but it is not similarly obvious that a block of marble, as conceived by the Cartesians, is an aggregate. Leibniz does not dispute the point that a block of marble is more tightly bonded than a flock of sheep, but he does wish to draw out the troublesome consequences of the fact that any Cartesian body is composed of other bodies (Bennett 1984: 58). Now these bodies are themselves entities whose essence is constituted by extension; so they are in turn aggregates which are composed of bodies and so on *ad infinitum*; nowhere in the Cartesian theory of the physical world does one come to entities which are not themselves aggregates. Now, for Leibniz, it is of the nature of aggregates that they presuppose true unities (WF 123); thus the Cartesians have a faulty understanding of the nature of aggregates. But for the purposes of understanding the present argument the important point is that any Cartesian body is an aggregate.

This argument is important, for it shows that Leibniz can draw on traditional resources in order to refute the Cartesian doctrine of extended substance. Some readers have been inclined to doubt that Leibniz has such resources available to him. Arnauld, for instance, supposed that Leibniz is conjuring a new definition of 'substance' out of thin air. Rightly noticing Leibniz's frequent insistence that any genuine substance is a true unity, and not a mere aggregate, Arnauld charges Leibniz with introducing a stipulative definition of 'substance' as 'that which has a true unity' in place of the traditional one deriving from Aristotle (WF 120). Arnauld believes, in other words, that Leibniz is seeking to refute the Cartesian doctrine of extended substance by means of the following argument:

1 Any entity whose essence is extension lacks genuine unity.
2 Any entity which lacks genuine unity is not a substance (by a stipulative definition of 'substance' as 'that which has true unity').
3 Therefore, any entity whose essence is extension is not a substance.

Leibniz's reply to Arnauld's criticism is highly instructive. Leibniz firmly denies that he is simply defining 'substance' as 'that which has true unity'. Nonetheless, he does recognize an equivalence between being a genuine unity and being an ultimate subject of predication; as Leibniz tells Arnauld:

> To cut the point short, I hold as an axiom the following proposition which is a statement of identity which varies only in the placing of the emphasis: nothing is truly *one* being if it is not truly one *being*. It has always been held that *one* and *being* are reciprocal things.
>
> (WF 124)

Thus Leibniz accepts the second premise of the argument, but he denies that it is true by virtue of a stipulative definition of the term 'substance'.

ACTIVITY: THE CRITIQUE OF OCCASIONALISM

The arguments which we have examined so far are directed against Descartes and Cartesian philosophy in general. Around the time of the *Discourse on Metaphysics* Leibniz is also concerned to argue against a highly unorthodox version of Cartesianism which was influential in his own age; this is the doctrine of occasionalism which is above all associated with the name of Malebranche. As a form of Cartesian philosophy, occasionalism, at least in its Malebranchean version, thus inherits the difficulties inherent in Descartes's notion of extended substance, but in Leibniz's eyes it is also subject to more specific difficulties of its own.

Occasionalism is a doctrine which, at least until recently, has tended to have a bad press in the English-speaking world; it has been unfairly represented as merely an ad hoc solution to the mind–body problem which Descartes is supposed to have bequeathed his successors. In fact, however, occasionalism is a doctrine of some power and sophistication which is also of wholly general application; it maintains that no created substance – that is, no body and no finite mind – can be a genuine cause. Rather, God alone is the one true cause who exercises his causal power on the occasion of events in the created world. To say this, as we shall see, is not to say that God intervenes in time to move one billiard ball when it collides with another or to raise my arm when I decide to scratch my nose; it is rather to say that from all eternity God has laid down laws of physics and of mind–body union (psycho-physical laws) in accordance with which creatures behave as they do. The arguments for occasionalism are varied and ingenious, and we cannot survey them here; but it is important to notice that at least one argument has clearly Cartesian roots: it consists in drawing out the consequences of the Cartesian conception of matter as a purely passive substance devoid of intrinsic force.[1]

From the time of his days in Paris, Leibniz found much to admire in the doctrine of occasionalism; he was particularly sympathetic towards the thesis that there can be no genuine causal interaction between minds and bodies as conceived by Descartes. In an early letter to Malebranche Leibniz writes: 'I am entirely of your opinion concerning the impossibility of conceiving that a substance which has nothing but extension, without thought, can act upon a substance which has nothing but thought, without extension' (L 209). But Leibniz could never reconcile himself to the core thesis of occasionalism that created substances are devoid of genuine causal powers; for Leibniz, it is of the very essence of substances to be sources of activity.

In a characteristic way, Leibniz criticizes occasionalism in many different places in his writings, and he does not always clearly mark the distinctions between his various criticisms. But his principal objections to the doctrine seem to be three. One objection is that, as a proposed solution to the mind–body problem, occasionalism really fares no better than Descartes's interactionist thesis, for 'it does not save the disturbance of the laws of nature' (H 157). Leibniz's point, then, is that occasionalism, like its Cartesian ancestor, violates the principle of the conservation of momentum, for it implies that when I raise my arm, a change of momentum occurs which is not counterbalanced elsewhere in the physical system. More generally, occasionalism violates a metaphysical principle to which Leibniz, like Spinoza, is deeply committed; this is the rather modern-sounding principle that the physical realm is causally closed; that is, every physical event has exclusively physical causes. Occasionalism, by contrast, maintains that some physical events like the movement of my arm when I will to raise it have mental events, such as volitions, at least as their occasional causes.

The first objection targets occasionalism simply as a proposed solution to the mind–body problem. A second objection is of more general application. The trouble with occasionalism is that it introduces perpetual miracles into the world, and that it is contrary to the divine wisdom to act in this way. Bayle, with his characteristic intelligence, voices a sense of puzzlement at this objection which will be shared by readers with at least a cursory knowledge of occasionalist teachings. Although Bayle focuses on the mind–body problem, he could just as well have drawn his examples from apparent interaction between bodies:

The reason why this clever man [Leibniz] finds the Cartesian [i.e. Malebranchean] system not to his taste seems to me to be based on a false supposition; it cannot be said that the system of occasional causes, with its reciprocal dependence of body and soul, makes the actions of God into the miraculous interventions of a *deus ex*

machina. For since God intervenes between them only according to
general laws, in doing so he never acts extraordinarily.

(WF 197)

In other words, Leibniz's objection seems to miss the mark, for
occasionalists such as Malebranche recognize that God acts through
general laws which are his general volitions. If a miracle is defined
as a violation of a law of nature, and if, according to occasionalism,
God's activity in the world is governed by laws, it cannot be correct
to object, as Leibniz does, that occasionalism introduces perpetual
miracles.

Leibniz's reply to Bayle's challenge is instructive, and comes in
several stages. First, he insists on defining a miracle, not as a violation
of a law of nature, but rather as an event which exceeds the causal
powers of creatures (WF 205). But, according to occasionalism,
creatures have no genuine causal powers of their own; thus all
events exceed their causal powers. It trivially follows, then, that for
occasionalism all events must be miraculous. Here Leibniz may
seem to be merely arguing past the occasionalists, for it is clear that
they will not accept the Leibnizian definition of 'miracle'; indeed,
for Malebranche, a miracle is an event which is produced by one of
God's particular volitions. Leibniz's second reply to Bayle cuts
deeper. Leibniz is prepared to concede that occasionalists recognize
the existence of regularities in nature, but he insists that such regularities are not sufficient to constitute genuine laws; for genuine
laws must be based on the natures – that is, the causal powers – of
creatures, and for occasionalists creatures have no natures in this
sense (WF 205). Even here Leibniz is in some danger of overplay-
ing his hand, for he complains that the divinely ordained regularities which occasionalists call laws are simply arbitrary. It is true
that, for Malebranche, the regularities which God ordains are not
grounded in the natures of things, but it does not follow that they
are arbitrary in the sense that God has no reason for choosing them.
On the contrary, Malebranche has a story to tell here which is very

much like Leibniz's own; God is guided in his choice of laws by considerations of what is best or most fitting. Despite this mistake on his part, Leibniz does at least succeed in isolating a central difference between himself and the occasionalists. For the occasionalists such as Malebranche scientific explanation is in terms of laws in the sense of regularities; for Leibniz, by contrast, scientific explanation is ultimately in terms of causal powers or forces. Here again Leibniz reveals his fidelity to the Aristotelian tradition.

Leibniz's final objection to occasionalism is that it leads to the Spinozistic heresy that God is the only substance. According to Leibniz, it is of the very essence of substances to be bearers of genuine causal powers; thus, on occasionalist teaching no created being can be properly regarded as a substance, since they are all devoid of such powers. Now, according to a shared ontology, everything is either a substance or a mode; since they are not substances, minds and bodies must be regarded by the occasionalists as modes of the one being which they do recognize as causally active and thus a genuine substance, namely God:

> This again shows that the doctrine of occasional causes which some defend can lead to dangerous consequences . . . though these consequences are doubtless not intended by its very learned defenders. Far from increasing the glory of God by removing the idol of nature, this doctrine seems, with Spinoza, to make God into the very nature itself of things, and to reduce created things to mere modifications of a single divine substance. For that which does not act, which has no active force, which is robbed of any distinguishing characteristic, and finally of all reason and ground of permanence, can in no way be a substance.
>
> (WF 221)

Leibniz is clear, then, that he is not charging Malebranche with crypto-Spinozism; he is simply pointing out that his doctrine of occasionalism, in conjunction with other commitments, entails the thesis that God is the only substance.

There is no record of any reply to this objection, either by committed occasionalists or fair-minded neutral parties such as Bayle. But it is interesting to note that occasionalists could easily have met this objection in the same spirit in which Arnauld responded to Leibniz's earlier charge that Cartesian bodies, by virtue of lacking any internal principle of unity, could not be genuine substances. It would be natural for an occasionalist to respond that once again Leibniz is simply introducing a stipulative definition of 'substance'; instead of defining it in the traditional manner as an ultimate subject of predication or that which is neither mode nor state, he is defining it as 'that which is genuinely active'. Indeed, in support of this charge it can be noted that on occasion Leibniz does appear to define 'substance' as a being capable of action (WF 258). But if Leibniz sometimes seems to define 'substance' in these terms, it is clear that in his view he also has the resources to respond to this criticism in the same way he did to Arnauld: that is, he is not introducing a new-fangled definition of his own; rather, he is drawing out the consequences of a more traditional definition. To understand more fully how this reply would go, we must turn to the positive arguments of the *Discourse on Metaphysics*.

THE LOGICIST STRATEGY

We saw in a previous chapter that the refutation of occasionalism and allied doctrines provided the stimulus for Leibniz's first mature statement of his positive case for his central metaphysical doctrines. In a section heading of the *Discourse on Metaphysics* Leibniz announces that, in order to distinguish the actions of God from those of creatures, it is necessary to explain the nature of an individual substance (DM 8, WF 59); that is, a proper understanding of this issue is essential in order to show the falsity of the occasionalist thesis that there is strictly no division of causal labour between God and creatures, and that everything is done by God. Now, as we have seen, in this section Leibniz expresses his approval of the Aristotelian thesis that substances are ultimate subjects of predication. But in the next breath he goes on to indicate that the Aristotelian analysis does not go deep enough: 'But that is not enough, and such an explanation is merely nominal'. Leibniz then states in what this deeper analysis consists:

> It is necessary, therefore, to consider what it is to be truly attributed to a certain subject. Now it is obvious that all true predication has some foundation in the nature of things, and when a proposition is not identical, that is to say, when the predicate is not expressly included in the subject, it must be virtually included in it. This is what philosophers call *in-esse*, and they say that the predicate *is in* the subject. So the subject term must always involve that of the predicate, in such a way that anyone who understood the subject notion perfectly would also see that the predicate belongs to it. This being so, we can say that the nature of an individual substance or of a complete being is to have a notion so complete that it is sufficient to include, and to allow the deduction of, all the predicates of the subject to which that notion is attributed.
>
> (DM 8, WF 59)

In the following sections of the *Discourse* Leibniz develops a distinctive strategy of argument which consists in drawing out the consequences of this last thesis so that the falsity of occasionalism is exposed.

If Leibniz is to refute occasionalism without appealing to a stipulative definition of 'substance', he must be in a position to say that the definition on which he draws is a traditional one. Leibniz seems to believe that he is doing just that, for he appears to regard the claim that individuals have complete concepts as offering a deeper analysis of Aristotle's definition of substance rather than a replacement for it. In one way Leibniz's claim that he is drawing on traditional resources is surprising, for it is clear that his analysis of the nature of individual substances is derived from a theory of truth, and this theory of truth is anything but traditional. The traditional theory of truth is surely a version of the correspondence theory; that is, truth consists in a relation of correspondence between propositions and states of affairs in the world. It is this theory that Aristotle seems to have had in mind when he defined truth as saying of what is that it is, and of what is not that it is not (*Metaphysics* 1011 b 27). For Leibniz, by contrast, truth consists not in a relation between propositions and states of affairs in the world but in a relation of containment between concepts. Although Leibniz hints at this theory of truth in Section 8 of the *Discourse on Metaphysics*, he states it best in the subsequent exchange of letters with Arnauld. 'In all true affirmative propositions, necessary or contingent, universal or singular, the notion of the predicate is always in some way included in that of the subject . . . – or I do not know what truth is' (WF 111–12). Let us call this 'the concept-containment theory of truth'.

Leibniz's concept-containment theory of truth is perhaps best understood as a bold generalization of a theory which seems natural in the case of universal truths. Consider the proposition: 'Gold is a metal'. It is plausible to say that what makes this proposition true is the fact that the concept expressed by the predicate term is contained in the concept expressed by the subject term; in other words, an analysis of the concept of gold reveals that the concept of metal is one of the constituent concepts. (Analysis is to be understood here in terms of replacing a given term by its definitional equivalent.) Leibniz now wishes to extend this theory so that it applies to singular propositions such as 'Julius Caesar crossed the Rubicon'. For Leibniz, a proper name is not an arbitrary label; like a general term, such as 'gold', it expresses a concept. Thus the proposition: 'Julius Caesar crossed the Rubicon' is true because the concept expressed by the predicate 'crossed the Rubicon' is contained in the subject concept expressed by the name 'Julius Caesar'. From the concept-containment theory of truth Leibniz's thesis that individual substances have complete concepts follows as a special case; by virtue of the general theory, all the predicates which are true of an individual substance are contained in its complete concept. (As we shall see in Chapter 5, this poses special, intractable problems for Leibniz's attempt to find room for contingent propositions in his philosophy.)

In subsequent sections of the *Discourse* the theory that individual substances have complete concepts not only serves as a springboard for exposing the falsity of occasionalism; it also serves as a basis for deriving some of the central doctrines of Leibniz's metaphysics. It is not surprising, then, that some commentators have spoken of Leibniz's strategy of deriving his metaphysics from his logic; that is, Leibniz seeks to derive his main doctrines about the properties of substances and their relations from his concept-containment theory of truth (via the thesis that substances have complete concepts). Whether, as Louis Couturat thought, this 'logicist strategy', as we may call it, is the key to Leibniz's metaphysical thought as a whole may be strongly disputed, but there is little doubt that it can be safely attributed to Leibniz on the basis of the *Discourse on Metaphysics*. It is possible to come up with slightly different lists of the doctrines that are so derived, but there are five major doctrines which are generally included:

1 The Identity of Indiscernibles: there cannot be two substances which are exactly alike.
2 The expression thesis: every substance expresses or mirrors the whole universe.
3 The denial of causal interaction between (created) substances.
4 Every substance is the causal source of all its (non-initial) states.
5 The hypothesis of concomitance (or what is later termed by Leibniz 'the pre-established harmony'): the states of substances are harmonized by God so that they give the appearance of causal interaction (the phrase 'pre-established harmony' is also sometimes used by Leibniz and commentators to refer to the conjunction of theses 3–5).

The relation of these doctrines to Leibniz's logic is more problematic in some cases than in others. In the case of (at least one version of) the Identity of Indiscernibles, the derivation is relatively straightforward. The complete concept of an individual substance is presumably a concept under which no more than one individual can fall. Thus if there were two substances exactly alike, there would be two substances with the same complete concept, which is impossible. It should be noted, however, that the complete concept theory seems to provide a basis only for a weak version of the Identity of Indiscernibles; for all the argument so far shows, the principle would be satisfied by two substances which differed solely in terms of their spatial relationships. However, for reasons which will become clearer, Leibniz in fact subscribes to a stronger version of the Identity of Indiscernibles to the effect that two substances cannot be exactly alike in terms of their intrinsic (i.e. non-relational) properties.

Leibniz's most popular statements about the Identity of Indiscernibles can be unhelpful. For example, Leibniz sometimes tries to provide a posteriori support for the principle by means of an anecdote; he tells how a courtier was challenged to find two leaves exactly alike, and how after a while he abandoned the search as fruitless (L 687). Picturesque as it is, this story is doubly misleading. First, insofar as it follows from the complete concept theory, the Identity of Indiscernibles is a thesis about substances. Strictly speaking, for Leibniz, as we shall see, dead leaves are not substances but at most aggregates of substances. Second, and more importantly, the Identity of Indiscernibles is not an empirical generalization but a necessary truth. The thesis is not that as a matter of contingent fact there are no two substances exactly alike, but that there could not be two such substances.

More serious problems are presented by the other main metaphysical theses 2–5. Different commentators tend to locate the main difficulties in different places, but they agree in the general diagnosis: Leibniz tends to slide from what is true at the level of concepts (in the mind of God) to what is true at the level of substances in the world. Leibniz may have been unwittingly encouraged in this tendency by the imprecision of his terminology; as used by Leibniz, terms such as 'subject' and 'predicate' are dangerously ambiguous. The word 'subject' for example is ambiguous between subject concept and the substance in the world which instantiates this concept; *mutatis mutandis* the word 'predicate' is similarly ambiguous. Bearing this ambiguity in mind, in the remainder of this section we shall, then, examine the problems presented by 2–4.

Despite the unusual terminology, on one level at least the expression thesis is straightforward. Leibniz was pressed by Arnauld as to what he meant by 'expression' and in reply he made clear that it was a technical term which he explained as follows: 'one thing *expresses* another (in my language) when there is a constant and ordered relation between what can be asserted of the one and what can be asserted of the other' (P 71). When Leibniz says that every substance expresses the whole universe, at least part of what he wants to say is that, given a complete knowledge of the concept of any individual substance, say Alexander, it is possible in principle to read off the predicates (i. e. the predicate-concepts) of every other substance. We can see that Leibniz must hold this by virtue of the fact that there are relational truths linking Alexander to everything else in the universe. It is a fact about Alexander, for example, that he was born so many years before George W. Bush became President of the United States of America. It follows, then, that all such relational predicates must be contained in the complete concept of Alexander, and so on for every other substance. Thus if one really knew the complete concept of Alexander, one would *ipso facto* also know everything there was to be known about the universe.

When Leibniz says every substance expresses the universe, he also wants to assert a more controversial and more metaphysical thesis. Leibniz claims that

> in the soul of Alexander there are for all time remnants of
> everything that has happened to him and marks of everything
> that will happen to him – and even traces of everything that happens

in the universe, although it is only God who can recognize
them all.

(DM 8, WF 60)

But of course it is not easy to see how from the fact that the concept
of Alexander timelessly includes the predicate of dying in 323 BCE,
it follows that there must be a mark of the event in Alexander's soul
before it happens. It has been suggested that Leibniz is thinking
along the following lines. Since it is a timeless fact about Alexander
that he dies in 323 BCE, throughout his history there must be
something about Alexander himself by virtue of which the proposition is true; there must be some persistent structural modification of Alexander corresponding to the fact of his dying. This
modification remains quiescent until the event when it bursts into
activity; subsequently it reverts to a state of quiescence (Broad ·
1975: 24).

Commentators have similarly stressed the difficulty of seeing
how theses 3 and 4 follow from Leibniz's logic. From the fact
that every individual substance has a complete concept Leibniz
infers that all the states of a substance are consequences of that
concept; from this he concludes, apparently, that there is no causal
interaction between created substances. But this argument seems
fallacious. Consider the proposition: 'Julius Caesar was killed by
Brutus and Cassius'. Here a causal relational predicate 'killed by
Brutus and Cassius' is truly ascribed to Caesar. This causal predicate
must be contained in the concept of Julius Caesar. But then it clearly
does not follow from the complete concept theory that there is no
causal interaction between created substances. Nor does it help
matters to point out that, though in the *Discourse*, Leibniz derives 4
from 3, he sometimes reverses the order of derivation. For if it is
difficult to see how 3 follows from the complete concept theory, it
is no less difficult to see how 4 follows from that theory.

One way of dealing with these problems is to suppose that the
derivation of thesis 3 from Leibniz's logic is mediated by a doctrine

that we have not so far discussed; this is the doctrine that 'there are no purely extrinsic denominations', which is itself a consequence of the 'marks and traces' version of the expression thesis (AG 32). The claim that there are no purely extrinsic denominations is one of Leibniz's more obscure doctrines, but is generally taken to assert the reducibility of relations; in other words, all relational truths about individual substances can be deduced from non-relational truths about those substances. For example, the relational proposition 'Smith is taller than Jones' is reducible in the sense that it can be derived from the non-relational propositions 'Smith is 6 feet tall' and 'Jones is 5 feet 10 inches tall'. Thus by virtue of the thesis that there are no purely extrinsic denominations, Leibniz would claim that the proposition 'Julius Caesar was killed by Brutus and Cassius' is derivable from propositions which ascribe only non-relational predicates to those individuals. But this approach does not really solve the problem. The thesis that there are no purely extrinsic denominations asserts at most that relational propositions are theoretically dispensable; it does not assert that such propositions are actually false. But it seems that it is the stronger thesis which is required if the claim that there are no purely extrinsic denominations is to provide a basis for 3; for Leibniz is committed by 3 to saying that propositions which assert causal relations between created substances are all of them, strictly speaking, false.

An alternative way of dealing with these problems is to reinterpret Leibniz's notion of a complete concept. One writer, in particular, has been impressed by those passages in which Leibniz tells Arnauld that the complete concept of an individual contains the laws of its world (Loeb 1981: 286). On this basis it has been suggested that a Leibnizian complete concept is constituted by a combination of basic (i.e. non-relational) predicates and laws – the laws of the universe. These laws are taken to include a law of succession for the states of the substance; such a law would imply that a substance's states causally depend only on itself. On this interpretation, then, there is no danger that the complete concept of Julius

Caesar, say, will contain causal predicates such as being killed by Brutus and Cassius; such a predicate must be excluded because it suggests of course that a state of Julius Caesar causally depends on other created substances. We may still wonder, however, whether this interpretation can do justice to the expression thesis, given that relational predicates are excluded from complete concepts. But here again the crucial point is taken to be that laws are built into complete concepts. The idea is that the concept of an individual substance contains non-causal laws of co-existence with other substances; from this it follows, as the expression thesis requires, that the predicates of all other substances can be deduced from the concept of a given substance. It is in this sense, then, that 'every individual substance contains in its perfect notion the entire universe' (AG 32). This interpretation is attractive, for it frees Leibniz's argument from its otherwise obvious invalidity. But as its proponent acknowledges, it does so at a heavy price; a complete concept turns out not to be a purely logical notion, for Leibniz has packed some of his metaphysics into it. Thus the difficulty now is not that Leibniz's argument involves a non sequitur but that it is effectively question-begging.

The weaknesses of such arguments have led some readers (such as Ayers) to question whether Leibniz does really seek to derive his metaphysical doctrines from his logic (Ayers 1978: 45). It has been suggested that Leibniz rather tailors his logic (i.e. his theory of truth) to a metaphysics to which he is independently attracted; perhaps Leibniz is in the grip of the time-honoured assumption that the structure of language mirrors the structure of reality. Yet it is clear that in a number of places Leibniz does employ the language of derivation; he speaks of 'several considerable paradoxes' (i.e. the central doctrines of his metaphysics) as following from the thesis that individual substances have complete concepts (DM 9, WF 60). Perhaps Leibniz himself may have become aware of problems with the logicist strategy, for it disappears from his later public presentations of his system.

Despite the apparent weaknesses of his arguments, it is easy to see why the logicist strategy must have appealed to Leibniz, for it seems to promise a way of achieving two important goals. In the first place, by means of this strategy Leibniz aims to refute the doctrine of occasionalism by showing that activity is indeed of the essence of substance in general. He also aims to extend and deepen our understanding of the way in which all created substances are mirrors of God. Created substances are not merely active in the sense of possessing the kind of causal powers which occasionalists deny them; they are also endowed with a degree of causal self-sufficiency which is as great as possible consistent with their status as creatures; they are thus mirrors of the divine perfection of omnipotence. Further, all substances express the universe according to their point of view; they thus mirror the divine perfection of omniscience.

CAUSALITY AND CREATION

One weakness of the logicist strategy is that it leaves at least one of Leibniz's doctrines concerning causality shrouded in mystery. Leibniz is committed not merely to the spontaneity thesis and to the denial of interaction between created substances, but to the further thesis that God acts causally on such substances. The logicist strategy provides no grounds for this last thesis, for the strategy depends on a theory of truth which is wholly general; it applies no less to true propositions about God than to true propositions about finite substances. The strategy is thus incapable of furnishing a basis for restricting the denial of causal interaction to the realm of created substances. From the point of view of the logicist thesis this restriction must appear wholly unprincipled and ad hoc. To say that God (alone) can act on created substances may be good theology, but it can receive no support from the theory of truth.

To see why Leibniz is not simply making an ad hoc exception in the case of God, it is necessary to look beyond the logicist strategy, and to understand what it is that Leibniz is attacking.[2] When Leibniz

denies that created substances can causally interact, he has a very
specific model of causality in mind: this is the 'influx' model which
Leibniz, rightly or wrongly, associates with the Scholastics such as
Suarez. (Although, as we have seen, Leibniz believed that there were
nuggets of gold in Scholastic thought, he also believed that there
was much dross as well.) According to the influx model, causal
transactions between substances in the world are understood as
involving a process of contagion, as it were; when substance A
causes a change of state in substance B, A infects B with one of its
properties, or strictly speaking, property-instances (tropes). Thus
when the kettle boils, the gas infects the water inside the kettle with
its own 'individual accident' of heat, in Leibniz's terms. In other
words, there is something which literally 'flows in' from substance
A to substance B; hence the term 'influx'. For Leibniz, such a model
of causality is deeply incoherent, for it involves the metaphysical
fiction that accidents can become detached from their own substances and wander over to other substances. As Leibniz says, 'no
created substance exerts a metaphysical action or influx on any
other thing . . . one cannot explain how something can pass from
one thing into the substance of another' (AG 33).

Leibniz sometimes speaks of God's action on creatures in terms
of influx or at least influence, but it is abundantly clear that he does
not conceive of divine causality in terms of the model described
above. For one thing, the process of influx is understood in terms of
one substance causing a change of state in another substance which
is already in existence; in other words, this second substance is not
supposed to depend causally for its existence on the first. By contrast, when God, for Leibniz, acts causally on creatures, he does not
send out causal influence into things which are independent of him
for their existence; rather, he acts on substances by conserving
them, and conservation, for Leibniz, is what it is for Descartes: it is
a process of continuous creation. In the 'New System', for instance,
Leibniz writes that 'all things, with all their reality, are continually
produced by the power of God' (WF 150). When Leibniz affirms

that God acts on creatures he is not making an ad hoc and unprincipled exception to his denial of causal interaction between substances, for what he ascribes to God is a form of action which is quite different from what he denies in the case of creatures. (In logical terminology, 'influx' or 'influence' is not a univocal term with respect to God and creatures.)

Divine causality, then, takes the form of conservation or continuous creation; it does not involve influx in the objectionable sense of the transfer of accidents from one substance to another. This distinction proves helpful in another way. Some readers have wondered whether Leibniz can consistently hold intrasubstantial causality (i.e. causality within the substance), while denying causal interaction between substances. The objection is that intrasubstantial causality might succumb to the same difficulties that infect the latter. We are now in a position to see how Leibniz would respond to this objection. For Leibniz has given arguments which seek to establish that all created substances are mirrors of God, and he wishes to extend this thesis to the causality of created substances; that is, such causality is modelled on the conserving and creative activity of God. Influx between substances is a metaphysical fiction, but for Leibniz, God's creative activity is not only possible but actual. There is thus strong reason to believe that any causality that is modelled on divine creative activity is also not only possible but actual.

The claim that the causality of creatures is modelled on divine creation may be greeted with some surprise. But it is important to remember what is at issue here. The claim is not that created substances are strictly creators (they do not for instance create *ex nihilo*); it is rather that their causality provides an analogy to divine creation. Created substances are not God, but they are mirrors of God. In fact, the analogy proves surprisingly strong. In the first place, as we have seen, substances cause new states in themselves by activating a disposition; a mark of a future state which was latent becomes actual. In a similar way when God creates the world he activates a disposition; God creates by activating a possible world, that is, a world which exists potentially in his intellect. Further, as we shall see in more detail in subsequent chapters, created substances are always striving to bring about what seems to them to be good. In a similar way God's creation is directed towards the good, for he creates the *best* of all possible worlds.

THE PROBLEM OF ONTOLOGY

In the first writings of his philosophical maturity, then, Leibniz is clear about the conditions for being a created substance: substances are genuine unities; they are genuinely active to the extent of being as causally self-sufficient as is consistent with their status as creatures; they express the whole universe, and thus reflect the divine perfection of omniscience. In all these ways substances are mirrors of God. Moreover, Leibniz is clear that they all satisfy the demands of the principle of the Identity of Indiscernibles. These themes are unambiguously present in these works, and are never abandoned or recanted by Leibniz in any of his subsequent writings. However, although he is clear about the conditions for substantiality, he is much less clear at this stage about what items in the world satisfy these conditions. In fact, it is striking that in the *Discourse on Metaphysics* Leibniz has not made up his mind on the issue whether any bodies qualify as substances. Leibniz's hesitation on this issue is evident in the drafts of the work:

> If bodies are substances their nature cannot possibly consist only in size, shape, and motion; there must be something else.
>
> (DM 9, WF 60)

> I believe that anyone who thinks about the nature of substance . . . will find [either that in metaphysical strictness bodies are not substances (as indeed was the view of the Platonists), or] that the whole nature of body does not consist solely in extension, that is to say, in size, shape, and motion.
>
> (DM 12, WF 63)

{Something I don't attempt to decide is whether, in metaphysical strictness, bodies are substances, or whether, like the rainbow, they are only *true* phenomena, and consequently whether there are substances, souls or substantial forms which are not intelligent.}

(DM 34, WF 86)

In the writings of the middle period Leibniz, it seems, is torn between the claims of two main theories about what items are truly substantial.[3]

One option that Leibniz seriously entertains at this stage is rather surprising. In the drafts of the *Discourse on Metaphysics* Leibniz is attracted by the idea that all substances, the basic building-blocks of the universe, are of the nature of minds or spirits. Thus Leibniz writes that minds 'are either the only substances there are in the world – if bodies are only true phenomena – or else at least they are the most perfect' (DM 35, WF 87). In other words, Leibniz was prepared to entertain a form of idealism which Berkeley was later to adopt wholeheartedly: the only true created things are minds, and bodies are merely phenomena or appearances. On this view, in perceiving the world of bodies each of us would, as it were, be really engaged in watching a private film.

One advantage of this theory is obvious; it does clear justice to the thesis that all substances are mirrors of God. For if all substances are minds or spirits, then they are all endowed with high-level cognitive capacities (perfections); they have reason, self-consciousness and a capacity for knowing the eternal truths of logic and mathematics. Moreover, all minds or spirits are at least in some degree endowed with virtues, and thus mirror the moral perfections of God. And of course there is scriptural warrant for the thesis; according to the Book of Genesis, God made man in his own image. For Leibniz, the class of created minds is not limited to human minds, but the Genesis text could be taken to apply with no less warrant to superior spirits.

But if the advantages of this theory are obvious, its disadvantages are no less so. At this stage such an uncompromising form of

idealism seemed needlessly paradoxical to Leibniz; certainly we
know that Berkeley encountered incredulity when he maintained
that the only genuine things are spirits, and that bodies are purely
mind-dependent. Further, at this stage Leibniz may not have seen a
way of giving a plausible account of the status of bodies within
such an ontology; a form of idealism which restricts substances to
minds encounters notorious difficulties in accommodating our
intuitions about bodies – for instance, that they have a continued
existence and that they are public objects which can be perceived
by different observers. More speculatively, Leibniz may have seen
no way of reconciling such an ontology with his attempt to provide
metaphysical foundations for physics. For as we know, Leibniz
wished to say that the physical forces of bodies are grounded in the
forces of substances, but it is hard, perhaps impossible, to make
sense of this claim if the only substances are minds or spirits.

It is not surprising, then, that by the time of the correspondence
with Arnauld, Leibniz no longer seems to entertain this option;
here he seems more attracted by an ontology of corporeal substances which has its roots in Aristotle's metaphysics. According to
this thesis in its purest form, it is living organisms which are the
fundamental building-blocks of the universe; every body is either
itself an organism or an aggregate of organisms. Such living bodies,
unlike inanimate objects – for example, tables, chairs, and computers
– satisfy the unity requirement for substances by virtue of possessing a soul or principle of life which animates them. The body,
considered in abstraction from the soul, is not a substance but an
aggregate of smaller corporeal substances which are themselves
informed by a soul; and these smaller corporeal substances in turn
have bodies which are aggregates of still smaller corporeal substances, and so on to infinity. At least according to the purest version of the theory, the soul is not a substance in its own right, but a
substantial form which organizes the matter of the body: 'Moreover, the soul, properly and accurately speaking, is not a substance
but a substantial form existing in substance, the first act, the first

active faculty' (AG 105). More typically, however, Leibniz is prepared to say that the soul is a genuine substance in its own right. In
that case, strictly speaking, there are two kinds of substances –
simple (souls) and corporeal or composite (organisms) – but there
is no suggestion that organisms are reducible to souls. Thus the
theory is not a form of idealism.

The theory of corporeal substances has some obvious attractions
which are quite different from those of the idealist theory of spirits.
For one thing, the theory maintains a real continuity with the
teachings of the Aristotelian–Scholastic tradition; for Aristotle, at
least in the *Metaphysics*, it is organisms which are the paradigm cases
of substances. Yet, equally, the theory is not simply an antiquarian
relic, for it could claim at least some empirical support from the
new science. The recent invention of the microscope had revealed a
mass of tiny living creatures where none are visible to the naked
eye. The theory of corporeal substances thus satisfied Leibniz's
characteristic desire to reconcile the teachings of the Ancients and
the Moderns.

More importantly, the theory of corporeal substances has significant philosophical strengths. It is plausible to maintain that if any
bodies satisfy the unity requirement for substances, then organisms
are the best candidates (Broad 1975: 74). Such bodies do indeed
seem to be endowed with intrinsic, non-conventional unity, and it
seems correct to locate the source of this unity, as Leibniz does, in
the soul or principle of life. We can see this most clearly in the case
of a human being. When I am engaged in writing, my hand is
closer to the paper than it is to my foot, but it is natural to say that
my hand and my foot belong together as parts of a genuine unified
whole in a way that my hand and the paper do not; this would
remain the case even if my hand and the paper were glued together
so that they were in permanent contact. I can, for example, feel pain
in my hand and my foot, but I cannot feel pain in the paper on
which I write. The presence of the soul seems to provide a wholly
non-conventional basis for grouping certain physical parts together.

Yet the theory is also subject to objections and difficulties some of which were raised by Arnauld. Arnauld was never made aware of Leibniz's flirtation with an idealist ontology of spirits, but he was given the opportunity to criticize Leibniz's doctrine of corporeal substances, and as a good Cartesian he made some familiar objections to the doctrine. The postulation of souls is superfluous for the purpose of explaining animal behaviour which, according to Descartes's teaching, can be fully explained in mechanical terms (WF 115). Moreover, the doctrine of animal souls raises embarrassing difficulties concerning the status of such souls after the destruction of their bodies; as Descartes had said, it seems more probable that gnats and caterpillars are mere machines than that they are endowed with immaterial, and hence immortal, souls (CSMK 366).

More tellingly perhaps, Arnauld raised an internal difficulty for Leibniz's doctrine of corporeal substances. It is Leibniz's contention that the unity of a substance entails its indivisibility (see DM 9, WF 60); thus he is committed to the thesis that any organism is in some sense indivisible. Arnauld, however, challenges the thesis that organisms enjoy any kind of privileged status among bodies in this respect; he cites the case of a worm, both parts of which, when cut in two, continue to move as before (WF 121). Arnauld's serious philosophical point here is that the chopping up of the worm seems in principle no different from the chopping up of a table; in both cases we are simply left with parts of the original body. In reply Leibniz seeks to reconcile the facts about the case of the worm with his thesis that animals are genuine substances, and hence endowed with both unity and indivisibility. From the fact that both parts of the worm continue to move after its body has been chopped in half, it does not follow that there are either two souls or none. The soul may continue to animate one of the parts, and it is with this 'part' that the worm is strictly to be identified. Although of course it suffers a loss of matter, the worm survives the act of chopping intact; unlike the table it is not decomposed into two parts neither of which has the character of the original entity. There is a sense, then, in which the worm is indivisible, and the table is not.

Leibniz thought he could answer Arnauld's objections to the doctrine of corporeal substance, but he may have been more troubled by a different aspect of the doctrine. We have seen that Leibniz is in search of an ontology which does justice to his conviction that created substances are all mirrors of God. The idealist theory of spirits satisfies this desideratum handsomely, but it is much less clear that the doctrine of corporeal substances does so. For on this doctrine there is a radical disanalogy between God and created substances. Although they are both supposed to satisfy the unity requirement for substances, created substances in being endowed with bodies are unlike God. Perhaps for this reason Leibniz could not be truly satisfied with an ontology of corporeal substances. In any case, whatever his deepest motivations, in his final metaphysics Leibniz returns to a form of idealism. This is the famous doctrine of monads.

SUMMARY

This chapter introduces the reader to some of the great constants of Leibniz's metaphysics: substances are genuinely unified, indivisible, and active. Concentrating on the writings of his middle period, such as the *Discourse on Metaphysics*, it shows how Leibniz offers positive arguments for these and other God-like properties of substances; it thus seeks to establish the thesis that, for Leibniz, all created substances are mirrors of God. The first two sections of the chapter examine Leibniz's criticisms of two leading metaphysical systems of the time for giving inadequate accounts of the nature of substance. Leibniz criticizes Descartes's doctrine of extended substance for violating the unity requirement for being a substance. According to Leibniz, Descartes fails to take seriously Aristotle's claim that a substance is an ultimate subject of predication; Cartesian bodies are mere aggregates, not true unities, and thus cannot be such ultimate subjects. In response to Arnauld's objection that he is introducing a stipulative definition of 'substance' as that which has true unity, Leibniz protests that he is simply recognizing the traditional equivalence of unity and being. The other metaphysical system in the period which Leibniz criticizes for offering an inadequate account of substance is the doctrine of occasionalism associated with Malebranche. As an unorthodox version of Cartesianism this system inherits all the difficulties of Descartes's concept of extended substance, but it also involves specific difficulties of its own. Leibniz has three main objections to occasionalism: first, it involves a disturbance of the laws of nature which causes problems in physics; secondly, it introduces perpetual miracles, and third, and perhaps most importantly, by failing to recognize the essential activity of substances, it leads to the Spinozistic heresy that God is the only substance. In the next section we see how Leibniz advances positive arguments for his own metaphysical doctrines which imply the falsity of occasionalism. In the *Discourse on Metaphysics* Leibniz develops a line of reasoning which is sometimes called the 'logicist' strategy inasmuch as it seeks to derive metaphysical doctrines from logical considerations about the nature of truth. In particular, beginning with his distinctive concept-containment theory of truth, Leibniz argues for the Identity of Indiscernibles and for the doctrine of the pre-established harmony. Leibniz's attempt to derive his metaphysics in this way is discussed in the light of the criticism that it conflates the level of concepts in God with the level of substances in the world. Whatever the validity of such criticisms, the limitations of the logicist strategy are apparent in its inability to explain why God alone acts on created substances. However, reasons are given for believing that this doctrine is not simply an ad hoc exception to Leibniz's denial of causal interaction between substances. In the final section of the chapter it is argued that although, in his middle period, Leibniz is clear about the conditions for being a substance, he is still unclear about what items in the world satisfy these conditions; in particular, Leibniz is undecided about whether any physical objects qualify as substances. Leibniz apparently oscillates between holding that organisms are genuine substances and holding that all substances are of the nature of spirits. Thus Leibniz has not yet arrived at his final metaphysical position, the theory of monads.

FURTHER READING

C.D. Broad (1975) *Leibniz: An Introduction*, Ch. 3. (Although somewhat dated, still valuable for its clear presentation of the issues.)

L. Couturat (1972) 'On Leibniz's Metaphysics,' Frankfurt (ed.), *Leibniz: A Collection of Critical Essays*. (A classic statement of the thesis that Leibniz derives his metaphysics from his logic.)

D. Garber (1985) 'Leibniz and the Foundations of Physics: The Middle Years,' Okruhlik and Brown (eds), *The Natural Philosophy of Leibniz*. (An important article emphasizing the development of Leibniz's views of the relations between physics and metaphysics.)

N. Jolley (1998) 'Causality and Creation in Leibniz'. (Argues that for Leibniz the causality of created substances is modelled on divine creation.)

L. Loeb (1981) *From Descartes to Hume*, Ch. 7. (Examines the problems in Leibniz's arguments for pre-established harmony.)

G.H.R. Parkinson (1965) *Logic and Reality in Leibniz's Metaphysics*. (A clear and judicious assessment of the relationship between Leibniz's logic and metaphysics.)

R.C. Sleigh (1990) *Leibniz and Arnauld: A Commentary on their Correspondence*, Chs. 5–7. (A penetrating analysis of the issues in the correspondence between Leibniz and Arnauld: highly recommended for the serious student.)

C. Wilson (1989) *Leibniz's Metaphysics: A Historical and Comparative Study*, Ch. 3. (Emphasizes the different strands in Leibniz's metaphysics during his middle period.)

R.S. Woolhouse (1988) 'Leibniz and Occasionalism,' Woolhouse (ed.), *Metaphysics and Philosophy of Science in the Seventeenth and Eighteenth Centuries*. (Helpfully examines the different arguments in Leibniz's critique of occasionalism.)

Three

The Theory of Monads

Since Plato, one of the recurrent themes in western philosophy is that there is a fundamental contrast between appearance and reality. Philosophers have often insisted that though the world appears to us as one of blue skies and green grass, these appearances are systematically misleading; the ultimate nature of reality can only be grasped by turning away from the senses and consulting instead the deliverances of pure reason. This tendency to emphasize the misleading nature of appearances is already evident in Descartes, who insists that the physical world is strictly devoid of sensible qualities such as colour, odour, and taste. The tendency is far more marked in Leibniz's theory of monads, which relegates even the physical world to the status of appearances.

At first sight in his final metaphysics Leibniz seems to have moved a long way from the philosopher who sought renewed appreciation of Aristotle's theory of substance as an ultimate subject of predication. It is certainly true that Leibniz arrives at a picture of the ultimate nature of reality which is very different from Aristotle's relatively down-to-earth account. But it is equally striking that, despite the changes in his metaphysical thought, Leibniz never abandons any of the core doctrines which we examined in the previous chapter; he continues to emphasize, no less strongly than before, that substances, the ultimate building-blocks of the universe, are genuine unities and sources of activity. But if he does not abandon these doctrines, he systematically reinterprets them within the framework of the theory of monads.

THE PROPERTIES OF MONADS

Perhaps the best way of introducing the theory of monads is to begin by noticing that it is a form of atomism; as Leibniz says in the *Monadology* monads are the 'true atoms of nature' (3, WF 268). Now it is one of the constants of Leibniz's thought, as we have seen, that nothing purely material can be indivisible; thus monads cannot be like atoms as they are traditionally conceived, that is, tiny, unsplittable bodies. Nonetheless, they play the same role in Leibniz's metaphysics that atoms have traditionally played in metaphysical systems; they are the basic building-blocks of which the universe is constituted. In what has come to be regarded as one of the canonical statements of his later metaphysics Leibniz tells the Cartesian Burcher De Volder : 'Indeed, considering the matter carefully, we must say that there is nothing in things but simple substances [i.e. monads] and in them, perception and appetite' (AG 181). To say that monads are simple is to say that they are without parts, and thus immaterial; for Leibniz, anything material consists of parts. The simplicity of monads is also the foundation for their indestructibility. According to an old tradition which Leibniz accepts, destruction consists in the dissolution of a thing into its component parts; thus where there are no parts to begin with, there can be no decomposition. As Leibniz says in the *Monadology*, in the case of monads there can be no dissolution to fear (4, WF 268). Monads can begin only by a miraculous act of creation and end only by a miraculous act of annihilation.

If monads are simple, immaterial, and indestructible, then it is clear that Leibniz has arrived at an ontology in which the building-blocks of the universe share certain properties with God. Leibniz reinforces the thesis that monads, the basic entities, are mirrors of God when he tells De Volder that they are all endowed with perception and appetite, or appetition. Leibniz defines perception as the expression of the many in the one, and we shall discuss this in more detail below, but here we can note that it is in terms of the concept of perception that Leibniz explains how all monads have the God-like property of expressing the universe; they thus all contain within themselves at least a shadow of divine omniscience. Appetite or appetition is the dynamic principle by means of which a monad moves from one perceptual state to its successor. Since it involves a kind of *conatus* or striving, it may seem that appetition is in no sense a God-like property. But this would be a mistake. For it is by virtue of having appetition that simple substances are sources of activity, like God; further, appetition is always directed towards the apparent good, and thus resembles the divine activity of creation. In the case of God the apparent good always coincides with the real good; in the case of created monads, however, the apparent good and the real good often diverge.

Leibniz's final metaphysics is thus a form of idealism in the sense that the basic building-blocks of the universe are all mental or soul-like in nature; monads may be atoms, but they are spiritual atoms. This idealism allows Leibniz to do more justice to the claim that all substances are God-like than was possible within the theory of corporeal substances. Yet no less striking than the novelty of Leibniz's commitment to idealism is his determination to preserve continuity with the themes of his earlier metaphysics. The continuity in Leibniz's thought about substances is most clearly signalled perhaps in his very choice of the term 'monad' for the basic building-blocks of reality. The term 'monad' derives from the Greek word for unity; thus substances continue to be conceived as entities endowed with genuine unity.

Within the idealistic framework of the monadology Leibniz continues to advance the central doctrines of the pre-established harmony. Indeed, the theory of monads even allows Leibniz to strengthen his case for these doctrines; it allows him, in particular, to advance a new argument against the causal interaction between created substances. For the fact that monads are simple and immaterial implies that they have no physical parts which could be re-arranged or transposed by the action of another substance; there can be no alteration of monads in this sense. Thus if there were causal interaction between monads it could only take the form of a transference or exchange of accidents. But Leibniz continues to hold that the transference of accidents is metaphysically impossible; properties, or rather property instances, such as perceptual states, are not the sort of entity that can become detached from the substances in which they inhere. Leibniz thus summarizes his negative teachings on this subject in a passage which introduces the famous claim that monads are 'windowless': 'Monads have no windows, through which anything could come in or go out. And accidents cannot detach themselves and stroll about outside of substances as the Scholastics' sensible species used to; so neither substance nor accident can come into a monad from outside' (*Monadology* 7, WF 268).

No less importantly, Leibniz is equally unwavering in his commitment to the principle of the Identity of Indiscernibles: though all monads express (perceive) the whole universe, no two are exactly alike; each has what Leibniz terms a point of view that is unique to it. Differences of point of view are to be analysed in terms of the distribution of clarity and distinctness over their perceptual states. Thus certain objects which are perceived with relative clarity and distinctness by one monad are perceived with relative obscurity and confusion by other monads, and conversely.

The notion of differences in the clarity and distinctness of perceptual states is crucial to understanding Leibniz's further thesis that there is a hierarchy of monads. The fact of such a hierarchy is clear, but the details of the picture are less so. On the face of it Leibniz seems to envisage the following picture. God is at the top of the hierarchy by virtue of possessing perceptions that are perfectly clear and distinct; thus, strictly speaking, God has no point of view. Human minds are somewhat lower down the hierarchy; they are high-quality monads by virtue of possessing not only the faculty of reason, which allows them to know the eternal truths of logic and mathematics, but also self-consciousness, or what Leibniz calls the ability to say 'I'. At the bottom of the hierarchy are what Leibniz terms 'bare monads'; such monads of course have perceptual states but these perceptual states are extremely obscure and confused; they fall well below the threshold of consciousness. As we shall see, bare monads play an important role in grounding inanimate bodies such as tables and chairs.

What accounts for the obscurity and confusion which are present in very different degrees in the perceptual states of all created simple substances? Leibniz attempts to answer this question by means of a rather strained adaptation of the traditional idea, deriving from Aristotle, that all created substances are compounds of matter and form. Since monads are immaterial entities, they cannot literally have a material component. But to the extent that they have a passive power, a kind of sluggishness, as it were, they have something analogous to matter which is traditionally supposed to be a purely passive entity. It is this component of the monad which Leibniz calls 'prime matter'. When Leibniz has his sights set on explaining this aspect of monads he even insists that the soul should be identified with the form factor of monads rather than with the monad itself. At other times, however, he is prepared to say, more straightforwardly, that monads are souls rather than that they are entities which have souls as a component.

Leibniz's account of the hierarchy of monads obviously gives a distinctive twist to the traditional idea that there is a Great Chain of Being which extends downwards from God to the lowest creature. Nonetheless, despite its respectable pedigree, Leibniz's version of the doctrine raises two problems which have their source in the attempt to combine traditional teachings with the distinctive principles of his philosophy. One such problem concerns the status of God. Whether God is the supreme monad is a basic issue on which Leibniz is surprisingly unclear, and statements can be found on both sides of the question. But if God is the supreme monad, then Leibniz faces a problem arising from his subscription to what he calls the Law of Continuity – the thesis that nature makes no leaps. For the Law of Continuity might be taken to imply that there should be monads immediately below God differing from him infinitesimally in terms of the clarity and distinctness of their perceptions. But of course any such monad would be a created substance, and there are obvious theological difficulties in allowing that any created substance might differ from God, its creator, only in this way; theological orthodoxy surely requires that there be a difference of kind between the Creator and his creatures. Perhaps Leibniz could say that the Law of Continuity commits him to holding only that all possible positions within the hierarchy are occupied, and that though we may speak of a position infinitesimally below God, we do not thereby succeed in identifying one that is logically possible. A similar problem is posed by the status of human minds within the hierarchy. As Donald Rutherford observes, Leibniz often writes as if the perceptual capacities of monads can be obtained by incremental addition in clarity and distinctness to those of lower monads. In the case of human minds, which are distinguished by the faculty of reason from lower substances, Leibniz seems committed to saying that this is not so; it seems as if the presence of the faculty of reason marks a difference of kind, not of degree (Rutherford 1995b: 143).

LEIBNIZ, SPINOZA, AND MONADS

However serious these problems may be, there is no doubt that Leibniz is deeply committed to the existence of a hierarchy of monads. The existence of such a hierarchy imposes obvious qualifications on the thesis that, for Leibniz, all monads are in a sense God-like. (By contrast, if Leibniz had opted for an ontology of spirits, few qualifications would have been needed.) Nonetheless, in spite of the huge gaps which separate higher from lower monads, it is still fair to say that, at least at the level of creatures, Leibniz's later metaphysics recognizes only one basic kind of substance. If Descartes's metaphysics of the created world is dualistic, then Leibniz's theory of monads is monistic. Although such labels are convenient, they are also potentially misleading. Leibniz's theory of monads is not monistic in the sense in which Spinoza's metaphysics is monistic; when Spinoza's philosophy is described in these terms what is at issue is a claim about the overall number of substances, not kinds of substances; for Spinoza, there is only the one substance, namely God or Nature. Far from being a monist in this sense Leibniz is an extreme and emphatic pluralist, for he holds that there is an infinity of simple substances or monads. Leibniz defends this thesis in correspondence with Des Bosses by saying that nothing less than an infinity of monads would be worthy of God's perfection (L 607).

The contrast with Spinoza's monism is revealing, for Leibniz's doctrine of monads may be regarded as an attempt to defeat Spinoza's objections to a plurality of substances. Although Leibniz is deeply at odds with Spinoza's pantheistic metaphysics, he pays it a back-handed compliment by recognizing that it is the only competitor to his own system; in a letter to Bourguet he remarks that if it were not for monads, Spinoza would be right (L 663). Leibniz is clear that he has the resources to defeat Spinoza's objections to pluralism, and it is instructive to see how.

In the Ethics Spinoza had first sought to show that any attempt to combine pluralism with regard to number, and monism with regard to kinds of substances, is doomed to incoherence. Spinoza argues from a version of the Identity of Indiscernibles to the conclusion that there cannot be two or more substances of the same nature or attribute (Ethics I P5). Leibniz of course accepts the principle of the Identity of Indiscernibles, but he argues that it does not have the consequences Spinoza claims for it. Although any two monads share the same abstract nature of perception and appetition, taken concretely they differ in terms of their properties. For while all monads perceive the whole universe, and thus in a sense agree in terms of the contents of their perceptions, they necessarily differ in terms of their points of view; that is, they differ in terms of the distribution of clarity and distinctness over their perceptual states. They thus satisfy the demands of the principle of the Identity of Indiscernibles.

Spinoza had further sought to demonstrate the incoherence of any form of pluralism which, like Leibniz's system of monads, seeks to accommodate the Christian doctrine of the creation. If, as Spinoza claims to have shown, there cannot be two or more substances of the same nature or attribute, then it is obviously true that any form of pluralism must maintain that substances must have different natures. Spinoza then appeals to the Causal Likeness Principle to show that such substances could not enter into any sort of causal relations; that is, he invokes the principle that there must be a similarity of nature between cause and effect. It follows, then, that one substance cannot be produced by another substance; the whole notion of created substance which stands at the heart of the Christian philosophical tradition is fundamentally incoherent. Spinoza concludes that any substance must enjoy unrestricted causal self-sufficiency; that is, it must be self-caused.

Once again Leibniz accepts a central Spinozistic principle; he agrees with Spinoza that substances are not only active but in a sense causally self-sufficient. But Leibniz parts company with Spinoza by refusing to admit that the causal self-sufficiency of substances is inconsistent with divine creation. Leibniz's refusal to admit this point may seem simply like a concession to Christian theology, and it would certainly have been so viewed by Spinoza. But we can perhaps come to Leibniz's philosophical defence here by saying that the causality of God and the causality of monads operate on different ontological levels. We can clarify this picture by means of a familiar analogy. Imagine an author writing a novel. Within the framework of the narrative there is a complete story to be told about the causal sequence of events; a character dies in a fire, and the fire is in turn caused by the deplorable state of the wiring in the house, and so on. But there is also a sense in which the author himself is a cause; it is he or she who made the causes cause. In this way we might seek to reconcile the causal self-sufficiency of monads with their status as substances created and conserved by God.

Leibniz thus believes that he has created conceptual space for his system of monads in the face of Spinoza's critique of substance pluralism. But it is one thing to show that monads are conceptually possible and thus escape Spinozistic criticisms; it is quite another to show that monads are actual. Part of the answer to the question of why Leibniz believes in monads should be already clear. For Leibniz, as we have seen, it would be shocking to reason, or at least to divine wisdom, if everything in the universe were composed of compounds whose components were themselves compounds, and so on to infinity; there must be ultimate building-blocks of the universe endowed with genuine unity. Further, these atoms cannot be purely material entities, for everything merely material lacks genuine unity, and is thus a compound of the sort just described.

It is still possible to ask, however, why Leibniz believes that the basic building-blocks must be purely spiritual atoms or monads. In the correspondence with Arnauld Leibniz had entertained the possibility that the ultimate building-blocks of the universe demanded by reason were corporeal substances – that is, they were organisms unified by the presence of a soul or substantial form. By the time he arrives at the doctrine of monads Leibniz continues to believe that matter is composed of organisms, but he no longer believes that such organisms are the basic building-blocks of the universe.[1] As we have seen, one reason for this change of mind may have been that organisms were poor candidates for mirrors of God. But it would be unlike Leibniz not to have more strictly philosophical reasons for his theories. It seems, then, that Leibniz must have become convinced that organisms do not possess the kind of intrinsic natural unity required for genuine substances, and in arriving at this conclusion he may have been influenced by Arnauld's criticisms of the doctrine.

THE STATUS OF BODIES

According to Leibniz, strictly speaking, there is nothing in the universe but simple substances, and in them perception and appetite.

But if this is the case, then it is natural to ask what becomes of the status of bodies or physical objects within such an ontology; some account must be given of the fact that we appear to live in a world of three-dimensional objects such as tables, chairs, and computers. Here Leibniz seems to be faced with a choice that anticipates modern philosophers who offer a materialist theory of mind. The contemporary materialist can adopt an eliminativist approach to the issue; that is, he can say that strictly speaking there are no such things as mental states. Alternatively, the materialist can adopt a reductionist approach; he can say that while there are mental states, they are identical with certain states of the brain; pain, for example, is the firing of certain neurons. Fortunately, Leibniz leaves the reader in no doubt about which of these two general approaches he prefers. In a remarkably modern-sounding passage Leibniz tells De Volder:

> I don't really eliminate [*tollo*] body but reduce it [*revoco*] to what it is. For I show that corporeal mass [*massa*], which is thought to have something over and above simple substances, is not a substance but a phenomenon resulting from simple substances which alone have unity and absolute reality.

> (AG 181)

Thus Leibniz clearly commits himself to a reductionist approach to the issue, one which is not contradicted elsewhere in his writings.

Leibniz, then, is in some sense a reductionist about bodies, but the nature of the proposed reduction is unclear. Leibniz's talk of bodies as phenomena or appearances has suggested to some readers that he is anticipating a phenomenalist theory of the kind adopted by Berkeley; that is, bodies are simply the contents of harmonized sets of perceptions in different monads. On this view, each soul or monad would be watching a private film, as it were, with nothing behind the images to back them up; the only sense in which there is a public world of bodies is that these private films have been coordinated by God so that their contents harmonize. Leibniz seems to have flirted with this phenomenalist approach on occasion. For instance, in correspondence with De Volder, he immediately follows up an uncompromising statement of his idealism with a phenomenalist account of matter and motion: 'Matter and motion are not substances or things as much as they are the phenomena of perceivers, the reality of which is situated in the harmony of perceivers with themselves (at different times) and with other perceivers' (AG 181).

And in correspondence with Des Bosses Leibniz expresses the same thesis in a more linguistic mode; he explains how statements about a public world of bodies can be analysed in terms of statements about appearances to perceivers:

> It is true that things which happen in the soul must agree with those which happen outside of it. But for this it is enough for the things taking place in the one soul to correspond with each other as well as with those happening in any other soul, and it is not necessary to assume anything outside of all souls or monads. According to this hypothesis, we mean nothing else when we say that Socrates is sitting down than that what we understand by 'Socrates' is appearing to us and to others who are concerned.
>
> (L 605)

As one writer has suggested, Leibniz seems remarkably well placed by features of his doctrine of monads to give a phenomenalist account of bodies, for he does not face a problem which confronts other phenomenalists, such as Berkeley, who recognize only a limited number of perceiving subjects (Furth 1972: 118–19). Such philosophers must concede that there are times when no finite mind is having perceptions of the 'tree in the quad'. Insofar as they do not simply appeal to God to plug the gaps in perception, they are driven to analyse statements about the continued existence of the tree in terms of statements about the possible perceptions of finite minds; to say that the tree in the quad exists when no one perceives it, is to say that if a finite mind were suitably located, it would have perceptions with the appropriate content. In other words, such philosophers are compelled to resort to subjunctive conditionals, in logical terminology. Leibniz, by contrast, is under no pressure to adopt this sort of approach, since he holds that the number of souls or monads is infinite, and that every possible point of view on the phenomena is occupied. Thus Leibniz can analyse all statements about the existence of physical objects in terms of other statements which are exclusively about the actual perceptions of monads.

In spite of the fact that Leibniz was well placed to do justice to such a theory, phenomenalism (in the style of Berkeley) does not seem to be Leibniz's considered position on the status of bodies. It is more characteristic of Leibniz to advance claims which have a decidedly non-phenomenalistic flavour: he writes, for instance, that 'mass is a being by aggregation, but from infinite unities' (G II 379). It has sometimes been supposed that in passages like these Leibniz is saying that bodies are aggregates of monads. If every body were indeed strictly to be identified with a certain aggregate of monads, then an obvious problem would arise. According to Leibniz's Law, if A is identical with B, then A and B share all their properties. It is clear that bodies have properties, such as size and shape, which no individual monad has. Now from the fact that no individual monad has size and shape, it does not of course follow that no aggregate of monads has these properties. Nonetheless, it is difficult to see how the mere aggregation of monads can give rise to properties such as size and shape which no individual monad possesses. Thus if Leibniz wishes to hold that every body is identical with some aggregate of monads, he has some explaining to do if he is to avoid running foul of the logical law that bears his name. But in fact Leibniz tends to say, not that bodies are aggregates of monads, but rather that they are aggregates which result from monads: he tells Des Bosses, for instance, that the consecrated bread in the Mass 'is a being by aggregation, that is, a substantiated thing resulting from innumerable monads' (G II 399). Such statements leave open, and indeed suggest, the possibility that while bodies result from monads they are not aggregates of them. But in that case the question arises as to what bodies are aggregates of.

The most natural way of answering this question is to invoke one of the themes of Leibniz's correspondence with Arnauld. For Leibniz in that document, every body is either itself an organism or an aggregate of organisms, and these organisms have bodies which are in turn aggregates of organisms, and so on to infinity. Thus if Leibniz is drawing on this thesis in his theory of monads, he would be advancing a claim that was restricted to inanimate bodies such as tables and chairs; such bodies are aggregates of organisms. In this way, then, one of the themes of the middle period would find a place within the new theory of monads. But it is also relevant to note that, for Leibniz, any body, considered in abstraction from souls or substantial forms, is an aggregate of extended parts, and so on to infinity. Thus there may be two distinct senses in which bodies are aggregates for Leibniz.

Leibniz's preferred view, then, is not that bodies are aggregates of monads but rather that they are aggregates which result from monads. But what exactly does it mean to say that bodies result from monads? It is helpful to begin by noticing ways in which this relation cannot be construed. First, resulting cannot be a causal relation; where monads are concerned the only causality at issue is internal to the monads themselves. Monads produce their perceptual states by means of striving or appetition; but they do not produce bodies. Second, the relation of resulting cannot be that of wholes to parts. Leibniz is insistent that bodies are not composed of monads; he is anxious to guard against the misunderstanding that if only bodies were divided up far enough, we should somehow encounter monads. In a key passage he explicitly contrasts resulting with the part/whole relation: 'Accurately speaking, matter is not composed of these constitutive unities but results from them. . . . Substantial unities are not parts but foundations of phenomena' (AG 179). Finally, as we have seen, the relation of resulting is not one of identity: Leibniz prefers not to say that bodies are identical with aggregates of monads.

It is tempting perhaps to say that the relation in question is one of supervenience; bodies supervene on certain sets of monads in the way in which the goodness of an apple supervenes on its physical properties such as its acidity content. Even this cannot be quite right, however, for it fails to do justice to the point that bodies are in some sense confused representations of monads which result from prime matter (the stuff-factor) in our mind. Indeed, a closer analogy would be with the redness of apples where this is understood as a property projected on to the fruit on the basis of its physical properties.

All things considered, the most promising approach is to fall back on Leibniz's notion of expression. To say that bodies result from monads is to say – in part at least – that monads express bodies; that is, it is in principle possible to read off the properties of the desk in front of me, for example, from the properties of a certain collection of monads. But this cannot be the whole story. For Leibniz seems to regard expression as a symmetrical relation; thus it will also be true to say that it is in principle possible to read off the properties of a certain collection of monads from the properties of the desk in front of me. But Leibniz would surely not want to say that monads result from, or are founded in, bodies. We can take care of this problem by adding that monads, by virtue of being substances, are ontologically more basic than the bodies which result from them. Thus, though expression is indeed a symmetrical relation, it is correct to say that bodies are founded in monads, but not conversely that monads are founded in bodies.

Despite the problems of interpretation which it involves, it is clear that 'the aggregate thesis', as we may call it, is different from the phenomenalist theory. The crucial difference between the two theories is that on the aggregate thesis each body stands in a privileged relationship to some subset of the totality of monads; this subset of monads has the job of well-founding it. On the phenomenalist thesis, by contrast, this appears not to be the case. According to phenomenalism, every statement about the tree in the quad, for example, is to be analysed in terms of other statements about all monads with the relevant perceptual content. Now since every monad perceives the whole universe according to its point of view, there will be no monad which will be excluded from the analysis: every monad will have some perception, however obscure, of the tree in the quad. Thus on the phenomenalist approach there will be no subset of monads which is singled out.

If the theories are different in this way, it is natural to ask why Leibniz preferred the aggregate thesis to the phenomenalistic approach; phenomenalism is at once more intelligible and more fruitful in the subsequent history of philosophy. The answer seems to lie in Leibniz's desire to provide metaphysical foundations for his physics; Leibniz wishes to argue that the physical forces in bodies, such as kinetic energy, are grounded in the primitive force of monads, namely appetition:

> In phenomena, or in the resulting aggregate, everything is explained mechanically, and so masses are understood to impel each other. In these phenomena it is necessary to consider only derivative forces, once it is established whence these forces arise, namely, the phenomena of aggregates from the reality of the monads.
>
> (L 529)

Such a grounding of physics in metaphysics seems to require that bodies stand in a privileged relationship to some subset of the totality of monads. On the phenomenalist approach this condition cannot be met.

Near the beginning of this section we saw that Leibniz stated that he was not seeking to eliminate bodies but rather to reduce them to what they really were. We have also seen that Leibniz is consistent in maintaining that he does not eliminate bodies: bodies are not illusions; they are well-founded phenomena (*phaenomena bene fundata*). But it is natural to wonder whether Leibniz's approach is really reductionistic in the modern sense. Modern reductive materialists are those philosophers who say that mental states are identical with states of the brain. Leibniz, however, does not seem to adopt a parallel position within the framework of his idealism. Although he may flirt with both views, he does not settle either on the claim that bodies are harmonized sets of perceptions (phenomenalism) or on the claim that bodies are aggregates of monads. By modern standards, then, Leibniz is not strictly a reductive idealist; that is, he does not hold that bodies are strictly identical with more basic, mental entities. But he is a reductive idealist in a looser sense perhaps. For in addition to claiming that there really are bodies such as tables and chairs, he holds that facts about such bodies can in principle be derived from facts about the monads, the only true substances in the universe.

CORPOREAL SUBSTANCE AND THE *VINCULUM SUBSTANTIALE*

In the correspondence with De Volder and elsewhere, then, Leibniz strongly suggests that his later metaphysics is a form of idealism; the only true substances are monads. But it has been noticed that in connection with organisms Leibniz continues to employ the language of corporeal substances; he tells Des Bosses, for instance, that he restricts 'corporeal, i.e., composite substance to living things alone, that is, to organic natural machines. Other things are, for me, mere aggregates of substances which I call substantiated things [*substantiata*]' (AG 206; translation modified). In the words of one writer, corporeal substances 'keep popping up' in Leibniz's later philosophy (Hartz 1998). This continuing talk of corporeal substances has led some readers to suppose that Leibniz is not really committed to idealism after all, but is still in the grip of a metaphysics inspired by Aristotle. Others have supposed that Leibniz is simply inconsistent; he both does and does not embrace a form of idealism which excludes the existence of corporeal substances.

The challenge is important, but it would be a mistake to jump to either of these conclusions too hastily. The fact that Leibniz continues to speak of corporeal substances does not necessarily mean that he is not committed to idealism, for he can be understood to be offering a reductionist approach to corporeal substances. In the same way the fact that modern materialist philosophers may be found speaking of pain sensations and thoughts does not necessarily mean that they have abandoned materialism, for they can be understood to be offering a reductionist account which identifies mental states with brain states. Indeed, the unity of organisms, which leads Leibniz to speak of corporeal substances, can be analysed in a way consistent with the hypothesis of mere monads, as he terms it. In the case of organisms, including of course human beings, there is one monad which is dominant with respect to the aggregate of monads which ground the body of the organism; the dominant monad is of course the soul which endows the corporeal substance with its unity. The dominance relation is to be spelled out in terms of the superior clarity and distinctness of perceptions.

It must be admitted, however, that Leibniz seems to voice some dissatisfaction with the 'hypothesis of mere monads' (L 607). He appears to doubt whether the pure doctrine of monads can really do justice to the unity of organisms which had impressed him so much in the correspondence with Arnauld that organisms came to be regarded as the paradigm substances. Towards the end of his life Leibniz develops the obscure theory of the *vinculum substantiale* as something over and above monads which unifies the monads of an organism into a substantial whole. The substantial bond is like a substratum of change inasmuch as it can survive the addition and subtraction of the monads which it unifies.

The theory of substantial bonds is one of baroque complexity and obscurity (cf. Rutherford 1995b: 162). It is not surprising, therefore, that some readers have doubted whether Leibniz ever really committed himself to the doctrine of substantial bonds. The serious scholarly basis for such scepticism is that Leibniz first proposed the theory in correspondence with Des Bosses, a Jesuit professor who invited him to explain how the doctrine of monads could accommodate the Catholic dogma of transubstantiation. It has thus been suggested that Leibniz put forward the theory to assuage a Jesuit's scruples without ever having a philosophical stake in the doctrine (Russell 1937: 152).

Plausible as it is, this account of what Leibniz is doing runs into difficulties. For one thing, Leibniz persists in developing the theory of substantial bonds in spite of a marked lack of encouragement or enthusiasm from Des Bosses who raised theological scruples against the doctrine. Moreover, the fit between the doctrine of substantial bonds and the dogma of transubstantiation is a strikingly poor one: substantial bonds are introduced to explain the unity of organisms; but the consecrated bread and wine are not organisms but at most aggregates of organisms. It is thus hard to see why Leibniz should propose a theory tailored to explaining the unity of organisms in order to accommodate a dogma concerned with the miraculous disappearance of bodies which are not organic at all. Finally, and most decisively, there is scholarly evidence that Leibniz was experimenting with the doctrine of substantial bonds before the topic of transubstantiation was first broached. In the draft of a letter to Des Bosses Leibniz writes:

> The union which I find some difficulty explaining is that which joins the different simple substances or monads existing in our body with us, such that it makes one thing [*unum*] from them, nor is it sufficiently clear how, in addition to the existence of individual monads, there may arise a new existing thing, unless they are bound by a continuous bond [. . .] which the phenomena display to us.
>
> (Rutherford 1995a: 277)

There is thus good reason to suppose that, though Leibniz was never more than tentative about the theory of substantial bonds, he was led to it by an independent train of thought about the unity of organisms; he then adopted it, rather clumsily perhaps, for the purposes of explaining transubstantiation.

SPACE, TIME, AND MONADS

Leibniz's adoption of the theory of the substantial bond may not have been motivated by a desire to assuage the concerns of a Catholic theologian, but there is no doubt that the correspondence with Des Bosses which lasted until the year of his death displays the eirenical side of Leibniz's philosophy. The other major philosophical exchange of letters of his last years reveals Leibniz in a decidedly less accommodating mood; this is his celebrated correspondence with Dr Samuel Clarke, a disciple of Sir Isaac Newton. As we saw in Chapter 1, by the final years of his life Leibniz's relations with Newton had deteriorated sharply as a result of the priority dispute over the differential calculus; this mood of bitterness is reflected in his letters to Clarke, which are nothing less than a full-scale assault on the alleged metaphysical foundations of Newtonian physics.

The philosophical debate between the two men ranges over a number of issues. As in the brilliant polemical paper 'The Anti-barbarian Physicist' Leibniz criticizes the Newtonian theory of universal gravitation for betraying the principles of the Scientific Revolution. The new mechanistic physics had proceeded on the twin assumptions that no body can act immediately on another except by impulse, and that physical explanations must be ultimately based on properties of bodies, such as size, shape, and motion, with which we are familiar in everyday experience. Newton, by contrast, seemed to Leibniz to be abandoning these principles by admitting action at a distance and by postulating gravitational force as a basic property of bodies in order to explain such action. In Leibniz's eyes he was thus guilty of reintroducing the occult (that is, hidden) qualities of the Scholastics which by common consent had been banished from physics in the age of the Scientific Revolution. But though in passing Leibniz touches on a number of alleged problems with Newtonian physics he focuses most of his attention on the issue of the ontological status of space and time. By this stage of his career Leibniz is in full possession of the theory of monads, but in correspondence with Clarke Leibniz does little to reveal the deep metaphysical underpinnings of his thought about the physical world. It is thus left largely to the reader to infer how his theory of space and time is related to the monadology.

Although it involves technical considerations concerning the nature of motion, the Newtonian theory of absolute space and time which Leibniz opposes is in outline rather intuitive. The basic thesis is that space and time are like containers for bodies and events respectively. That is, if there were no bodies space would still exist; if there were no events time would still exist; in logical terminology, space is logically prior to bodies, and time is logically prior to events (Broad 1981: 158). A further element of the theory is that these containers, unlike what they contain, are infinite; the material universe, like the series of events, is of only finite extent.

In his letters to Clarke Leibniz offers two main arguments against the Newtonian theory. The first argument is from the Principle of Sufficient Reason. This principle is formulated in many different ways in Leibniz's philosophy, but here it can be understood to mean simply that there must be a reason for God's choice. The argument takes the following form. On the Newtonian theory of absolute space, the parts or regions of space are qualitatively indistinguishable. Thus, if God created a material world he could have no reason for choosing to create it at one location in space rather than some other. But if God could have no reason for such a choice, then since he never acts without a reason, he would not create at all. But we know that God has created a material world. It follows, then, that the theory of absolute space is false. *Mutatis mutandis* the argument can be directed against the theory of absolute time (AG 325).

Leibniz's second argument has proved to be of greater philosophical interest in our own time. The argument depends on a version of the Identity of Indiscernibles which, as various writers have noted, is really tantamount to the modern verificationist principle. According to Leibniz, the Newtonians are committed to saying that God could, for example, move the whole universe a few miles to the west while keeping its internal structure unchanged. Leibniz has no patience with such suppositions. If God were to do such things, no change would be observable even in principle. In a remarkable passage Leibniz then states the verificationist objection:

> Motion indeed does not depend on being observed; but it does depend on its being possible to be observed. There is no motion where there is no change that can be observed. And when there is no change that can be observed, there is no change at all.
>
> (AG 340-1)

The supposition in question can thus be dismissed as meaningless, or, as Leibniz sometimes says, as an impossible fiction.

Ever since Clarke, Leibniz's readers have been bothered by an apparent inconsistency in his position. The first argument seems to assume that, though absolute space and time are contrary to the divine wisdom, they are at least logically possible; the second argument, by contrast, seeks to establish a stronger claim: the theory of absolute space and time is an impossible fiction. Relatedly, there seems to be an inconsistency in Leibniz's claims about the Identity of Indiscernibles. Sometimes he says that to suppose two indiscernible entities or states of affairs is to suppose two things under the same name; at other times he says that, though logically possible, the existence of two indiscernible entities would be contrary to the divine wisdom. The problem of interpretation, however, is not really a serious one; it can be solved by assuming that Leibniz is mounting a two-pronged attack on the Newtonian position. Leibniz's main argument turns on the claim that the Identity of Indiscernibles is a necessary truth: on this argument the supposition of two indiscernible entities is indeed an impossible fiction. But Leibniz is also prepared to argue in a more concessive vein: even if it is granted that two indiscernible entities are logically possible, it can still be shown that they would never obtain because they are contrary to the divine wisdom.

In correspondence with Clarke, then, Leibniz offers several

intriguing arguments against the Newtonian theory of absolute space and time. And in the same correspondence Leibniz defends as much of his positive teachings on the topic as he can explain without disclosing the deep metaphysics of monads. The main thesis of which he seeks to persuade Clarke is that space and time are relational; opposing what he sees as the metaphysical extravagance of the Newtonian theory Leibniz argues that 'space is an order of co-existences; time an order of successions' (AG 324). That is, to say that bodies are in space is not to say that there is some further ontological entity over and above the bodies; it is simply to say that they are related in certain ways (for example, that body A is to the left of body B). Once again, *mutatis mutandis*, the same story can be told about time and events. From the relational theory Leibniz derives a further thesis to the effect that space and time are ideal. Strictly speaking, this thesis does not follow from the relational theory alone; it follows from that theory in conjunction with Leibniz's general ontological doctrine that only substances are fully real, everything else – including relations – being only an *ens rationis* or mental construct.

There is a final main component in Leibniz's positive teachings about space and time which he does not disclose in the letters to Clarke: this is the thesis that space and time are phenomenal.[2] That is, space and time belong to the realm of appearances only; they have no place at the ground floor of Leibniz's metaphysics, the level of monads. Here of course it is important not to be misled by Leibniz's claim that monads have points of view. This claim should not be interpreted literally as implying that they are in space. Rather, the picture that Leibniz wishes to defend is that, in modern jargon, space is a logical construction out of the points of view of monads where these are analysed in terms of the distribution of clarity and distinctness over perceptual states. That is to say, the system of spatial relations of physical objects in the phenomenal world can in principle be derived from the properties of monads. The point can be made in theological terms. By knowing all the facts about the relevant monads, God can read off, for example, how the desk in front of me is spatially related to the other physical objects in my study.

The thesis that space and time are phenomenal is one that Leibniz could not explain without revealing the doctrine of monads; for this reason it makes little or no appearance in the exchange of letters with Clarke. By contrast, Leibniz was able to defend the thesis that space and time are ideal without showing much of his monadological hand, so to speak, for despite what is suggested by the terminology, there is no tight logical connection between the ideality of space and time and the idealism implicit in the doctrine of monads. The absence of a tight logical connection is suggested by reflection on the content of these two theses. To say that Leibniz is an idealist is to say that simple substances, the basic building-blocks of the universe, are all mental or at least quasi-mental in nature. To say that space and time are ideal for Leibniz is to say that they are mental constructs which are neither substances nor properties of substances but rather projected on to the phenomena.

We can bring the issue to a sharp focus by attending, as commentators tend to do, to the case of space. The core thesis of monadology – there is nothing in the world except simple substances, and in them perception and appetite – does not entail that space exists as ideal, that is, as a mental construct. Consistently with his theory of monads, Leibniz could maintain that there are no bodies at all; the realm of bodies, together with their spatial relations, could be an entire illusion. It might be thought that the core thesis of the theory of monads at least entails the weaker thesis that if space exists, it exists as ideal. But even this would be a mistake. As we have seen, to derive this result Leibniz avails himself not just of his thesis that space is relational but of his further, wholly general thesis about the ontology of relations: relations are all mental constructs.

There is thus no very direct route from monadology to the ideality of space. There is no very direct route in the other direction either:

the ideality of space does not entail the core thesis of monadology. Indeed, the ideality of space and time is consistent with the realist, quasi-Aristotelian ontology of corporeal substances of the kind Leibniz envisages in his correspondence with Arnauld. Even if such a form of realism were true, it would still be the case that space was relational, and hence ideal. The thesis of the ideality of space thus has no tendency to discriminate between the idealism of the monadology and the realism of the theory of corporeal substances.

We can conclude this chapter by reflecting on one of the consequences of Leibniz's theory that space and time are merely phenomenal: monads, like God, are outside space and time altogether. We thus encounter further reasons for thinking that even in the theory of monads Leibniz remains committed to the thesis that all substances are mirrors of God. It is true that Leibniz tends to play down this theme in his official pronouncements on the subject in his later writings; and it is not difficult to see why he should have felt some reluctance to say expressly that bare monads are mirrors of God. But though Leibniz may change the emphasis, he never really recants the thesis of the *Discourse on Metaphysics*. Here the constants of Leibniz's metaphysics play an important role. Even within the severely hierarchical world of the monadology, it is still true to say, as Leibniz does in the *Discourse*, that 'each substance in some way carries the imprint of the infinite wisdom and omnipotence of God, and imitates them in so far as it is capable of it' (DM 9, WF 61). For in addition to being outside space and time, all substances including the barest monads have a kind of causal self-sufficiency and perceive the whole universe according to their point of view. And they all share with God the properties of simplicity, unity, and natural indestructibility. In the next chapter we shall focus on one kind of substance whose God-like status is not open to question: this is the human mind.

SUMMARY

Since Plato a recurrent theme of western philosophy is the contrast between appearance and reality: the nature of reality can be grasped only by turning away from the senses and consulting the intellect. This theme is present in Descartes's philosophy, but it is developed much further by Leibniz in his theory of monads, the metaphysics of his final years. The first section argues that Leibniz's theory of monads can perhaps be best understood as a form of atomism. Like traditional atoms monads are the basic building-blocks of reality, but unlike them they are spiritual, not physical in nature: the basic properties of monads are perception and appetite. The second section addresses the nature of Leibniz's monism by way of a comparison with Spinoza. Leibniz's final metaphysics is monistic in the sense that, although monads are hierarchically ordered, there is only one basic kind of substance. Spinoza's metaphysics, by contrast, is monistic in the sense that it recognizes the existence of only one substance, God. Indeed, Leibniz's theory of monads can be regarded as an attempt to refute Spinoza's objections to a plurality of substances. If successful, Leibniz's refutation of Spinoza's objections thus creates conceptual space for monads – monads are at least possible – but it still leaves open the question of why monads are actual. It is shown that Leibniz's arguments for monads turn on the need for basic substances which are not mere composites, and on the infinite divisibility of matter. The next section addresses a pressing question: if, as Leibniz says, there is strictly nothing in the universe but monads or simple substances, what is the status of bodies or physical objects? It is clear that Leibniz opts for a reductionist rather than an eliminativist approach to this issue: there are bodies, but they are not metaphysically basic entities. The nature of Leibniz's reductionism about bodies is controversial. Although Leibniz flirts with it in places, phenomenalism is shown not to be his preferred solution to the problem; instead Leibniz's official position is that bodies are aggregates which result from monads: the concept of resulting here is best analysed in terms of

Leibniz's technical concept of expression. Leibniz's preference for the aggregate thesis over phenomenalism is probably best explained by his desire to provide a metaphysical foundation for his physical theory of force. The next section examines a further problem in Leibniz's final metaphysics posed by his apparent continuing recognition of the existence of corporeal substances. It is argued that such a commitment to corporeal substances can be understood in a way consistent with the idealism of the theory of monads. However, the obscure theory of the substantial bond (*vinculum substantiale*) which Leibniz entertains in his late writings suggests some dissatisfaction with 'the hypothesis of mere monads'; Leibniz is concerned whether this hypothesis can do justice to the unity of organisms. The concluding section of the chapter examines Leibniz's doctrine of space and time which, like the theory of monads, finds its classic exposition in the writings of his final years. Against Newton's theory of absolute space and time, Leibniz argues for three main connected theses: space and time are relational, phenomenal, and ideal. It is argued that despite appearances there is no tight logical connection between the idealism of the doctrine of monads and the ideality of space and time.

FURTHER READING

R.M. Adams (1994) *Leibniz: Determinist, Theist, Idealist*, Chs. 9–13. (A magisterial study which argues for the continuity of Leibniz's commitment to idealism; highly recommended for the serious student.)

C.D. Broad (1981) 'Leibniz's Last Controversy with the Newtonians,' Woolhouse (ed.), *Leibniz: Metaphysics and the Philosophy of Science*. (A very clear and helpful account of the main issues in the Leibniz–Clarke correspondence.)

M. Furth (1972) 'Monadology,' Frankfurt (ed.), *Leibniz: A Collection of Critical Essays*. (An illuminating article which argues for Leibniz's commitment to phenomenalism in his later metaphysics.)

G. Hartz and J. Cover (1988) 'Space and Time in the Leibnizian Metaphysic'. (Criticizes the view that for Leibniz space and time are phenomenal.)

N. Jolley (1986) 'Leibniz and Phenomenalism'. (Criticizes the phenomenalist interpretation of the later Leibniz.)

L. Loeb (1981) *From Descartes to Hume*, Ch. 7. (Endorses Furth's phenomenalist interpretation.)

D. Rutherford (1995a) *Leibniz and the Rational Order of Nature*, Chs. 8–9. (A scholarly discussion which emphasizes the different levels of Leibniz's metaphysics.)

D. Rutherford (1995b) 'Metaphysics: The Late Period,' Jolley (ed.), *The Cambridge Companion to Leibniz*, Ch. 4. (A valuable survey of Leibniz's later metaphysics.)

Four

Mind, Knowledge, and Ideas

Writing to a correspondent Leibniz criticized his great contemporary Locke for having an inadequate appreciation of 'the dignity of our mind'.[1] In context it is reasonably clear what Leibniz means by this charge; he is thinking above all of Locke's famous denial of innate knowledge: as Leibniz puts it, Locke fails to recognize that the principles of necessary truths are latent in our mind. But it is also clear that, for Leibniz, there is a metaphysical dimension to a proper appreciation of our mind's dignity: it involves the recognition that the mind is an immaterial substance, and that it is as causally self-sufficient as is consistent with its status as a creature. In all these respects the human mind is, as Leibniz is fond of expressing it, 'like a little divinity' (*Monadology* 83, WF 280). In this chapter we shall explore how Leibniz develops this theme in his metaphysics and epistemology. We shall also take up the question of how far Leibniz's ontological claims about the human mind have implications for his famous theory of innate ideas and knowledge.

THE IMMATERIAL MIND

Throughout his philosophical career Leibniz scarcely wavered in his commitment to the thesis that the human mind is an immaterial substance. When Locke, for example, put forward the suggestion that matter might think, Leibniz was implacable in his opposition to the claim; indeed, in a letter he explained to a correspondent that his main purpose in the *New Essays on Human Understanding* was to vindicate the immateriality of the soul (i.e. the human mind) against Locke's scepticism about the doctrine (G III 473). Leibniz's apparent dogmatism on this topic has excited some surprise on the part of his modern readers. John Cottingham, for example, has observed that Leibniz's conception of matter as a being endowed with active force gave him the resources to develop an alternative to the dogmatic conception of the mind, which he shared with Descartes, as an immaterial substance, and he wonders why Leibniz did not exploit these resources: why should Leibniz not say that 'mental states (thought, perception, consciousness) arise from the "dance of activity", as it were, of the countless monads composing the brain or nervous system of man – all acting spontaneously yet in perfect harmony?' (Cottingham 1988: 140). But in fact what is really surprising is the surprise of such writers at Leibniz's failure to advance such a theory. Leibniz may indeed have had the resources to develop a materialist theory of the human mind, but there is no mystery as to why he did not. If the human mind were identical with the human brain, it could hardly be maintained that it is a mirror of God (even if the brain is grounded in immaterial monads), and as we have seen, this is a non-negotiable commitment in Leibniz's philosophy. Moreover, Leibniz further thinks that it is an advantage of the immaterialist theory that it offers a secure foundation for the Christian doctrine of personal immortality. Thus, provided an immaterialist theory of the human mind is coherent, Leibniz will regard it as obviously preferable to any rival theory.

Because of his most basic commitments, then, Leibniz was clearly predisposed in favour of the thesis that the human mind, like God, is an immaterial substance. Yet such a predisposition in favour of the doctrine did not blind Leibniz to the weaknesses of fashionable arguments for it. In his 'Critical Comments on Descartes's *Principles of Philosophy*' (1691), for instance, Leibniz is scathing in his assessment of one of Descartes's arguments for the real distinction of mind and body:

It is not valid to reason: 'I can assume or imagine that no corporeal body exists, but I cannot imagine that I do not exist or do not think. Therefore I am not corporeal, nor is thought a modification of the body.' I am amazed that so able a man could have based so much on so flimsy a sophism. . . . No one who thinks that the soul is corporeal will admit that we can assume that nothing corporeal exists, but he will admit that we can doubt (as long as we are ignorant of the nature of the soul) whether anything corporeal exists or does not exist. And since we nevertheless see clearly that our soul exists, he will admit that only one thing follows from this: that we can still doubt that the soul is corporeal. And no amount of torture can extract anything more from the argument.

(L 385)

Superficially it may seem that Descartes's inference is valid, for it appeals to Leibniz's Law (as explained in the previous chapter). Yet, as Leibniz implicitly recognizes, the logical law which bears his name has limited scope: it does not apply in contexts, such as the present one, in which the property ascribed or not ascribed consists only of what can be doubted, assumed, or imagined.[2] In short, there can be no valid inference from a state of subjective uncertainty to what is objectively the case.

Leibniz, then, can be acute in diagnosing the weaknesses of fashionable arguments for the thesis that the mind is an immaterial substance. Leibniz's acumen in this respect needs to be borne in mind when we turn to his positive arguments for an immaterialist theory of mind. Consider, for instance, the famous 'mill argument' in the *Monadology* where Leibniz invites us to perform a thought experiment:

Everyone must admit that *perception*, and everything that depends on it, is *inexplicable by mechanical principles*, by shapes and motions, that is. Imagine there were a machine which by its structure produced thought, feeling, and perception. We can imagine it as being enlarged while maintaining the same relative proportions, to the point where we could go inside it, as we would go into a mill. But if that were so, when we went in we would find nothing but pieces which push one against another, and never anything to account for a perception. Therefore, we must look for it in the simple substance and not in the composite, or in a machine.

(17, WF 270)

The thought experiment is obviously striking, but Leibniz's use of it has been sharply criticized. Leibniz has been taken to argue here that if we imagine a machine (such as the brain) blown up to the size of a mill, we would never catch sight of anything that resembled mental states or consciousness: all we would observe is parts of machinery pushing against one another. The argument is then dismissed on the ground that it overlooks the fact that we might simply lack the understanding or knowledge to see that consciousness is in fact present in the machine (Lodge and Bobro 1998: 554–5). Thus the argument falls far short of its goal of refuting materialism.

The fact that the argument is supposed to succumb to this objection gives us reason to doubt that it has been reconstructed correctly. For Leibniz himself makes just the same objection to a Cartesian argument for substantial dualism. Adopting the role of devil's advocate Leibniz writes:

[Malebranche's spokesman] holds that thoughts are not relations of distance because one cannot measure thoughts. But a follower of Epicurus will say that this is due to our lack of proper knowledge of them, and that if we knew the corpuscles that form thought and the motions that are necessary for this, we would see that thoughts are measurable and are the workings of some subtle machines.

(AG 263)

It is scarcely credible that, speaking in his own voice, Leibniz himself should have endorsed an argument of whose weaknesses he was perfectly aware.

One feature of the argument that is overlooked in standard reconstructions is its emphasis on explanation: there is something about mental life or consciousness which machinery cannot explain. And though Leibniz is not as forthcoming on the point as one could wish, it is natural to suppose that the feature in question is the unity of consciousness. Thus Leibniz is implicitly drawing our attention to the fact that our mental life is not compartmentalized: when I am engaged in writing a letter, for example, one and the same self is conscious of a slight ache in the wrist, the colour of the paper, and the noise of the radio, and so on. On such a reconstruction Leibniz does not seem vulnerable to the objection that on his principles one could similarly argue that clockwork machinery could never explain time-keeping or that water molecules could never explain liquidity: for unity is in a wholly different category from these properties. Moreover, it is not, I think, fair to say that Leibniz is still offering us an invalid argument from ignorance – that is, he is inferring fallaciously from the fact that we find no explanation in the machine to the conclusion that no explanation could be given. Rather, the thesis that machinery could never in principle explain the unity of consciousness is a basic premise of the argument against materialism.

The idea of the unity of consciousness seems to be invoked in another striking passage which also tends in the direction of an immaterialist theory of mind. The thesis of the following fragment needs only to be supplemented by the further premise that all substances are immaterial to yield an argument against materialism:

> That we are not substances is contrary to experience, since indeed we have no knowledge [*notitiam*] of substance except from the internal experience of ourselves when we perceive the I [*to Ego*], and on that basis we apply the term 'substance' to God himself and other monads.
>
> (Gr II 558)

If we ask how 'internal experience' is supposed to assure us that we are substances, it is natural to answer by appealing to the unity of consciousness. Indeed, Leibniz is suggesting that our internal experience of ourselves is the only direct experience we have of substantial unity.

The human mind is not only a simple, immaterial substance; it is also naturally immortal. It is tempting to suppose that, for Leibniz, the immortality of the mind follows from the fact of its simplicity; as we have seen, Leibniz accepts the Platonic thesis, going back to the *Phaedo*, that where there is no composition, there can be no dissolution or destruction. Leibniz may sometimes write as if the immortality of the mind follows from its simplicity, but we know that this is not his considered view: for Leibniz, the simplicity which the mind shares with all souls or monads entails only that it is naturally indestructible. True immortality – that is, the personal immortality that is relevant for ethics – involves more than mere indestructibility; it involves memory and self-consciousness (which Leibniz sometimes calls apperception), and these properties belong only to spirits.[3] For Leibniz, it is by virtue of possessing memory and self-consciousness that human minds are moral beings, capable of reward and punishment.

Leibniz's insistence that personal immortality involves memory has a clear polemical intent; it is directed against the views of Descartes and Spinoza. Leibniz argues that, in their rather different ways, these philosophers hold out the prospect of a sham or at least impoverished immortality which can have no significance for ethics; by conceding that the human mind which survives death will have no recollection of its actions or experiences in this life they effectively deprive the doctrine of personal immortality of its motivational force, for immortality without memory would be in no way desirable. Leibniz seeks to persuade us of this point by means of one of his most intriguing and memorable thought-experiments:

Suppose that someone could suddenly become the King of China, but only on condition of forgetting what he had been, as if he had just been born all over again. Would it not in practice or in terms of perceivable effects [*dont on se peut appercevoir*] be the same as if he had been annihilated and a King of China had been created at the same instant in his place? And that is something which that individual could have no reason to want.

(DM 34, WF 86)

Leibniz's King of China example offers a striking anticipation of the thought-experiments conducted by some modern philosophers, who similarly explore the importance of memory for personal identity.[4]

MIND, BODY, AND THE PRE-ESTABLISHED HARMONY

One of the leading characteristics of Leibniz's philosophy is that certain themes and principles remain constant despite changes in the basic ontology. In his later philosophy, for example, the unity and activity of substances come to be reinterpreted within the setting of the idealist doctrine of monads. But it is not only certain themes and principles which remain constant; so too do certain of Leibniz's claims to have solved philosophical problems which embarrassed his predecessors. We have seen that in the 'New System' Leibniz drew attention to Descartes's inability to solve the problem of 'explaining how the body can make something pass over into the soul or vice versa. . . . As far as we can see from his writings, Descartes gave up the game at this point' (WF 149). From the time of the *Discourse on Metaphysics* to the end of his life Leibniz maintains that it is one of the great advantages of his system that it solves Descartes's problem for him. In the *Discourse* he writes that his system offers

an explanation of the great mystery of *the union of the soul and the body*, that is to say, how it comes about that the passive and active states of the one are accompanied by active and passive states, or by suitable phenomena, in the other.

(DM 33, WF 85)

Nearly thirty years later, in the *Monadology*, Leibniz is still writing in the same vein: 'these principles gave me a way of providing a natural explanation of the union, or the conformity, of the soul with the organic body' (79, WF 279).

At each stage of his career the solution is supposed to be furnished by the doctrine of the pre-established harmony: the human mind and its body have been so programmed by God that they appear to interact causally with one another. In the language which Hume was later to employ, there is a constant conjunction between decisions to raise my arm and cases of my arm going up; that is to say, at least in a healthy body events of the first type are regularly followed by events of the second type. And in the other direction, there is a constant conjunction between bee stings and sharp, stabbing sensations of pain in the mind. The existence of such constant conjunctions leads the philosophically unwary to infer that there is genuine causal interaction between mind and body. But this inference, tempting as it may be, is strictly unwarranted. The metaphysical truth of the matter is that in the first kind of case the body, acting in accordance with physical laws, executes the movement when the mind, acting in accordance with laws of final causality, forms the volition in question; to say the mind acts from final causality is to say that its behaviour is always directed towards a goal. *Mutatis mutandis* the same story holds in the opposite direction of apparent interaction.

Leibniz's theory of the pre-established harmony between mind and body is very familiar, but it is difficult to know what to make of it. For one of the disturbing features of Leibniz's presentations of the doctrine is that he tends to play down just how far he has abandoned the Cartesian metaphysical framework. Indeed, it is not even clear that the problem of mind–body union, at least in its classical form, really arises in his philosophy (cf. Loeb 1981). In Descartes's philosophy the problem is traditionally taken to arise from his subscription to two metaphysical assumptions: mind and body are both substances, and their natures are completely heterogeneous: the nature of mind consists wholly in thinking, and the nature of body consists wholly in being extended. It has thus seemed difficult to Descartes's readers, from his time to the present day, to see how there could be any union or interaction between such different kinds of substances. By contrast, unlike Descartes's unorthodox disciple Malebranche, Leibniz never really accepts the fundamental assumptions which generate the mind–body problem in its pure Cartesian form.

One Cartesian assumption that Leibniz fails to share is that the human mind and the body are both substances. Although, on at least one occasion, Leibniz says that the human mind is more strictly a substantial form than a substance, he is generally committed to holding that it is an immaterial substance. But at no point in his career does Leibniz hold that the human body, considered in abstraction from the mind, is a substance in its own right. According to the doctrine of corporeal substances that Leibniz entertains in correspondence with Arnauld, the human body is an aggregate of corporeal substances, that is, living organisms such as cells. When, in his later philosophy, Leibniz comes to embrace the doctrine of monads, the status of the human body and of bodies in general is in some respects less clear. According to some readings it is an aggregate of monads; according to the view proposed in the preceding chapter it is an aggregate of bodies which is grounded in the reality of the only true substances, namely, monads. But on either reading the human body is an aggregate, and therefore a phenomenon; it is emphatically not a substance.

The classical problem of understanding the union of two heterogeneous substances, mind and body, cannot arise within Leibniz's philosophy. It may be objected, however, that Leibniz shares one central assumption with Descartes and the occasionalists; even if he does not hold that both are strictly substances, he agrees that mind and body are in a sense heterogeneous: in his later philosophy the human body may be grounded in immaterial souls or monads, but it is not itself immaterial. But even if Leibniz does face a problem of understanding the union of mind and body, it is not clear that he is entitled to appeal to the doctrine of pre-established harmony to solve it. The doctrine of pre-established harmony is introduced as a general thesis about the relations between created substances; it says that no such substances interact and that they have all been programmed with their states by God. But if the human body is not a substance, then the doctrine has no obvious bearing on its relationship with the human mind. It is true of course that there is a pre-established harmony between the mind and all the substances which either constitute or ground the aggregate in which the human body consists. But it cannot be validly inferred from this that the mind is in harmony with the body: to draw such an inference would be to commit the fallacy of composition, that is, the fallacy of inferring from what is true of each of the items in a group to what is true of the group as a whole. (For example, from the fact that Mary loves each soldier in a platoon it does not follow that she loves the platoon.) We can bring out Leibniz's problems here by pointing out the way in which he is at a disadvantage compared with Malebranche. Malebranche shares the Cartesian assumption that mind and body are both substances; he can thus invoke occasionalism as a solution to the mind–body problem regarded as a special case of a more general problem concerning the relations between substances. Because of his rejection of Cartesian onto-logical assumptions Leibniz, by contrast, is not entitled to appeal to his doctrine of pre-established harmony in the same way.

The fit between Leibniz's general metaphysical doctrines and his approach to 'the great mystery' of mind–body union is thus not a very close or comfortable one. In any case Leibniz is led, like Spinoza, to the position that the human mind and the human body are causally insulated from one another; each of my mental states is caused by a prior state of my mind, and each state of my body is caused by a prior physical state. To say this, however, is not to say that there is no interesting positive relationship between mind and body. As Leibniz tells Arnauld, the human mind expresses its body in the technical sense of the term explained above; indeed, it expresses it better than it expresses anything else in the universe. In response to Arnauld's query Leibniz explains that he does not mean by this that our mind has clearer thoughts of, say, the activity of its lymphatic glands than of the satellites of Jupiter; he means rather that given a complete knowledge of my mental states a supermind would find it easier to read off truths about my physical states than about the celestial bodies (P 73). But Leibniz does not stop here, as he might have done; he further claims that the human mind expresses its body by perceiving it, perception being a species of expression. As we shall see in the last section of this chapter, this claim provides the basis for an argument for the existence of unconscious perceptions.

THE CASE FOR NATIVISM (1): INNATE IDEAS

The human mind, then, for Leibniz is an immaterial substance which is causally independent of its body and indeed of all bodies. Such metaphysical considerations concerning the human mind are highly relevant to understanding Leibniz's doctrine of innate ideas; for, as we shall see, one of Leibniz's main arguments for innateness, or nativism as it is sometimes called, turns on the fact that the human mind is causally independent of all other substances except God. Nonetheless, it would be a mistake to suppose that Leibniz's revival of the ancient Platonic doctrine of innate ideas and knowledge is fuelled simply by such metaphysical doctrines. As we shall see, Leibniz, like Plato and Descartes before him, is driven to invoke innate ideas to solve problems in the philosophy of mathematics; in particular, Leibniz appeals to innate ideas to explain how a priori knowledge of mathematical truths is possible.

It is natural to approach Leibniz's theory of innate ideas by asking: 'What is an idea?', a question which itself forms the title of one of Leibniz's own essays (L 207–8). The term 'idea' had become central in early modern philosophy as a result of the teachings of Descartes, who explained to Hobbes that he had adopted it for the contents of the human mind because it was the term traditionally used for the forms of divine perception (CSM II 127–8). Leibniz must have been sympathetic to the implicit suggestion that the human mind is a God-like entity, but his conception of an idea differs in significant ways from that of his great predecessor.

In the first place, Leibniz is much clearer, or at least more consistent, than Descartes in holding that the term 'idea' is to be understood in a dispositional, not an episodic or occurrent, sense. To say that I have an idea of x is to say that I have a mental disposition to think of x in such and such circumstances; the idea is thus to be distinguished from the actual thinking of x. As Leibniz says in 'What is an Idea?', an idea consists not in some act, but in a faculty of thinking (L 207). In terms of this analysis Leibniz can do justice to the ordinary language claim that I may be said to have the idea of an elephant even when I am not actually engaged in thinking of elephants. As we shall see in a later section, the dispositional nature of ideas plays an important role in Leibniz's defence of nativism against the objections of both Locke and Malebranche. Second, Leibniz is more consistent than Descartes in upholding the intellectual status of ideas. An idea is a disposition to think of x where thinking is understood to be a strictly intellectual activity. To insist on this as a point of difference from Descartes may seem surprising, for it is generally agreed that, for Descartes, the paradigm examples of ideas are intellectual items; they are thoughts with mathematical and metaphysical content such as those of God and triangles. But it is also well known that Descartes tends to use the term 'idea' very broadly, and that he is prepared to speak of even pain sensations and sense perceptions as ideas, albeit confused ones. A third and final difference between the two philosophers is one that Leibniz is prepared to exploit for the purposes of criticizing Descartes. In the *Discourse on Metaphysics* Leibniz insists that a certain restriction must be placed on the content of ideas. To have an idea is not just to have a mental disposition towards (intellectual) thoughts: ideas necessarily take possible entities as their objects. Thus from the fact that I can think of x it does not follow that I have an idea of x; we have no idea of a round square, for example. Leibniz exploits this condition on ideas for the purpose of criticizing Descartes's ontological argument for the existence of God. This is the proof that seeks to infer God's existence from the fact that the property of existence is built into the very idea of God as a being possessing all perfections. Alluding to the recent debate between Malebranche and Arnauld about 'true and false ideas', Leibniz writes:

> When we reason about something, we imagine we have an idea of it, and on this basis some ancient and modern philosophers have grounded a very imperfect proof of God. Thus, they say, it is certain that I have an idea of God or of a perfect being because I can think about him, and one cannot think without an idea. Now the idea of this being involves all perfections, and existence is one of them – consequently, it exists. But we often think of impossible chimeras – for example, of the greatest speed, or the largest number, or the meeting of a conchoid with its base or rule, so this reasoning will not do. In this sense, therefore, we can say that there are true and false ideas, according to whether the thing in question is possible or not. And we can boast of having an idea of the thing only when we are assured of its possibility. So the above argument proves that God exists necessarily if he is possible. It is indeed an excellent privilege of the divine nature to need only its possibility or essence in order actually to exist – exactly what is called an *ens a se*.
>
> (DM 23, WF 76)

As the passage shows, Leibniz is far from being hostile to the Ontological Argument in principle; he is not to be numbered among those philosophers – such as Aquinas, Gassendi, and Kant – who complain that it misguidedly tries to 'define God into existence'. But he does believe that Descartes's version of the proof is seriously vitiated by its unwarranted assumption that we have an idea of God in Leibniz's sense.

On the basis of this conception of ideas, then, Leibniz advances a strongly metaphysical argument for nativism. In the *Discourse on Metaphysics* Leibniz reminds the reader of the metaphysical doctrines of the pre-established harmony which he claims to have demonstrated: the human mind, in common with all other substances, is a causally self-sufficient entity. From this premise, in conjunction with his theory of ideas, Leibniz seeks to infer the innateness of all ideas:

> In fact our soul does always have in it the ability to represent to itself any nature or form when the occasion for thinking of it arises. And I believe that ability of our soul, insofar as it expresses some nature, form, or essence, is properly called an idea of the thing, and it is in us, and is always in us, whether we are thinking of the thing or not. For our soul expresses God and the universe, and all essences as well as all existences. This fits in with my principles, for nothing naturally enters our mind from outside, and it is a bad habit of ours to think of our soul as receiving messenger species, or as if it had doors and windows. We have all these forms in our mind and indeed always have had; because the mind always expresses all its future thoughts, and is already thinking confusedly of everything it will ever think clearly.
>
> (DM 26, WF 78)

Such an argument for innate ideas from the causal independence of the mind may seem distinctively Leibnizian, and it certainly appeals to the doctrines of the pre-established harmony, but in fact it is reminiscent of a non-standard argument which Descartes advances in the *Comments on a Certain Broadsheet* (1647):

> Nothing reaches our mind from external objects through the sense organs except certain corporeal motions. . . . But neither the motions themselves nor the figures arising from them are conceived by us exactly as they occur in the sense organs, as I have explained at length in the *Optics*. Hence it follows that the very ideas of the motions themselves and of the figures are innate in us. The

ideas of pain, colours, sounds, and the like must be all the more innate, if on the occasion of certain corporeal motions, our mind is to be capable of representing them to itself, for there is no similarity between these ideas and the corporeal motions.

(CSM I, 304)

Here Descartes is helping himself, as Leibniz does, to the thesis that nothing comes into the mind from outside; he also appeals to the Causal Likeness Principle which states that there must be a similarity in nature between cause and effect. On Descartes's austere new picture of the physical world there is no such similarity between sensory perceptions and bodies; hence by the Causal Likeness Principle, such perceptions cannot be caused by such objects.

The strongly metaphysical argument from the causal independence of the mind which Leibniz advances licenses the conclusion that no mental state is externally caused, but does it really amount to an argument for innate ideas? Part of the answer to this question is straightforward: ideas are mental dispositions, and such dispositions are mental states; thus, since no mental state is externally caused, no idea is externally caused. But it is natural to object that talk of what is innate has a temporal dimension: to say that x is innate in the mind is to say not just that x is not caused by anything external to the mind but that x has been present in the mind at least since birth. The defence of Leibniz against this objection is, I think, a little different from what might be expected, for it is the notion of a disposition which plays the vital role. For Leibniz, it seems, dispositions are not just persistent properties of the things which have them; they are permanent properties. Thus it is the status of ideas as dispositions rather than their status as innate which guarantees that ideas are present in the mind at least since birth; Leibniz's argument for innateness is strictly an argument concerning causal origins. Thus, for Leibniz, while all mental states – including fleeting items, such as perceptions – are innate in the causal sense, it is only ideas which are innate in the richer temporal sense which is standard today.

We are now in a position to understand a second, rather puzzling argument for innate ideas which is most fully presented in the *New Essays on Human Understanding*. In the Preface to that work Leibniz seizes on Locke's admission that there are ideas which the mind acquires from reflection – that is, introspection – and argues that this is tantamount to the admission of innate ideas:

> Perhaps our gifted author will not entirely disagree with my view. For after devoting the whole of his first book to rejecting innate illumination, understood in a certain sense, he nevertheless admits at the start of his second book, and from there on, that ideas that do not originate in sensation come from reflection. But reflection is nothing but attention to what is within us, and the senses do not give us what we carry with us already. In view of this, can it be denied that there is a great deal that is innate in our minds, since we are innate to ourselves, so to speak, and since we include Being, Unity, Substance, Duration, Change, Action, Perception, Pleasure, and hosts of other objects of our intellectual ideas?
>
> (NE, Preface RB 51)

It is tempting to suppose that the argument from reflection is simply an expression of Leibniz's characteristic eirenical desire to find common ground with his opponents wherever possible, and that it strikes no deep roots in his philosophy. But this supposition would be mistaken; the argument from reflection is found, in its essentials, twenty years earlier in the *Discourse on Metaphysics* (27, WF 79).

The argument from reflection for innate ideas has tended to have a bad press from commentators, and it is not difficult to see why. In the first place, it has been objected that on this argument to say that an idea is innate is simply to say that it is non-sensory in origin; this, it is said, is an impoverished conception of innateness which allows ideas to count as innate that are acquired in the course of the mind's development. It can also be objected that the argument from reflection can establish at most the existence of a small class of ideas — those which pertain to metaphysics; it is powerless to show that mathematical ideas are innate, yet these have characteristically figured among the nativist's prize exhibits. This second objection must be conceded, but the first objection can be met by clarifying the role of reflection. It is plausible to suppose that, for Leibniz, reflection on the mind's properties, such as unity and identity, is not strictly the means by which an idea is acquired; it serves rather as the stimulus which activates the dispositional property of the mind in which the relevant idea consists. Thus what happens in post-natal acts of reflection is that the mind first comes to conscious awareness of an idea which it has always possessed.

THE CASE FOR NATIVISM (2): INNATE KNOWLEDGE

The two arguments for nativism which we have examined both have precedents in Descartes. In the *Discourse on Metaphysics* Leibniz supplements these arguments for nativism with a very different line of reasoning which is even more traditional: Leibniz, like Plato before him, believes that it is possible to mount an argument for nativism from our capacity for knowing necessary truths in geometry. Leibniz himself claims no originality for this argument; he acknowledges that he is essentially recycling Plato's case for reminiscence in the *Meno* while purging it of the extravagant thesis that in knowing geometrical truths the mind is remembering a previous existence in which such truths were actually known.

[Plato] confirmed his opinion [of reminiscence] by a beautiful experiment. He introduces a small boy whom he gradually leads to very difficult geometrical truths about incommensurables, without telling him anything, only asking him a sequence of appropriate questions. This shows that our souls have virtual knowledge of all these things, and that to grasp these truths they only need to have their *attention* drawn to them. Consequently, they have at least the ideas on which those truths depend, and we can even say that they

already possess these truths, if we consider them as relations
between ideas.

(DM 26, WF 78–9)

Here Leibniz offers a fair summary of Socrates' technique of cross
examination (*elenchus*) and of his claim to act simply as a midwife to
the truth.

Leibniz's fullest presentation of the argument from mathematical
knowledge occurs not in the *Discourse on Metaphysics*, but in his
response to Locke, the *New Essays on Human Understanding* written nearly
twenty years later. But in the latter work Leibniz seems to be offering a significantly different version of the argument; certainly the
emphasis has changed in two apparently related ways. In the first
place, Leibniz is more dogmatic now about what the argument is
supposed to establish. In the *Discourse on Metaphysics* Leibniz is clear
that the argument stops short of establishing Plato's extravagant
theory of reminiscence; it establishes only a dispositional or virtual
form of innatism. But Leibniz betrays some uncertainty on the issue
of whether he is advancing simply another argument for innate
ideas: the Platonic argument shows that the mind has *at least* the
ideas on which the truths depend. Less confidently Leibniz claims
that there is a sense in which the argument shows that the mind
already possesses these truths. In the Preface to the *New Essays*, by
contrast, Leibniz shows no such hesitation; the argument is
intended to establish that there are principles (i.e. basic truths)
which are innate in the mind.

The second way in which the argument of the *New Essays* differs
from its Platonic predecessor in the *Discourse* is arguably more far-
reaching; it concerns the manner in which the argument is supposed to work. In the *Discourse on Metaphysics* it is natural to suppose
that what is at issue is a psychological question about the origin of
various cognitive states. The slave boy comes to have full consciousness of what is for Leibniz a necessary geometrical truth; since he
was neither instructed in the truth by Socrates nor performed any

measurements or experiments, we can conclude, by an argument by elimination, that he must have had at least the ideas on which these truths depend in his mind all along. The theory of innate ideas is thus supposed to offer the only psychological explanation of the slave boy's coming to have an explicit belief. In the *New Essays* Leibniz again offers an argument by elimination, but what is at issue now is not a problem of explanation but a problem of justification. According to Leibniz, it is characteristic of mathematics in general that we make knowledge claims to the effect that necessarily p; we claim to know that it is necessarily true that $2 + 2 = 4$ or in Socrates' example that a square is doubled by squaring the diagonal. But such claims to universal necessary knowledge cannot be justified by an appeal to the evidence of the senses:

> Although the senses are necessary for all our actual knowledge, they are not sufficient to provide it all, since they never give anything but instances, that is to say, particular or singular truths. But however many instances confirm a general truth, they do not suffice to establish its universal necessity, for it does not follow that what happened will always happen in the same way. . . . From this it appears that necessary truths, such as we find in pure mathematics, and particularly in arithmetic and geometry, must have principles whose proof does not depend on instances, nor, consequently, on the testimony of the senses, even though without the senses it would never occur to us to think of them.
>
> (NE Preface, RB 49–50)

In this argument it is clear that innate principles play a normative role, not an explanatory one.

The argument from the Preface to the *New Essays* thus seems different from its predecessor in the *Discourse*, but it is not obvious that it represents an improvement over its predecessor. It may indeed be appropriate to appeal to innate ideas to account for the possession of certain beliefs, like those of the slave boy; it is less clear that it is appropriate to do so when what is at issue is a question about justification. For it is natural to ask what reason there is to suppose that the innateness of a principle would be any guarantee of its truth; in the words of one writer, why should not a pack of lies be inscribed on our minds?[5] Ironically, Descartes may seem to be in a better position than Leibniz to answer such a question, since he at least tries to show that whatever propositions are innate in our mind have been implanted by God who is not a deceiver; for Descartes, it is this divine benevolence that provides innate principles with their epistemological credentials. But one of the things which Leibniz most disliked in Descartes's theory of knowledge was his habit of appealing to God's goodness to solve epistemological problems. Thus this avenue is not really open to Leibniz.

Once again it is natural to take our cue from Leibniz's thesis that the human mind is the mirror of God. Leibniz himself provides the warrant for this approach when he says that the divine mind is 'the pattern for the ideas and truths which are engraved on our souls' (NE IV.xi.14, RB 447). Elsewhere in the *New Essays* Leibniz elaborates this theme by saying: 'And when God displays a truth to us, we come to possess the truth which is in his understanding, for although his ideas are infinitely more perfect and extensive than ours, they still have the same relationships that ours do' (NE IV.v.2, RB 397). The idea here seems to be that our innate beliefs have the same structure as the eternal truths in the divine mind, and that it is this identity of structure that guarantees the truth of the beliefs in question. Thus whereas Descartes appeals to divine benevolence to justify our innate beliefs, Leibniz appeals to the isomorphism between the human mind and the mind of God.

DISPOSITIONS AND THE DEFENCE OF NATIVISM

During Leibniz's lifetime the doctrine of innate ideas and knowledge came under siege not only from the empiricist Locke but also from Leibniz's fellow-rationalist, Malebranche. Locke and Malebranche launch their attacks from general philosophical positions which could hardly be more different; for whereas Locke holds that the mind starts out as a blank slate on which experience subsequently writes, Malebranche is committed to the view that the mind achieves knowledge by being illuminated by divine ideas. Curiously, however, some of their specific objections to the doctrine of innate ideas are not dissimilar. Moreover, in their very different ways Locke and Malebranche challenge Leibniz's overall picture of the mind as a cognitively self-sufficient entity. We shall see that Leibniz's dispositional version of nativism provides him with the resources to respond to the objections of both philosophers.

In the first book of the *Essay Concerning Human Understanding* Locke confronts the defender of nativism with an important dilemma. Like other critics he is troubled by the fact that it is not clear just what nativists wish to assert. A defender of the doctrine is either asserting the existence of actual knowledge and concept possession, or he is asserting merely that the mind is born with the potential to acquire such knowledge and concepts. But Locke then argues that if the nativists embrace the first horn of the dilemma, they are saying something which is empirically false, for new-born children show no signs of actually knowing the truths of logic and mathematics or of possessing the metaphysical concepts of substance and identity. On the other hand, if the nativists grasp the second horn of the dilemma, then they are committed to saying something trivially true, for all the knowledge and concepts which we ever come to possess will be innate. The doctrine is thus either reduced to triviality or to the absurd thesis that all knowledge and ideas are innate.

Leibniz's dispositional defence of the doctrine of innate ideas and knowledge allows him to go through the horns of Locke's dilemma; in the Preface to the *New Essays* Leibniz seeks to show that there is a third possibility which Locke has overlooked, and which is not vulnerable to his criticisms. To say, as Leibniz does, that ideas and truths are innate in us as 'inclinations, dispositions, tendencies and natural virtualities' is to assert something less than actual knowledge, as Locke understands it; the child may indeed not be able to assent to the law of non-contradiction or consciously think of, say, God or infinity. But it is also to assert something more than the claim that the child has the bare potential to understand logical laws or to engage in abstract thought. The claim that Leibniz wishes to defend is the claim that the human mind from birth has a certain natural grain to it, as it were; it is differentially predisposed towards employing certain principles and thinking in some ways rather than others. Leibniz expresses the idea that the human mind has a certain natural grain to it by means of the kind of picturesque analogy which has often been seen as a characteristic of the debate over innate ideas. Leibniz opposes Locke's image of the *tabula rasa* with one of his own:

> I have also used the analogy of a veined block of marble, as opposed to an entirely homogeneous block of marble, or to a blank tablet, what the philosophers call a *tabula rasa*. For if the soul were like such a blank tablet, then truths would be in us in the same way as the shape of Hercules is in a piece of marble when the marble is entirely neutral as to whether it assumes this shape or some other. However, if there were veins in the block which marked out the shape of Hercules rather than other shapes, then that block would be more determined to that shape, and Hercules would be innate in it, in a way, even though labour would be required to expose the veins, and to polish them into clarity, removing everything that prevents their being seen.
>
> (NE, Preface, RB 52)

Leibniz's point is again anticipated by Descartes, who employs a different and perhaps even more helpful analogy: ideas are innate in us

> in the same sense as that in which we say that generosity is innate in certain families or that certain diseases such as gout or stones are innate in others; it is not so much that the babies of such families suffer from these diseases in their mother's womb, but simply that they are born with a certain faculty or disposition to contract them.
>
> (CSM I 304)

Strictly speaking, the two philosophers are making rather different points. Leibniz's example focuses on the second horn of Locke's dilemma: the dispositional is more than the potential. Descartes's example focuses on the first horn of the dilemma: the dispositional is less than the actual. Yet Descartes's example easily lends itself to making Leibniz's point as well, for to say that a child has a certain genetic predisposition to contract heart disease, for instance, is clearly to say more than that the child has the capacity or potential to contract such a disease. Thus it is clear that Leibniz and Descartes have the same conception of a disposition and of the role that it can play in the defence of innate ideas.

Leibniz and Descartes are right that it is possible to go through the horns of Locke's dilemma in this way. Nonetheless, the strategy is better adapted to a defence of innate ideas than to a defence of innate truths or principles; it is significant perhaps that Descartes, unlike Leibniz, focuses exclusively on items of the former sort. In the context of innate ideas the dispositional thesis has a certain plausibility. To say that we have an innate idea of substance, for example, is to say that we are innately programmed to carve up the world in terms of things rather than clusters of features: it is more natural for us to respond to cats rather than instances of furriness. But it is not similarly clear how we are to unpack such claims regarding differential predispositions when logical or mathematical principles are at issue, for it is obscure what the terms of the contrast are supposed to be. If, for example, Leibniz claims that the rules of the propositional calculus work with the grain of the mind, as it were, it is open to Locke to reply that most people's reasoning is fallacious much of the time.

By appealing to the notion of a mental disposition, then, Leibniz is able to respond effectively at least to Locke's objections against the doctrine of innate ideas. Leibniz can also say that a proper understanding of the nature of dispositions provides him with the resources to reply to Malebranche's rather different objections. Unlike Locke, Malebranche is not worried that nativism is threatened with triviality; he is not bothered by the claim that all ideas might turn out to be innate. Indeed, unlike Locke, Malebranche is prepared to grant implicitly that talk of dispositions does not simply collapse into talk of capacities and potentialities. Nonetheless, he objects that appealing to the notion of a disposition will not save the doctrine, for it is now threatened from a new angle: it is explanatorily empty (*The Search After Truth*, Elucidation X, LO 622). According to Malebranche, the doctrine of innate ideas is supposed to offer an explanation of the occurrence of certain episodic thoughts, but in fact it is incapable of doing so, for it is threatened with the same weakness as infects Scholastic explanations in terms of dormitive powers: thus philosophers such as Descartes are inconsistently accepting an explanatory model in the case of the mind which they rightly reject in the case of bodies. To bring out Malebranche's point we can appeal to a dispositional property such as fragility. Suppose, in Scholastic style, we seek to explain the breakage of a set of glasses by invoking the fact of their fragility. Now to say that a physical object is fragile is to say roughly that it would break if it were dropped in such and such conditions (on a stone floor, for example). So if we explain the glass's breaking on a stone floor by citing the fact of its fragility, our explanation is merely circular; it broke when dropped on the stone floor because it has the property that when dropped in such circumstances it breaks. Analogously, if we explain an episodic thought (say, of a triangle) by citing an innate disposition, our explanation is merely circular; the mind thought of a triangle on a certain occasion, because its nature is such that it thinks of a triangle given a certain stimulus. Making Malebranche's point in this way by reference to the example of fragility serves to show how his objection is logically distinct from Locke's dilemmatic argument, for fragility is a paradigm example of a dispositional property. To say that an object is fragile is obviously to say more than that it has the capacity to break.

Leibniz does not respond directly to Malebranche's objection as he does to Locke's argument, but his philosophy clearly has the resources for such a reply; the resources in fact are furnished by his anti-Cartesian innovations in the philosophy of mind. Here it is important to note that, for Leibniz, mind and body run parallel not just in the familiar sense that mental states can be mapped on to physical states and conversely, but that certain metaphysical principles apply to both. For Leibniz, physical dispositions are not free-floating; they are grounded in the non-dispositional, structural properties of bodies. So too mental dispositions such as innate ideas need to be grounded in the non-dispositional, structural properties of minds. The parallel between the mental and the physical realms extends even further to what plays the role of grounding. Just as physical dispositions are grounded in microstructural properties of bodies, so too mental dispositions are grounded in a kind of microstructure, but what is at issue is of course not the tiny corpuscles which interest the physicist; it is rather what Leibniz calls minute perceptions (*petites perceptions*) (NE, Preface, RB 56). Unlike the corpuscles studied by the physicist, the perceptions are minute in terms of their intensive, not extensive, magnitude; that is to say, they are too low in intensity to cross the threshold of consciousness.

By means of his theory of *petites perceptions*, then, Leibniz is able to answer Malebranche's objection of explanatory circularity. Leibniz can agree with Malebranche of course that it is circular to offer an ultimate explanation of the behaviour of bodies in terms of dispositional properties: Leibniz is not advocating a return to the Scholastic model of explanation. Nonetheless, he would point out that such dispositions are simply place-holders for the structural, non-dispositional properties to be discovered by science. So too Leibniz can concede to Malebranche that if philosophers offer an ultimate explanation of the occurrence of episodic thoughts in terms of innate ideas, they are indeed guilty of circularity. Nonetheless, innate ideas, by virtue of being mental dispositions, are place-holders for *petites perceptions*. Thus when we understand how these innate ideas – such as the idea of a triangle – supervene on minute perceptions, we shall see that the doctrine of innateness is not threatened with explanatory circularity.

We can conclude this section by noticing that Leibniz is committed to a three-tiered model of the human mind. The top tier is occupied by episodic conscious thoughts and sensory perceptions; these include such items as my conscious thought of God and my visual experience in seeing a tree. The second tier is occupied by innate ideas which, as we have seen, are dispositional items on a par with fragility and solubility in the physical realm. The third and bottom tier is occupied by the minute, unconscious perceptions. By recognizing the existence of this lowest tier Leibniz is making a radical break with Descartes's model of the mind according to which it is transparent to itself; as Descartes puts it, there is nothing in the mind of which we are not conscious (AT III 273). We must therefore turn to the issue of why Leibniz thought it was necessary to recognize the existence of such a bottom tier.

THE CASE FOR UNCONSCIOUS PERCEPTIONS

In the Preface to the *New Essays* Leibniz says that there are thousands of indications in favour of unconscious perceptions (RB 53). Obviously there is a strong element of hyperbole in this claim, but it is true that Leibniz deploys a battery of arguments of different types in favour of this anti-Cartesian doctrine. At least some of these arguments strike deep roots in Leibniz's metaphysics. Here is one clear case where Leibniz's metaphysics of substances has implications for his psychology and theory of knowledge.

Leibniz tends to present the doctrine of minute or unconscious perceptions as if it were original with him, and it is certainly true that he is the first philosopher to articulate it and defend it fully. But one argument for this thesis has a clear precedent in Spinoza's philosophy. In the *Ethics* Spinoza holds, by virtue of the strict parallelism between mind and body to which he is committed, that to every state of the human body a mental state corresponds; any change in blood pressure or in my lymphatic system, for example, will have a mental correlate. In the *Ethics* Spinoza draws out the consequences of this thesis by saying that 'whatever happens in the body is bound to be perceived by the mind' (II P 12). As we have seen, within his own metaphysical framework Leibniz is led to agree with Spinoza's thesis. But whereas Spinoza does nothing to dispel the air of mystery surrounding this proposition, Leibniz is clear as to how it should be solved. Since, as Leibniz would admit, there are many states of the body which are not consciously perceived by the mind, the states in question must occur below the threshold of consciousness. Thus while Spinoza had left it to the reader to infer a commitment to unconscious perception, Leibniz leaves us in no doubt on the matter.

In the Preface to the *New Essays* Leibniz offers other arguments for his theory of unconscious perceptions which strike similarly deep roots in his metaphysics. One such argument is from the Identity of Indiscernibles. This principle straightforwardly applies to human minds by virtue of their status as substances: thus there are no two minds which differ only numerically. From this Leibniz seeks to infer that the individuating characteristics required by the principle must occur below the threshold of consciousness:

> This knowledge of insensible perceptions also explains why and how two souls of the same species, human or otherwise, never leave the hands of the Creator perfectly alike, each of them having its own inherent relationship to the point of view which it will have in the universe. But that follows from what I have already said about two individuals, namely that the difference between them is always more than numerical.
>
> (NE, Preface, RB 58)

If intended to be demonstrative rather than hypothetico-deductive, this argument goes by rather quickly. It is not obvious why the demands of the Identity of Indiscernibles could not be satisfied without departing from the Cartesian assumption that there is nothing in the mind of which we are not conscious. Leibniz of course cannot say that minds are individuated in terms of mental content since he is committed on metaphysical grounds to the thesis that each mind perceives the whole universe according to its point of view; in a real sense all minds have the same content. But there is no a priori reason why minds should not be individuated in terms of the clarity and distinctness of their conscious perceptions. The truth seems to be that though the argument appeals to the Identity of Indiscernibles, it is not wholly a priori, for Leibniz is helping himself to an empirical or factual assumption; there are times in its history when the mind is without conscious perceptions. Hence, there must be unconscious perceptions.

The addition of the empirical premise certainly strengthens the argument, but it would still fail to move the philosophers who are its principal targets. Descartes, for example, would simply dispute Leibniz's empirical assumption about the mind; even within the mother's womb, the mind is never without conscious experiences, though all of these are subsequently forgotten. Locke, by contrast, against whom the argument is explicitly directed, would not be troubled by Leibniz's empirical claim, but he would challenge the argument at an earlier stage. For even if he accepts the Identity of Indiscernibles, he can challenge its application to the present case. For Locke, it is possible, for all we know, that the human mind is not a substance but a process of thinking superadded by God to another substance, the brain ('some systems of matter suitably disposed'); if the relevant substance, then, is not the mind but the brain, there can be no argument from the Identity of Indiscernibles to the existence of unconscious perceptions.

Perhaps Leibniz's most interesting argument for unconscious perceptions is what we may call the argument from attention, which may be explained by means of the following scenario. Suppose that two people, Smith and Jones, are having a conversation and that, throughout, a drill has been operating in the background; Smith has not been conscious of the noise, but he now suddenly has his attention drawn to it by Jones. Leibniz argues that in the act of attention Smith is really remembering a past perception of the noise. But *ex hypothesi* this earlier perception was not a conscious one, and must therefore have been minute or unconscious. This argument clearly depends on the premise that attention involves memory (NE, Preface, RB 54), and Leibniz does little in context to explain or support this premise. But what he seems to have in mind is that attention is essentially a second-order mental state: to attend is to reflect on another perception where this first-level perception is already past even though the interval is infinitesimally small.

Leibniz's doctrine of unconscious perceptions has rightly been seen as a bold and brilliant stroke of innovation in psychology, but it is also in the service of major metaphysical doctrines. Consider, for instance, a strange irony regarding the polemical role of the doctrine. As we have seen, the theory of unconscious perception marks one of Leibniz's major breaks with Descartes's philosophy of the mind, but in the *New Essays* it is deployed, against Locke, in order to rehabilitate the Cartesian thesis that the mind always thinks; it always thinks, that is, not in the sense of always having conscious experiences but in the sense of never being without some perceptual states, conscious or unconscious. Leibniz's defence of this thesis is in turn in the service of a larger ambitious metaphysical goal: this is the vindication of an immaterialist theory of the mind against what he sees as Locke's insidious attacks on this doctrine. For Leibniz, the immaterial nature of the mind entails that it is naturally immortal; this in turn entails that it always perceives. And for Leibniz, as we have seen, the defence of an immaterialist theory of the mind is absolutely central to his whole vision of the world, for without it, human minds could hardly be said to be made in the image of God.

SUMMARY

Leibniz criticizes his contemporary Locke for failing to appreciate 'the dignity of our mind'. In this chapter we see that there is both a metaphysical and an epistemological component to Leibniz's conception of the mind's dignity. The metaphysical component is the thesis that the mind is a simple, immaterial, and naturally immortal substance which is causally self-sufficient. The epistemological component is the thesis that the mind is innately endowed with ideas and propositional knowledge. In the course of his career Leibniz scarcely wavers in his commitment to the thesis that the human mind is an immaterial substance. Such a commitment has puzzled some of Leibniz's readers, but it is not surprising in view of his Neoplatonic claim that the mind is like a little divinity. Leibniz is clearly predisposed by his idealist commitments in favour of the thesis that the mind is an immaterial substance, but he is also aware of the weaknesses in fashionable seventeenth-century arguments for the thesis: Leibniz detects a fallacy in one of Descartes's famous arguments for it. Leibniz's awareness of such fallacies must be borne in mind when evaluating his 'mill argument' in the *Monadology*: it is shown that this argument turns on the alleged inability of mechanism to explain the unity of consciousness. In addition to claiming that the mind is an immaterial substance Leibniz holds that it is naturally immortal: such immortality, unlike mere indestructibility, does not follow strictly from the mind's simplicity or immateriality. The second section of the chapter explores Leibniz's well-known claim that he has solved the problem of mind–body union which defeated Descartes. Leibniz insists that his doctrine of pre-established harmony solves the problem, but it is difficult to evaluate this claim, for the problem of mind–body union, as found in Descartes, hardly arises in Leibniz's philosophy. Moreover, it is not clear that without fallacy Leibniz can appeal to his general doctrine of pre-established harmony to argue that the human mind and its body do not causally interact. The fit between Leibniz's general metaphysics and his approach to the issue of mind–body union is thus not a close one. The next two sections examine Leibniz's arguments for innate ideas and knowledge respectively. Leibniz's theory of innate ideas is introduced by clarifying his conception of an idea. Leibniz offers a more consistent theory of ideas than Descartes does: ideas, for Leibniz, are mental dispositions; they are intellectual items; and they take logically possible entities as their objects. This last claim about ideas serves as a basis for a critique of Descartes's ontological proof of the existence of God. We then see how Leibniz advances a strongly metaphysical argument for innate ideas from the causal self-sufficiency of the human mind; he also offers a more puzzling one from introspection, or the mind's reflection on its own nature. Leibniz's arguments for innate ideas have precedents in Descartes; his arguments for innate mathematical knowledge are even more traditional: they go back to Plato's dialogue, the *Meno*. Leibniz offers significantly different versions of these arguments in the *Discourse on Metaphysics* and the *New Essays on Human Understanding*. In the next section it is argued that Leibniz's dispositional version of the doctrine of innateness, or nativism, allows him to defend it against two of its seventeenth-century critics, Locke and Malebranche. In response to Locke, Leibniz goes through the horns of the dilemma that any doctrine of innate ideas and knowledge must be either empirically false or trivially true. In response to Malebranche, Leibniz argues that, unlike Scholastic faculty explanations, the doctrine of innate ideas is not condemned to explanatory emptiness or circularity: innate ideas are mental dispositions which are grounded in unconscious or minute perceptions which play a role in psychology analogous to that played by tiny particles in physics. The final section of the chapter analyses and evaluates Leibniz's various arguments for the existence of unconscious perceptions. It is shown that this important break with Descartes's psychology is in the service of defending a metaphysical theory of the human mind.

FURTHER READING

N. Jolley (1984) *Leibniz and Locke: A Study of the* New Essays on Human Understanding. (Emphasizes the metaphysical motivation of Leibniz's critique of Locke's theory of knowledge.)

N. Jolley (1990) *The Light of the Soul: Theories of Ideas in Leibniz, Malebranche, and Descartes.* (Places Leibniz's theory of ideas in general and his defence of innate ideas in relation to the views of Descartes and Malebranche.)

M. Kulstad (1991) *Leibniz on Apperception, Consciousness, and Reflection.* (A careful, analytic study.)

P. Lodge and M. Bobro (1998) 'Stepping Back inside Leibniz's Mill'. (Offers a reconstruction of Leibniz's argument against materialism.)

R. McRae (1976) *Leibniz: Perception, Apperception, and Thought.* (An important and sometimes controversial study.)

A. Simmons (2001) 'Changing the Cartesian Mind: Leibniz on Sensation, Representation, and Consciousness'. (A penetrating study which emphasizes the anti-Cartesian nature of Leibniz's theory of mind.)

M. Wilson (1999) *Ideas and Mechanism.* (Contains a number of valuable essays about Leibniz's philosophy of mind.)

Five

Human and Divine Freedom

Perhaps no topic mattered more to Leibniz throughout his philosophical career than the nature of human and divine freedom. For Leibniz, as for other philosophers, it was of the utmost importance to be able to show that God and human beings are free in a way that allows them to be morally responsible for their actions, and thus subject in principle to praise and blame. Once again Leibniz's treatment of the issues is constrained by his conviction that human minds are mirrors of God; as he says in a note, 'the root of contingency in man is the divine image' (Gr I 298).[1] Accordingly, Leibniz seeks to develop an analysis of freedom which applies to God and to human beings alike.

'It is a very old doubt of mankind,' Leibniz writes in a paper entitled 'On Freedom', 'how freedom and contingency can be reconciled with the series of causes and with providence' (P 106). In this passage Leibniz does more than reveal his awareness that the philosophical problem of freedom, and human freedom in particular, has a long history; he also indicates, implicitly at least, that there are two distinct causes of philosophical perplexity about the issue. One such source of perplexity is reflection on the 'series of causes'. To many philosophers it seems obvious that human actions are events, and that, like all events, they are embedded in a causal chain or nexus; such philosophers are thus led to embrace a form of causal determinism. But if determinism is true, then it is not causally possible for human beings to act in a way other than that in which they act. Intuitively, however, the causal possibility of acting otherwise seems to be a necessary condition of freedom and moral responsibility. The other source of perplexity is reflection on divine providence or foreknowledge. If God foreknows that I shall go to Los Angeles tomorrow, it may seem that I am not free in respect of going to Los Angeles tomorrow. The problem of divine providence or foreknowledge is really a theological version of a problem that goes back to Aristotle's famous discussion of the sea battle tomorrow in De Interpretatione (c. mid 4th century BCE); the underlying issue is whether statements about the future have determinate truth values. Thus philosophical speculation about freedom has been fuelled by concerns not only about causality but also about truth. It is fair to say that Leibniz was much more interested in the threat to human freedom posed by the nature of truth than by causal determinism, and in this respect he was more in line with ancient and medieval philosophers than with contemporaries such as Hobbes. Yet, as we shall see, especially in the final section of this chapter, Leibniz does also address the relevance of causal determinism for human freedom, and like other philosophers in the period he advocates a compatibilist solution. Human freedom is consistent, or compatible, with causal determinism.

Leibniz was never in danger of underestimating the difficulties surrounding the nature of human and divine freedom. In a famous passage in the Theodicy, anticipated in the essay 'On Freedom', he characterizes human freedom in particular as one of the two great labyrinths in which our mind gets lost (H 53; cf. P 107).[2] But, at least by the time of his philosophical maturity, Leibniz was confident that he had found a way of leading people out of the labyrinth. Leibniz's confidence, however, has impressed few of his readers; his theory of freedom has generally been regarded as highly ingenious and intriguing, but less than fully satisfying. As we shall see, some of Leibniz's most basic philosophical commitments raise special obstacles in the way of a satisfactory account of freedom.

BACKGROUND: DESCARTES AND SPINOZA

Speculation about human and divine freedom had been one of the hallmarks of philosophy throughout the middle ages; Christian philosophers, in particular, had been concerned with the problem of whether and how human freedom could be reconciled with divine foreknowledge and predestination. Among seventeenth-century philosophers Leibniz was unusually well versed in medieval discussions of the problems, and more than most of his contemporaries he tended to accept the terms in which medieval philosophers had framed the issues and even to adopt their method and strategies for solving them. Yet problems about the nature of human and divine freedom had also figured prominently in the works of Descartes and Spinoza who are no less an important part of the philosophical background. Although Leibniz joined in the general chorus of condemnation of Spinoza's work, ironically he is closer to him in spirit on this issue than to the more orthodox Descartes. Indeed, ever since his correspondence with Arnauld, it has been Leibniz's fate to be accused of coming perilously close to Spinoza's doctrine that every truth is a necessary truth.

We have seen that on the issue of free will Leibniz is fully commit-ted to the thesis that human minds are made in the image of God. At first sight Descartes might seem to endorse such an analogy, for in the Fourth Meditation Descartes's enquirer discovers that it is 'above all in virtue of the will that I understand myself to bear in some way the image and likeness of God' (CSM 2 40). Descartes justifies this claim by saying that human beings possess an infinite will; that is, like God, they are endowed with an unlimited power of choice. But further analysis suggests that Descartes recognizes key disanalogies between God and human minds. In the case of human beings, for instance, Descartes says that liberty of indifference is the lowest kind of freedom. When Descartes writes in this way it is tempting to suppose that he is taking up a stand on the issue of causal determinism, for 'liberty of indifference' has often been employed as a phrase to mean contracausal freedom, that is, a kind of freedom which implies the absence of all causes. But it is probably a mistake to suppose that this is what Descartes has in mind here. When Descartes says that in the case of human beings liberty of indifference is the lowest kind of freedom, he can be understood to be talking about indifference in respect of reasons rather than causes. We can do justice to Descartes's position by means of a contrast between an expert and a novice bridge player. The freedom enjoyed by the novice is liberty of indifference; that is, it is the freedom of one who is indifferent between playing the ace of spades and the king of diamonds in the sense that he or she can see no reason for playing one card rather than the other. Such a kind of freedom is clearly different from, and inferior to, the kind of freedom enjoyed by the expert who sees that in order to make the contract there is overwhelming reason to play, say, the ace of spades. Descartes's point in saying that liberty of indifference is the lowest grade of freedom is thus clearly neutral on the issue of causal determinism.

Liberty of indifference may be the lowest grade of freedom for human beings who should ideally be guided in their choices by a perception of the good. But in the case of Descartes's God, things are very different. Descartes is emphatic that God is endowed with an indifferent will, which is not guided in its choices by an independent faculty of intellect. And yet, according to Descartes, in the case of God such indifference is not a sign of imperfection but rather of perfection. It is clear, then, that despite his remarks in the Fourth Meditation Descartes is in fact committed to a crucial disanalogy between God and human beings in respect of the power of choice. On these issues Leibniz will strongly disagree with Descartes by maintaining that 'any will implies some reason for willing, and that this reason is naturally prior to the will' (DM 2 WF 55). For Leibniz, it is of the nature of the will, whether divine or human, to be guided by the intellect, and its perfection consists in being guided by perceptions of the intellect that are clear and distinct. Thus unlike Descartes Leibniz will insist that human freedom mirrors divine freedom.

Whether Descartes recognizes contracausal freedom in the case of human beings is unclear and has been disputed; indeed, Descartes is perhaps not much troubled by this issue. Spinoza, by contrast, was centrally concerned with this problem, and his position is quite uncompromising: contracausal freedom is an illusion. For Spinoza, all events in the universe, including human choices, are part of a causal chain or nexus which stretches back to infinity. But Spinoza is not merely a strict determinist; on standard readings at least, he is also a strict necessitarian who holds that every truth is a necessary truth; this is equivalent to claiming that the actual world is the only possible world.[3] Such a theory leaves no room for saying that it was logically possible for me to do otherwise than begin writing at nine o'clock this morning. Leibniz is determined to resist Spinoza's extreme theory of necessitarianism since he rightly supposes that it is inconsistent with any traditional conception of freedom. Nonetheless, in some respects Leibniz is closer in spirit to Spinoza than he is to Descartes. For one thing, though they may not agree over the analysis of the concept of freedom, they agree that freedom can be predicated of God and human beings in the same sense. Moreover, Spinoza and Leibniz are equally committed to holding that freedom is a matter of degree, and that as people become more free, they become more godlike. Finally, and most importantly, Leibniz and Spinoza are both compatibilists of a sort. Unlike Spinoza, Leibniz wants to insist that freedom excludes strict necessitarianism, but he agrees implicitly with Spinoza that it is compatible, or consistent, with determinism.

FREEDOM: THE GENERAL ANALYSIS

Perhaps Leibniz's most important statement on freedom or liberty is found in the Theodicy of 1710, the one philosophical book that he published in his lifetime. Here Leibniz offers a definitive analysis of the concept which shows how freedom can be predicated of God and human beings in the same sense. In this work Leibniz identifies three conditions which are, in logical terms, individually necessary and jointly sufficient for free agency (that is, for an action to count as free it must clear each hurdle, and if it clears them all, it counts as free). Freedom, for Leibniz, is constituted by intelligence, spontaneity, and contingency (H 303). The first two conditions are strikingly and obviously satisfied in the case of God, whereas their application to human beings is more problematic. The third condition, however, is problematic in the case of God and human beings alike; indeed, there is room for disagreement over whether it can be satisfied in either case.

Intelligence, the first of the three conditions, is also the most important, for according to Leibniz it is the 'soul of freedom', whereas the other two are said to be its body and basis. Leibniz defines 'intelligence' as a 'distinct knowledge of the object of deliberation' (H 303); this presumably implies a correct estimate of the value of the competing courses of action among which the agent chooses, and of the consequences of such possible choices. Clearly such a necessary condition of freedom is satisfied straightforwardly in the case of divine agency: God perfectly understands the value of the alternative possible worlds among which he chooses, and in the case of each world, he perfectly understands the consequences of deciding to actualize it. Now Leibniz holds that human beings are often not in possession of such distinct knowledge; they lack such knowledge, for example, when they are in the grip of the senses or of the passions. We might expect, then, that Leibniz would say that persons who are subject to the senses or the passions fail to possess intelligence, and thus fail to satisfy a crucial necessary condition for free agency. But in fact Leibniz does not say that; he seems to hold rather that freedom is a continuum concept – that is, one that admits of degree – and that though people who are subject to the passions lack fully distinct knowledge of the object of deliberation, their knowledge is distinct enough to count as intelligent. On reflection it is easy to see why Leibniz is driven to adopt such a position. For freedom, according to Leibniz, as for most philosophers, is a necessary condition of moral responsibility; thus, unless human beings satisfy the intelligence condition, they are not morally responsible for their actions. But obviously Leibniz does not want to say that a person who is in the grip of the passions lacks moral responsibility for his or her actions; the miser or the adulterer cannot get off the hook so easily. Such a concession would be fatal to the whole purpose which Leibniz's conceptual analysis of freedom is supposed to serve. In this respect Leibniz's position is strikingly at odds with Spinoza's; Spinoza equates freedom with acting under the guidance of reason, but he does not face Leibniz's problem, since in his philosophy freedom plays a very different role: it serves as a goal which we should strive to achieve rather than as a necessary condition of moral responsibility.

Spontaneity, like intelligence, is a condition of freedom which is satisfied straightforwardly in the case of God. For in the Theodicy Leibniz defines 'spontaneity' in terms of having the principle of action in oneself; that is, a person is spontaneous just in case he or she is the causal source of his or her actions (H 303). Clearly God is spontaneous in this sense, for he enjoys unrestricted causal self-sufficiency; he can never be acted upon by anything external to him. But again, the application of this condition to human beings is more troublesome. And the issue is complicated by Leibniz's distinctive metaphysical commitments regarding substances. Now Leibniz is at least right that, intuitively, spontaneity in his sense is a necessary condition of free agency. If, for example, I am standing in a queue for the cinema, and I shove the person in front of me because I in turn was shoved from behind, then we would naturally say that the principle of action does not lie in myself, and my action is not spontaneous, and hence, on Leibniz's general analysis, not free. Now Leibniz pays lip service to the commonsensical way of drawing the distinction between spontaneous and non-spontaneous actions, but he also points out that, according to his metaphysics, there is a sense in which all human actions are spontaneous; as Leibniz says in the Theodicy, our spontaneity 'admits of no exception at all, and external things have no physical influence on us at all, to speak in philosophical rigor' (H 304). Thus, on Leibniz's interpretation the spontaneity condition seems useless for the purpose of distinguishing free from unfree actions, since his metaphysics implies that this condition is always necessarily satisfied. Leibniz is right of course that his metaphysics implies that in this respect human beings are always like God, but he seems to have paid a high price for this result in terms of giving a convincing analysis of human freedom.

We may be tempted to try to rescue Leibniz by saying that the spontaneity condition applies to choices, not actions; freedom of action implies that our choices are spontaneous. Leibniz would then be saying that it is this condition which is always satisfied: the causal source of choices is always internal to the agent. But this defence seems unsatisfactory on two counts. First, we tend to recognize the existence of cases of psychological as well as physical coercion; the highwayman who says 'Your money or your life' does not physically force his victims to hand over their purses, but he coerces them by offering a choice in which one of the alternatives is extremely unattractive. Thus even to say that all our choices are spontaneous will still run counter to our intuitions, for we seem to admit the existence of cases where our choices are determined, at least in part, by external forces. Second, there is textual evidence against such a view: Leibniz is explicit that it is actions, not choices, which are in question in his analysis; we are always spontaneous in the sense that our actions always spring from an internal source or principle.

If, on Leibniz's analysis, the spontaneity condition seems to let in too much, his third and final condition on freedom raises the opposite problem: it is in danger of letting in too little, or even nothing at all. At first sight this is a surprising judgement, for contingency seems to be a rather minimal condition. In the Theodicy Leibniz defines 'contingency' in terms of the exclusion of logical and metaphysical necessity (H 303). With this condition Leibniz is imposing the seemingly innocent requirement that true propositions describing human actions not be on a par with the strictly necessary truths of logic and mathematics. But, as we shall see in the next section, there are aspects of Leibniz's general philosophy which make this seemingly innocent or minimal condition hard to satisfy. Indeed, contingency is such a source of problems for Leibniz's whole account of freedom that it demands treatment at length in the next two sections.

Before we turn to an analysis of such problems, we should not overlook one of the most remarkable features of Leibniz's discussion. As we have seen, Leibniz is intent on offering a compatibilist analysis of freedom; that is, freedom is consistent with the causal determination of actions. To say that an action is spontaneous is not to say, as we might suppose, that the person must be indifferent in the sense of being causally undetermined; it is simply to say that the cause of the action lies within the agent himself. And to say that the action (or strictly the proposition describing it) must be contingent is simply to say that it excludes necessitarianism; it does not exclude the thesis that every event is determined by prior causes. Leibniz's analysis of freedom may be a source of problems, but it is still an outstanding contribution to compatibilist approaches to the issue of free will.

CONTINGENCY AND HUMAN FREEDOM

The problem which Leibniz faces in accommodating contingency in his philosophy is easily stated; it arises, most obviously at least, from his distinctive theory of truth. As we have seen in Chapter 2, Leibniz analyses truth in terms, not of correspondence, but of concept-containment; according to this theory a proposition is true just in case the concept of the predicate is contained in the concept of the subject. Thus to employ the terminology later made famous by Kant, all true propositions are analytic. Yet, as we have seen, Leibniz also wishes to recognize a key distinction between necessary and contingent truths. According to Leibniz's standard account, a truth is necessary if and only if its opposite implies a contradiction

(DM 13 WF 64): thus the truths of mathematics are necessary in this sense, since it is self-contradictory to deny, for example, that two plus two are equal to four. By contrast, a truth is contingent if and only if its opposite does not imply a contradiction. In the class of contingent truths Leibniz places such singular factual propositions as 'Julius Caesar crossed the Rubicon'. Although the proposition is true, it might have been false; Julius Caesar might have refrained from crossing the Rubicon. Now to many readers it has seemed obvious that all analytic truths are necessary; that is to say, if the concept of the predicate is contained in the concept of the subject, then the proposition in question cannot be denied without contradiction. It is thus difficult to see how Leibniz's theory of truth leaves room for contingency. Leibniz himself was on occasion perfectly capable of articulating the problem, for in the *Discourse on Metaphysics* he spells out the apparent consequences of his theory of truth for contingency and hence freedom: 'But it seems that this means that the difference between necessary and contingent truths will be destroyed, and that there will no longer be any room for human freedom, and an absolute fate will reign over all our actions, as well as over all the rest of the events in the world' (DM 13, WF 64). Thus despite his later protests in correspondence with Arnauld, Leibniz was well aware of the objection that the concept-containment theory of truth seems to leave no room for contingency.

The problem of accommodating contingency in Leibniz's philosophy should be sharply distinguished from the issue of certainty. According to Leibniz, the proposition 'Julius Caesar crossed the Rubicon' is not a necessary truth; nonetheless, Leibniz is perfectly happy to say that it is certain. In other words, God knows with certainty from all eternity that Julius Caesar will cross the Rubicon. (Strictly speaking, what God knows is a proposition, expressed in the timeless present, of the form: Julius Caesar crosses the Rubicon at t). Indeed, God knows the truth of this proposition a priori by inspecting the complete concept of Julius Caesar which he finds in his intellect, and by seeing that the relevant predicate concept is contained in the concept of the subject. Unlike us, then, God does not have to discover the truth of this proposition by waiting to see what Julius Caesar will do or by relying on the reports of eye-witnesses or historians. But Leibniz is clear that there is nothing objectionable in such claims about the certainty of such propositions, for they amount to no more than an affirmation of the traditional doctrine of divine foreknowledge. Thus what is at issue is not an epistemological claim about certainty; it is a modal claim about the contingency of singular analytic truths.

The problem of interpreting Leibniz's attempts at accommodating contingency in his philosophy is one of the most difficult and controversial in Leibniz scholarship. It seems, however, that he entertains at least two main strategies, both of which are found in the correspondence with Arnauld. As we have seen, in the *Discourse on Metaphysics* Leibniz is able to state the problem lucidly, but he is curiously ambiguous about how he proposes to solve it. By contrast, in the subsequent exchange of letters with Arnauld Leibniz's strategies for solving the problem emerge more clearly.

One basic strategy for solving the problem is suggested by Leibniz's slogan: 'existence is the root of contingency'. It is a version of this strategy at least which Leibniz deploys in response to Arnauld who, like others since, had effectively objected that Leibniz's concept-containment theory of truth introduces 'a more than fatal necessity' (WF 98). At the heart of this approach is the time-honoured distinction between absolute and hypothetical necessity, which Leibniz charged Arnauld unfairly with ignoring (WF 99). We can best bring out the nature of the distinction by considering a true conditional proposition such as 'If John is a bachelor, he is unmarried'. The whole proposition is absolutely necessary: by virtue of the meanings of the terms, it is logically impossible that John should be a bachelor without being unmarried. But the consequent of the conditional – 'he [John] is unmarried' – is only hypothetically necessary; that is, John's being unmarried is simply logically implied by his being a bachelor. But to say this of course is not to say that John might not have married. Hypothetically necessary truths are thus strictly contingent (DM 13, WF 64); indeed, there is a sense in which the term 'hypothetical necessity' is something of a misnomer.[4]

In terms of this distinction Leibniz seeks to show that the doctrine that individuals have complete concepts does not entail that singular true propositions about these individuals are necessary truths. We can best explain the role that this distinction plays by considering the following argument:

1 Adam exists.
2 Necessarily, if Adam exists, then Adam eats the apple.
3 Therefore, Adam eats the apple.

When deploying the present strategy Leibniz is prepared to concede that the conditional second premise is absolutely necessary. For the sake of argument, at least, he is prepared to put it on a par with propositions such as: 'If John is a bachelor, he is unmarried'. In logical terms Leibniz is committed to affirming the necessity of the consequence; that is, it is logically impossible that Adam exist without eating the apple just as it is logically impossible that John should be a bachelor without being unmarried. But to affirm the necessity of the consequence in this way is not the same as, nor does it commit one to, affirming the necessity of the consequent – that is, 'Adam eats the apple', which figures as the second clause of the conditional proposition. It is thus only hypothetically, not absolutely, necessary that Adam eats the apple. Now the first premise of the argument, 'Adam exists', is supposed to be contingent since it is equivalent, for Leibniz, to the proposition 'God creates Adam', which depends on God's free will; it follows, then, that the conclusion, 'Adam eats the apple', is also contingent. By contrast, if the first premise were necessary, the conclusion of the argument would also be necessary, for it is uncontroversial that if both premises of an argument are necessary, the conclusion is necessary. Thus, for the purposes of this argument it is crucial that Adam's existence is only contingent. In this way, then, Leibniz seeks to show that his theory of truth, and the complete concept thesis which it implies, does not destroy the contingency of singular factual propositions about individuals.

Leibniz's second strategy for accommodating contingency locates it at the level of concepts rather than existence. When confronted with Leibniz's first defence of contingency Arnauld protested that he had not been guilty of confusing absolute and hypothetical necessity; on the contrary, he had been concerned with hypothetical necessity all along. What gives him trouble, Arnauld insists, is Leibniz's commitment to saying that all the predicates of Adam, such as eating the apple, follow from his complete concept in the same way and with the same necessity as it follows from the axioms and definitions of Euclidean geometry that the internal angles of a triangle are equal to the sum of two right angles. That is, although Arnauld deploys the geometrical analogy here, he is also committed to protesting against the suggestion that 'If Adam exists, Adam eats the apple' is strictly on a par with 'If John is a bachelor, he is unmarried'. In response to Arnauld's concerns, Leibniz now seeks to deny that the parallel holds; that is, he denies that the conditional proposition concerning Adam is by itself absolutely necessary. On the contrary, it is only when God's decrees or laws of nature are factored in that the conditional proposition is absolutely necessary:

> I therefore think that there are only a few free primitive decrees that regulate the course of things, decrees that can be called laws of the universe and which, joined to the free decree to create Adam, bring about the consequence.
>
> (AG 71)

One might suppose that the laws of the universe are already contained in the complete concept of Adam, and thus that there is nothing that can be added to the antecedent of the conditional.

But Leibniz anticipates this objection and replies that though the complete concept of Adam contains the laws of the universe considered as possible, it does not contain them considered as actual. In any case, whatever the merits of this reply, Leibniz's main point is clear: eating the apple does not follow from Adam's complete concept in the same way that geometrical theorems follow from the axioms and definitions of Euclidean geometry. On this strategy there are contingent connections at the level of concepts.

Another Leibnizian strategy for accommodating contingency, which is at least suggested in the correspondence with Arnauld, draws on his famous or notorious theory of possible worlds. As we shall see in Chapter 6, the doctrine of possible worlds is prominent in Leibniz's response to the problem of evil, but it also plays an important role in his theory of freedom and contingency. In the essay 'On Freedom' Leibniz candidly remarks that at one time he 'was not far from the view of those who think that all things are absolutely necessary', but that he 'was dragged back from this precipice by a consideration of those possibles which neither do exist, nor will exist, nor have existed' (P 106). Following Leibniz's lead, we might introduce the notion of a possible world by appealing to literary fiction; we might say that Tolstoy's novel *Anna Karenina* describes a possible world. A world in which a Russian noblewoman has an adulterous affair with a cavalry officer named Vronsky and subsequently commits suicide by throwing herself under a train is a world which might have existed; it is possible in the sense that it is internally consistent. However, such a world, though possible, is not actual; as Leibniz would say, it is not the world which God decided to create.

In terms of the theory of possible worlds Leibniz can offer an analysis of the distinction between necessary and contingent truths. Necessary truths, such as those of logic and mathematics, are true in all possible worlds; there is no possible world in which it is false to say that two plus two are equal to four. Contingent truths, by contrast, are false in at least one possible world. How Leibniz is justified in claiming that a singular proposition such as 'Julius Caesar crossed the Rubicon' is contingent on this analysis is a controversial issue. It has been suggested that Leibniz at least has the resources to offer the following account.[5] A proposition is false if its subject term fails to denote, that is, fails to pick out an individual. Now there are possible worlds in which the term 'Julius Caesar' does indeed have no denotation; an uncontroversial example would be the case of a possible world in which there are no human beings at all. It follows, then, that 'Julius Caesar crossed the Rubicon' is not true in all possible worlds, and is, thus, on this analysis, contingent.

The theory of possible worlds thus offers an apparatus for accommodating contingency. But though it may show how the proposition 'Julius Caesar crossed the Rubicon' could have been false, does it provide a way of showing that Caesar could have done otherwise? At first sight, Leibniz's theory of possible worlds may seem tailor-made for such a purpose: to say that Julius Caesar might have failed to cross the Rubicon is to say that there is a possible world in which he fails to take this proverbially decisive step. But further reflection suggests that in Leibniz's philosophy matters are not nearly so straightforward. For it follows from his theory of complete concepts that each individual expresses its whole world; by virtue of this concept it is related to all other individuals in its universe. Thus an individual who did not cross the Rubicon would not be Julius Caesar but someone else. The most that Leibniz can say is that there is another possible world containing a counterpart of Julius Caesar – that is, someone very like our Julius Caesar – who fails to cross the Rubicon. Leibniz may seek to analyse 'Julius Caesar might have done otherwise than cross the Rubicon' in terms of this doctrine of counterparts in other possible worlds, but few are likely to accept that the analysis is satisfactory.

The 'possible worlds' approach to the problem of accommodating contingency may thus not represent a fully novel strategy; it may be a disguised version of the first strategy according to which exist-ence is the root of contingency. To say that the proposition 'Julius

Caesar crossed the Rubicon' is contingent is really to say that Julius Caesar might not have existed. Similar questions can be raised about one final approach to the problem which Leibniz entertains in some of his writings. According to Leibniz, the contrast between necessary and contingent truths is to be understood in terms of the distinction between two kinds of analysis: necessary truths have a finite analysis whereas contingent truths have an infinite analysis. Leibniz's account of necessary truths in these terms is clear: necessary truths are susceptible of finite analysis in the sense that they can be proved in a finite number of steps by means of the laws of logic and the substitution of definitional equivalents. To take an extreme case, 'Gold is a metal' is proved by replacing the subject term with its definition and thus revealing explicitly how the concept of the predicate is contained in the concept of the subject; this is what Leibniz also calls reducing the proposition to an explicit identity. But in the case of contingent truths no such analysis is possible. Contingent truths have an infinite analysis in the sense that though the predicate concept is included in the subject concept, the inclusion or containment cannot in principle be revealed by any finite proof:

> But in the case of contingent truths, even though the predicate is in the subject, this can never be demonstrated of it, nor can the proposition ever be reduced to an equation or identity. Instead, the analysis proceeds to infinity, God alone seeing – not, indeed, the end of the analysis, since it has no end – but the connection of terms and the inclusion of the predicate in the subject, for he sees whatever is in the series.
>
> (P 109)

One may suspect that the theory of infinite analysis does not represent a fully novel approach to the problem of contingency. But even if one suspects that it collapses into one of the strategies already discussed, it is by no means clear to which of these it is equivalent. A case can indeed be made for saying that by means of infinite analysis Leibniz may well be expressing his second strategy in more technical terms; that is to say, the notion of infinite analysis captures Leibniz's claim made to Arnauld that the complete concept of Adam does not logically imply the predicate concept of eating the apple; there are contingent connections at the level of concepts. But a case can also be made for supposing that the doctrine of infinite analysis is a technical version of the first strategy. For the proposition 'Adam eats the apple' is true only if Adam exists, and to ask whether Adam exists is to ask whether he belongs in the best possible world. But this can be determined only by a comparison of the infinitely many possible worlds that God finds in his intellect.

Leibniz, then, has several approaches to the problem of reconciling contingency with his theory of truth. We are now in a position to see how Leibniz would defend the claim that he can find room for human freedom in his philosophy; indeed, he would claim to have a theory that accords with our intuitions about which actions are free. Consider again the case of Adam eating the apple: Adam was punished by God for this disobedient action, and thus, on the assumption that the punishment was just, the action was a free one. Leibniz can agree that it was, for it was intelligent, spontaneous, and contingent; these conditions, as we have seen, are individually necessary and jointly sufficient for freedom. But of course there will be lingering doubts about Leibniz's theory. It is possible to mount an external critique of the theory by objecting to its very compatibilist character; a free action, it may be said, is one that it was causally possible for the agent not to perform, and Leibniz's analysis does not impose this condition. But it is also possible to accept Leibniz's compatibilist approach and still criticize his theory of human freedom on internal grounds. According to Leibniz, a proposition is contingent if and only if its opposite does not imply a contradiction. But here our earlier worry resurfaces: if the property of eating the apple is contained in the complete concept of Adam, then it cannot be the case that 'Adam eats the apple' can be denied without contradiction: Adam would not be Adam, it seems, if he did not eat the apple. Leibniz of course claims to have established that this proposition, though analytic, is indeed contingent, but he has persuaded few of his readers.

CONTINGENCY AND DIVINE FREEDOM

True to his general thesis that they are mirrors of God, Leibniz seeks to show that human beings are free in the same sense as their creator. It is sometimes said that Leibniz succeeds better with respect to divine freedom than human freedom. We shall see, however, that once again Leibniz faces problems in showing how the contingency condition is satisfied; indeed, Leibniz faces special problems in showing how God's actions are contingent.

Although much of their correspondence centres on human freedom, it was in fact divine freedom which was the topic of Arnauld's initial objections to Leibniz's teachings. In response to article 13 of the *Discourse on Metaphysics* Arnauld is prepared to allow that Leibniz's God is free to create or not to create Adam (WF 98), but he worries that Leibniz's theory that individuals have complete concepts has other damaging consequences for God's freedom. On Arnauld's reading, as we have seen, all the facts about Adam's posterity and the subsequent history of the world are straightforwardly implied by the complete concept of Adam. Thus by his initial decision to create Adam God logically ties his hands, as it were; he destroys his freedom in respect of the subsequent history of the universe. If Arnauld had been more familiar with the foundations of Leibniz's thought about contingency, he might have been more reluctant to concede that Leibniz's God is free in respect of his decision to create Adam, for he would then have seen how Leibniz derives his doctrine that created individuals have complete concepts from a general theory of truth; this concept-containment theory, as we have seen, poses problems for accommodating contingency and freedom in general. But setting aside the issues raised by Leibniz's theory of truth, we can still ask whether Arnauld is right to concede that Leibniz's God is free to create or not to create Adam.

At first sight the answer to this question is clearly 'yes'. According to Leibniz, God is confronted with an infinity of possible worlds which he finds in his intellect; each possible world is a kind of blueprint for a possible act of divine creation. Out of this infinity of possible worlds God chooses to create the best – the world which contains Adam and his posterity. This choice is clearly intelligent, for it is based on a perfectly distinct knowledge of each possible world and its relative value. The choice is also clearly spontaneous: the principle of action is internal to God, who cannot be acted upon or coerced by anything external to him. And by Leibniz's lights it would seem to be contingent, for he holds that there is no contradiction in denying the proposition that God creates the best. Thus, on the face of it, Leibniz is wholly successful in his goal of putting a distance between his God and Spinoza's God, who seems to be paradigmatically unfree. Spinoza's God is not a person, and thus cannot choose; moreover, there are no alternatives from which a choice can be made: the actual world, for Spinoza, is the only possible world. Leibniz's God is a person and an agent who chooses among an infinity of possible worlds.

Unfortunately, for Leibniz, however, the situation is not quite so straightforward. For although Leibniz seeks to maintain the contingency of God's choice, he comes under philosophical pressure to deny it; as we have seen, if God's choice is not contingent, he is not a free agent. Ironically, perhaps, the problem which Leibniz faces arises from reflection on God's goodness. The proposition that God is good is clearly a necessary truth: God, by definition, is a being possessing all perfections, and benevolence is one of the perfections. But it would seem that God's very goodness must compel him logically to create the best of all possible worlds; in other words, the conditional proposition: 'If God is good, he creates the best of all possible worlds' would seem to be a necessary truth. But in that case Leibniz is in trouble, for he is committed to the following argument:

1   Necessarily, God is good.
2   Necessarily, if God is good, he creates the best of all possible worlds.
3   Therefore, necessarily, God creates the best of all possible worlds.

Thus, starting from premises which can both seem intuitive, Leibniz is led to the conclusion which denies the contingency of God's creation. Indeed, the conclusion seems tantamount to the Spinozistic thesis that the actual world is the only possible world.

We saw that, despite his defensive reaction in correspondence with Arnauld, Leibniz was well aware that his theory of truth appeared to undermine contingency in general. Leibniz is equally well aware of the threat to divine freedom posed by the argument above. At various times in his life he seems to have entertained different strategies for countering the threat.

One strategy for rescuing God's freedom is to deny that both premises of the argument are strictly logically or metaphysically necessary. Now the necessity of the first premise, for Leibniz, is non-negotiable: God's goodness follows straightforwardly from his essence. But it seemed to Leibniz that he was under no such pressure to accept the logical necessity of the second, conditional premise. That is, consistently with his necessary goodness, God could have failed to create the best of all possible worlds. Thus, in the vivid words of one writer, Leibniz is tempted to squeeze in contingency in the narrow slit between God's character and his actions (Bennett 1984: 116). It may seem that this strategy is contradicted by the *Discourse on Metaphysics* where Leibniz inveighs against such philosophers as Malebranche who deny that God creates the best of all possible worlds; in response to such philosophers Leibniz seems to insist that God is obliged by his goodness to create the best (DM 3, WF 55–6). But there need be no inconsistency involved. In the first place, Leibniz never disputes the claim that in some sense God's goodness obliges him to create the best; what is at issue is whether the necessity is of the strong kind which attaches to logical and mathematical truths. Moreover, Leibniz's denial of the necessity of the second premise is consistent with upholding the necessity of the weaker thesis: If God is good, then if he creates at all, he creates the best. Consistently with his essential goodness, God might never have created at all; but it follows from this essential goodness that if he creates, he does the best job open to him. It is possible that in the *Discourse on Metaphysics* Leibniz is committed only to the weaker thesis.

A more subtle approach to the problem would accept that there is a sense in which it is necessarily true that God chooses the best of all possible worlds. But it would add that there is also a sense in which it is only contingently true. In other words, this approach seeks to exploit an ambiguity in the phrase 'the best of all possible worlds'. In technical terms, the ambiguity in question is between referential and attributive uses of this phrase. The phrase is understood in the referential sense when it is used simply to pick out a particular possible world; by contrast, it is used in the attributive sense when it means 'the best possible world, whichever it may be'. We may clarify the distinction between the two senses by means of a more mundane example. Someone might use the phrase 'the winner of the 2001 British General Election' simply as a way of picking out a particular individual, i.e. Tony Blair. But now imagine someone speaking before the event who says: 'The winner of the 2001 British General Election will face tough economic challenges'. This speaker is most naturally understood as using the phrase in the attributive sense: the winner, whoever it may be, will face tough economic challenges. Making use of this distinction, then, Leibniz can argue that the proposition 'God chooses the best of all possible worlds' is a necessary truth when understood in the attributive sense but not when understood in the referential sense. That is, it is not logically necessary that God chooses this particular world which is, as a matter of fact, the best of all possible worlds.

The strategy faces an obvious problem. At least on any ordinary understanding of contingency it is clearly a contingent fact that Tony Blair satisfies the description: 'the winner of the 2001 British General Election'; Leibniz himself must regard it as contingent, even though it is difficult for him to establish its contingency. It is less clear how it could be a contingent fact that the actual world, the world in which we live, satisfies the description 'the best of all possible worlds'. Leibniz's best hope of upholding the contingency of such a claim seems to lie in appealing to the machinery of infinite analysis. Here the fact that there is an infinity of possible worlds clearly works to Leibniz's advantage. For to establish with regard to a particular possible world that it is the best involves a comparison with infinitely many other possible worlds. The truth of this proposition thus cannot be demonstrated in a finite number of steps; it requires an infinite analysis, and is therefore contingent.

The two approaches to the problem are obviously different, but they agree in one important respect; properly interpreted at least, the proposition that God creates the best of all possible worlds is not a logically necessary truth. Sometimes, however, at least in his early writings, Leibniz is prepared to bite the bullet; that is, he is prepared to concede the logical necessity of the proposition that elsewhere he is anxious to deny. Leibniz's willingness to bite the bullet in this way is based on his estimate of what is required to avoid Spinozism. Leibniz can insist that, even if God is logically necessitated to choose the best, his position does not collapse into Spinoza's thesis that the actual world is the only possible world. Leibniz's point here is that other worlds remain possible in their own nature. A possible world is one that is internally consistent, and the internal consistency of a world cannot be affected by the necessity of God's choice. A world in which events unfold according to the plot of Tolstoy's *Anna Karenina*, for example, is still possible in its own nature, however God chooses.

Whether we judge such an approach to be successful depends on what we take Leibniz's goal to be. If Leibniz's goal is simply to avoid Spinozistic necessitarianism, then the 'possible in its own nature' defence, as we may call it, is sufficient for this purpose; Leibniz is right that, on this view, the actual world is not the only possible world. But if Leibniz's goal is to show how God is a free agent on his analysis, then the 'possible in its own nature' defence is not adequate.[6] For Leibniz is clear that freedom involves contingency, and according to the 'possible in its own nature' defence, God's action in creating the world is not contingent. Since this defence makes no provision for the contingency of God's actions, it can find no room for the freedom of divine agency. And thus it would not be true to say that 'the root of freedom in man is the divine image'.

LAWS, EXPLANATIONS, AND FINAL CAUSES

We saw in the previous section that Leibniz offers a compatibilist account of human and divine freedom. Contingency of course is a necessary condition of free action in general, but according to the teachings of the *Theodicy*, contingency excludes only logical and metaphysical necessity; it is compatible or consistent with the causal determination of human choices by motives, desires, and the like. Unlike some philosophers, then, Leibniz is not worried that 'the series of causes' poses a threat to freedom and contingency. But Leibniz is not simply committed to saying that freedom is theoretically consistent with causal determination; he is committed to saying that such causal determination is actual as well. Thus Leibniz is a determinist as well as a compatibilist. Now the human mind resembles the divine mind in that it always chooses under the aspect of the good (*sub ratione boni*); they differ here only in that, whereas the human mind is often mistaken about the real good, the divine mind is always enlightened. But Leibniz wants to say more than that human choice is teleological in the sense that it is always directed towards the good; he claims that human choice is always governed by *laws* of final causality. Although Leibniz is vague about the details, he is committed to holding, with Spinoza, that just as there are laws of physics, so too there are laws of human psychology.[7]

On at least one occasion, however, the doctrine that human minds are mirrors of God seems to lead Leibniz in a different direction; that is, it appears to lead him towards the advocacy of liberty of indifference or contracausal freedom. In a paper entitled 'On Necessary and Contingent Truths' (1686) Leibniz contrasts human minds with the behaviour of bodies which are bound by the laws of nature such as the law of gravity:

> But free or intelligent substances possess something greater and more marvellous, in a kind of imitation of God. For they are not bound by any certain subordinate laws of the universe, but act as it were by a private miracle, on the sole initiative of their own power, and by looking towards a final cause they interrupt the connection and the course of the efficient causes that act on their will. So it is true that there is no creature 'which knows the heart' which could predict with certainty how some mind will choose in accordance with the laws of nature; as it could be predicted (at any rate by an angel) how some body will act, provided that the course of nature is not interrupted. For just as the course of the universe is changed by the free will of God, so the course of the mind's thoughts is changed by its free will, so that in the case of minds no subordinate laws can be established (as is possible in the case of bodies) which are sufficient for predicting a mind's choice.
>
> (P 100–1)

Leibniz goes on to say that the mind does not always choose what appears the better course, for it can suspend judgement.[8] Such an argument seems curious, for it seems open to the objection that suspending judgement is itself what seems best to a mind at a certain time. Thus it seems that the phenomenon of suspending judgement could be easily accommodated within the theory that the human mind always chooses what seems best to it.

'On Necessary and Contingent Truths' is certainly a puzzling text, but there are some aspects of Leibniz's intentions in this work which should not puzzle us. For one thing, it seems clear that in this work Leibniz is displaying the accommodationist side of his thought. We have seen that it is characteristic of Leibniz to seek to do justice wherever possible to the views of other philosophers. One idea that Leibniz finds in the philosophical tradition is that freedom is accompanied by indifference; Leibniz seeks to show that there is something right about this idea, at least when it is properly interpreted or 'given a good sense', as he would say. Further, Leibniz is clearly keen in this work to distinguish two issues concerning human freedom: the issue of the causality of human choices must be separated from the issue of divine foreknowledge. Thus Leibniz insists that even though there is a sense in which human choices cannot be predicted in accordance with causal laws, this fact has no tendency to undermine divine foreknowledge. God can know a priori how human beings will choose simply by inspecting the complete concepts of individuals which he finds in his understanding; it is in this way, for instance, that he knows that Julius Caesar will decide to cross the Rubicon. But in fact, despite his apparent willingness to countenance freedom of indifference, there is no compelling reason to suppose that Leibniz is abandoning in this work the determinism that he embraces elsewhere. Indeed, there are two possible ways in which we might seek to mitigate the appearance of deep inconsistency with Leibniz's standard teachings on the issue of human freedom.

One apparently promising approach to the issue of consistency is suggested by Leibniz's insistence that minds look towards final causes in their choices of courses of action. Leibniz may seem to be simply drawing out the implications of saying that human minds are governed by laws of final causality, not efficient causality. In other words, it is a mistake to suppose that a human mind is determined by motives in the way that a balance is determined by weights. In these terms we might try to make sense of Leibniz's claim that 'the human mind is not even subject to physical necessity'. Leibniz, then, is not denying that minds are governed by laws of final causality; he is simply warning against a crude assimilation of final causality to the model of the efficient causality of a mechanism.

Unfortunately, there is a problem with this approach. For Leibniz says that it is a matter of physical necessity that God should do everything in the best way possible. Thus he is not, it seems, saying that a kind of category mistake is involved in trying to understand the choices of human minds in terms of physical necessity. Moreover, Leibniz here rejects the view that minds always choose whatever seems best to them. Yet the thesis which Leibniz here denies seems central to his understanding of what it is for minds to be governed by laws of teleological causality.

It is more fruitful, I think, to focus on Leibniz's claim that human minds act by a private miracle. For we can understand this claim in the light of one of Leibniz's definitions of 'miracle': an event is miraculous just in case it surpasses the understanding of creatures. The fact that Leibniz is working with this definition of 'miracle' here is suggested by his subsequent claim that 'no universal reason or law of nature is assignable from which any creature, no matter how perfect and well informed about the state of this mind, can infer with certainty what the mind will choose' (P 102); that is, human choices cannot be predicted by created minds. One writer has suggested that what may be at issue here is the complexity or inaccessibility of the laws of nature which determine human choices; it is one, or perhaps both, of these features that makes prediction in such cases impossible for created minds (Davidson 1998: 391). Since human choices thus surpass the understanding of creatures, they are on this definition miracles. And they are private miracles because, as mental events, they are not public phenomena on a par, say, with Christ's walking on the water.

This approach is surely the most promising one, but it raises questions about what specifically prevents us from being able to predict human choices. The relevant factor may be less the complexity of the laws of nature than the fact that they are teleological, not efficient, in character. In the case of bodies we know not only that they are governed by laws of efficient causality; we know also in some detail what these laws are; we know, for instance, that the behaviour of falling bodies is governed by the law of gravity (to cite the example that Leibniz himself gives in the paper). In the case of human choices, by contrast, we know that they are governed by laws of final causality, but we do not know what these laws are; we are incapable of stating any laws of psychology to match our impressive body of laws of physics. Thus it may be the inaccessibility of the laws due to their teleological character, rather than their complexity, which puts prediction of human choices beyond our reach.

To say that the laws need not be complex is not to say that there is no relevant role for complexity to play in Leibniz's account; complexity may enter in at a different level. Here we must consider the form that perfect explanations of human choices would take. The explanation will surely be constituted by the conjunction of a law of human psychology (i.e., a law of final causality) and a statement of the antecedent conditions; the antecedent condition in question will be a state of the human mind. Now it is natural to think of such psychological states in terms of motives, desires, and the like; in Dostoevsky's *Crime and Punishment* Raskolnikov chose to murder his aunt because he desired to inherit the old lady's money. But Leibniz cannot take a simple view of the nature of motivational states, for he is committed by his theory of unconscious perception to holding that any motivational state will be infinitely complex: even if it is conscious, it will be composed of an infinity of unconscious or minute perceptions. Such infinite complexity suggests that, as created minds, we are unable to formulate statements of the antecedent conditions which should figure in the explanation of human choices. In this way, then, the doctrine of unconscious perceptions helps us to see why human choices cannot be predicted by human beings, and are therefore miraculous. To say this is not, of course, to exclude an approach which emphasizes the inaccessibility and perhaps even the complexity of the laws of final causality. The important point is that Leibniz's system has the resources to show why human choices are in a sense private miracles. There is no need to suppose that Leibniz has abandoned the commitment to determinism which is such a hallmark of his standard teachings on the issue of human freedom.

SUMMARY

Perhaps no topic mattered more to Leibniz during his philosophical career than the nature of human and divine freedom. Leibniz was particularly concerned to develop an analysis of such freedom which shows how God and human beings can be free in the same sense, and in a way which allows for moral responsibility. Leibniz was in no danger of underestimating the difficulty of the task; he even claims that human freedom is one of the two labyrinths in which the mind gets lost. Although he is aware that 'the series of causes' seems to some to pose a threat to freedom, he is more interested in the threat posed by divine foreknowledge, and, more fundamentally, by the nature of truth. After a section surveying the teachings of Descartes and Spinoza, the chapter turns to an examination of Leibniz's general theory of freedom in the *Theodicy*. For Leibniz, an action is free if and only if it satisfies three conditions: intelligence, spontaneity, and contingency. Although, as understood by Leibniz, the first two conditions pose problems in their application to human beings, they are clearly satisfied in the case of God. By contrast, the third condition – contingency – raises serious problems in its application to human and divine actions alike. In the case of human beings, the problem of accommodating contingency in Leibniz's philosophy arises from his distinctive concept-containment theory of truth. If, as Leibniz holds, all true propositions are analytic (in Kant's language), then it is difficult to see how he can find room for the distinction he wishes to draw between necessary and contingent truths: it seems that a singular proposition such as 'Julius Caesar crossed the Rubicon' must be a necessary truth. It is shown that Leibniz adopts several strategies for solving the problem of how such truths can be contingent. Leibniz variously appeals to the distinction between absolute and hypothetical necessity, between finite and infinite analysis, the apparatus of possible worlds, and the existence of contingent connections at the level of concepts. One problem addressed is whether these four approaches represent logically distinct strategies. In the case of God, the problem of accommodating contingency arises chiefly from his essential goodness. This thesis, to which Leibniz is committed, seems to imply that God could not do otherwise than create the best of all the infinitely possible worlds he finds in his intellect. But if this is so, then the actual world is the only possible world – a conclusion which Leibniz wishes to avoid. Once again it is shown that Leibniz adopts various strategies for solving the problem. One strategy denies that it is an absolutely necessary truth that if God is good, he creates the best of all possible worlds; a second strategy exploits an ambiguity in the phrase 'the best of all possible worlds'; a third strategy appeals to the fact that, however God chooses, other possible worlds remain possible in their own nature. The final section of the chapter examines Leibniz's compatibilist thesis that human freedom is compatible, or consistent, with causal determinism. It is shown that Leibniz not merely regards such determinism as consistent with freedom; he holds that it is actual as well; all human actions are causally determined by prior motives. It is argued that, despite one superficially troublesome text, Leibniz is consistent in his commitment to both these doctrines.

FURTHER READING

R.M. Adams (1972) 'Must God Create the Best?' (A penetrating analysis.)

R.M. Adams (1982) 'Leibniz's Theories of Contingency', Hooker (ed.), *Leibniz: Critical and Interpretive Essays*. (A classic study of Leibniz's various positions; highly recommended for the serious student.)

R.M. Adams (1994) *Leibniz: Determinist, Theist, Idealist*, Chs. 1–3. (Incorporates and expands on themes in 'Leibniz's Theories of Contingency'.)

D. Blumenfeld (1982) 'Superessentialism, Counterparts, and Human Freedom,' Hooker (ed.), *Leibniz: Critical and Interpretive Essays*. (A careful, analytic account.)

J. Davidson (1998) 'Imitators of God: Leibniz on Human Freedom'. (Argues for the consistency of Leibniz's commitment to determinism.)

D. Fried (1981) 'Necessity and Contingency in Leibniz', Woolhouse (ed.), *Leibniz: Metaphysics and Philosophy of Science*. (Criticizes Mates's account of how Leibniz could solve the problem of contingency.)

J. Hostler (1975) *Leibniz's Moral Philosophy*. (Helpfully places Leibniz's views on freedom and contingency in relation to his moral theory.)

B. Mates (1986) *The Philosophy of Leibniz: Metaphysics and Language*, Ch. 6. (A classic discussion of the issues; highly recommended for the serious student.)

M. Murray (1995) 'Leibniz on Divine Foreknowledge and Future Contingents'. (An important but controversial article which questions Leibniz's commitment to compatibilism.)

G.H.R. Parkinson (1970) 'Leibniz on Human Freedom'. (A helpful survey of Leibniz's views.)

R.C. Sleigh (1990) *Leibniz and Arnauld: A Commentary on their Correspondence*, Ch. 4. (A penetrating and sometimes controversial account of the issues; highly recommended for the serious student.)

Six

The Problem of Evil

In 1710 Leibniz published his one philosophical book, the *Essays in Theodicy on the Goodness of God, the Freedom of Man and the Origin of Evil*. The term 'theodicy' (*theos* = God; *dike* = justice) was Leibniz's own coinage; because of an ambiguity in the French, the word even misled some of Leibniz's earliest readers into supposing that it was the author's pseudonym; thus they interpreted the title to mean 'Essays by a Theodicean' (G II 428). But if the term was new, the project of the book was not; it marked a new departure neither in the history of philosophy nor in terms of Leibniz's philosophical career. Indeed, the *Theodicy* simply represents the culmination of Leibniz's lifelong concern with defending God's character and justice before the bar of reason. And (as the full title indicates), the project of the work is also continuous with that of the last chapter. As we have seen, central to the defence of divine freedom is the claim that God makes a contingent, spontaneous, and intelligent choice among an infinity of possible worlds. At the heart of the defence of God's character is the claim that the world which God freely chooses is the best.

Ever since Voltaire's devastating satire in *Candide* Leibniz's thesis that the actual world is the best of all possible worlds has been notorious; to many readers it has seemed to exhibit a callous disregard for the facts about sin and suffering in our world. Some philosophers, such as Nicholas Rescher, have accordingly attempted to come to Leibniz's defence by saying that Voltaire's critique is wide of the mark; they have argued that Leibniz's 'optimism' (the thesis that the actual world is the best of all possible worlds) is a technical thesis which has nothing to do with issues concerning human happiness (Rescher 1967: 19). It is true that Leibniz does advance a criterion of value for possible worlds which seems to have no relevance for happiness, but the claim that Voltaire's satire is wide of the mark is itself wide of the mark. At least as early as the *Discourse on Metaphysics* Leibniz does wish to maintain that the happiness of minds is God's primary goal in creation, even if he seeks to realize other, possibly conflicting goods as well. Indeed, it should not surprise us that Leibniz's God makes the happiness of minds his principal goal, for this thesis is rooted in Leibniz's further thesis that minds are made in the image of God.

'EPICURUS'S OLD QUESTIONS' IN A NEW SETTING

The problem of evil – that is, the problem of reconciling the existence of evil in our world with the attributes of God – is an old one in the history of philosophy. In Hume's famous *Dialogues Concerning Natural Religion* Philo remarks that the problem has remained unsolved since the time of the Greeks: 'Epicurus's old questions are yet unanswered. Is [God] willing to prevent evil but not able? Then is he impotent. Is he able but not willing? Then is he malevolent. Is he both able and willing? Whence then is evil?' (Hume, *Dialogues*, Part X).[1] (The last phrase recalls the full title of the *Theodicy*.) The difficulty can be formulated in terms of an apparently inconsistent triad of propositions. (For the sake of simplicity, we will assume that the subject term in the first two propositions denotes an existent entity.)

1 God is omnipotent.
2 God is just and benevolent.
3 Evil exists in the world.

In other words, for a theist such as Leibniz each of these propositions would seem to be intuitive, but it is difficult to see how all three of them can be true. The problem of consistency should be sharply distinguished, as it is by Hume himself, from the problem of inference: this is the problem of inferring moral attributes in a deity from the facts of our world which include such things as sin and suffering. The problem of consistency, by contrast, arises for a philosopher who is, as Hume says, antecedently convinced of the existence of a God who is at once omnipotent, just and benevolent. In his writings on theodicy Leibniz is almost exclusively concerned with the problem of consistency rather than the problem of inference.

In Leibniz's time the problem of evil (understood as the problem of consistency) became particularly pressing as a result of the Scientific Revolution. The new scientific picture of the world accustomed people to regard the universe as a vast and intricate machine governed by the laws of physics; the admirable order disclosed by Galileo, Descartes, and later Newton, seemed to provide clear evidence of intelligent design. But when people reflected on the moral world they were struck by the appearance, not of order, but of chaos; in our world little children die of hideous diseases such as meningitis and leukemia, and in the words of the Psalmist, the ways of the wicked prosper. The very triumphs of the Scientific Revolution thus conspired to throw the problem of evil into relief.

At least by the time of Leibniz's maturity the problem of evil had acquired a new urgency for Christian philosophers as a result of the pointed challenge thrown down by Spinoza. In the Ethics Spinoza in effect dissolves the problem of evil in the same way in which he dissolves other philosophical problems; he denies at least one of the central assumptions which give rise to it. According to Spinoza, as we have seen, God is not a person but nature itself; he is thus not the sort of entity to which moral predicates such as 'is just' and 'is benevolent' can possibly apply. Thus in Spinoza's philosophy the traditional problem of reconciling the facts of evil in our world with the existence of an omnipotent, just and benevolent God simply cannot get off the ground. We can make the point by returning to the seemingly inconsistent triad of propositions.

Spinoza's attitude to (1) and (3) is subtle and complex, but there is no doubt that he straightforwardly rejects (2). Thus Spinoza could claim that it was a great strength of his philosophy that it dissolves the problem of evil which had baffled Christian philosophers for centuries.

In Leibniz's time Christian philosophers tended to react to Spinoza's challenge in one of two very different ways. Fortunately for our purposes the contrasting approaches are represented in the writings of the two philosophers who did most to stimulate Leibniz's own interest in theodicy: the writings of Malebranche and Bayle embody the rationalist and fideist strategies respectively. As a rationalist in theodicy Malebranche refuses to concede to Spinoza that Christian philosophers are devoid of resources for solving the problem of evil; as we shall see, Malebranche in fact draws his inspiration from the Scientific Revolution itself by making the concept of law central to his whole project of theodicy. God acts through general laws not only in the natural world but also in the distribution of grace: the results may sometimes be less than fully optimal, but God is obliged by concern for his glory to act in accordance with laws. Bayle, by contrast, is prepared to concede to Spinoza that the problem of evil admits of no rational solution, but he insists that faith must lead us where reason cannot. As we should expect, Leibniz is far closer in spirit to Malebranche than he is to Bayle whose fideistic writings, as we have seen, provided the immediate stimulus for the composition of the *Theodicy*. But despite their common commitment to a broadly rationalist approach to the problem of theodicy, there are differences of emphasis between Leibniz and Malebranche. Neither philosopher of course would agree that the three propositions above constitute an inconsistent triad, but each is prepared to give ground a little, though in different places. It is fair to say that Malebranche tends to soft-pedal divine benevolence, whereas Leibniz tends to soft-pedal both divine omnipotence and the reality of evil.

THE BEST OF ALL POSSIBLE WORLDS

Perhaps the key to understanding Leibniz's theodicy is to see that it comes in at least two distinct stages. The first stage in the defence of God's character against the charge of injustice consists in maintaining the thesis that God has created the best of all possible worlds; that is, God has done the best job open to him. This thesis must of course be clarified by way of explaining the criteria in terms of which possible worlds are evaluated. The second main stage consists in defending this 'optimistic' thesis against obvious objections. Critics like Voltaire will protest that the actual world surely cannot be the best possible world in view of all the various kinds of evils which it contains; surely other, better worlds are conceivable than the one which we inhabit. As we shall see, Leibniz ingeniously deploys some of the basic principles of his philosophy to show how the Voltairean objection is misguided.

To say, as Leibniz does, that God has created the best of all possible worlds is not to say that the world is absolutely perfect; Leibniz may talk of the various perfections of this world, but he is clear that it stops short of absolute perfection. Indeed Leibniz can say that it is a necessary truth that if God creates a world, it is less than absolutely perfect; for otherwise it would simply collapse back into God himself (Ross 1984: 103). In Leibniz's time, in particular, such a pantheistic thesis was maintained by Spinoza who holds both that the world is identical with God and that it is supremely perfect; the world only appears imperfect when it is judged by irrelevant anthropocentric standards. Thus, if Leibniz is to avoid the Spinozistic thesis and to maintain that the world is ontologically distinct from its Creator, he must admit that the world is in some degree imperfect; it must have some degree of what Leibniz calls 'metaphysical evil'. Nonetheless, although it falls short of absolute perfection, the actual world is the best of all possible worlds.

For Leibniz, the actual world is not merely the best of all possible worlds; it is also the best of all possible worlds in an absolute, and not a relative, sense. Here Leibniz seeks to put a distance between himself and Malebranche, his fellow Christian rationalist in the approach to theodicy. Malebranche's God resembles the Leibnizian deity inasmuch as he is a personal God who discovers 'in the infinite treasures of his wisdom an infinity of possible worlds' (*Treatise on Nature and Grace*, Part I, XIII). However, unlike Leibniz's God, the God of Malebranche chooses the world which is best relative to certain non-negotiable constraints on his choice:

> Thus, do not imagine, that God willed absolutely to make the most perfect work possible, but only the most perfect in relation to the ways most worthy of Him. For what God wills uniquely, directly, absolutely in His plans is always to act as divinely as possible. It is to make his action as well as His work bear the character of His attributes, it is to act exactly according to what He is and according to all that He is.
>
> (*Dialogues on Metaphysics* IX.x, JS 163)

Malebranche's God is thus like a student who is assigned the task of writing a paper within a strict time limit. If the student had all the time in the world to write the paper, he could do a better job of it; nonetheless, he does the best that he can within the time-constraints over which he has no control. Of course the analogy is by no means exact. The constraints to which Malebranche's God is subject are not temporal ones and they are in a sense not external to him; they are in some sense imposed by his very nature. God is morally obliged to act for his glory, and this means that he must create a world which honours him by the ways in which events are brought about; in particular, God is obliged to create a world which is governed by simple and fecund laws, even when these laws result in the production of mutants and the destruction of innocent people. Nonetheless, in spite of the points of disanalogy, Malebranche's God resembles our conscientious student in one key relevant respect: if he were not subject to certain constraints, he would have been able to produce a more perfect work.[2]

The idea that the actual world is only relatively the best in this way is anathema to Leibniz; he denounces it early in a section of the *Discourse on Metaphysics* entitled 'Against those who think God could have done things better' (2, WF 55). Nonetheless, though Leibniz's opposition to Malebranche's thesis of relative perfection is real, he opposes it in a characteristically subtle and accommodating way; he proposes a seemingly minor but far-reaching amendment to the Malebranchean theory. Leibniz is prepared to agree with Malebranche that God cares about excellence of means; in particular, he cares about the simplicity and fecundity of laws. But Leibniz insists, against Malebranche, that simplicity and fecundity of laws should not be treated as side-constraints on God's maximization of perfection; rather, they should be seen as entering into the very criteria by which possible worlds are evaluated. In this way Leibniz is able to rescue the thesis that God creates the best of all possible worlds in an absolute, and not merely relative, sense.

THE CRITERIA OF VALUE

From Leibniz's revision of Malebranche's teachings it is natural to infer that the criteria in terms of which possible worlds are evaluated are exclusively physical; the criteria concern such things as the properties of laws and the range of phenomena to be explained in terms of those laws. Such an assumption has indeed been made by many readers of Leibniz, especially those who are concerned to defend him against Voltaire's satire in *Candide*. But, although it is easy to sympathize with the motives which underlie it, such an assumption is clearly mistaken. For in fact there is another dimension to Leibniz's quarrel with Malebranche. Not merely does Leibniz seek to find ways of opposing his thesis of relative perfection; he also seeks to argue against him that the happiness of minds is a primary goal of God's in creation. Indeed, Leibniz seeks to ground this claim in his strongly anti-Malebranchean conception of the excellence of minds which we examined in Chapter 4. In the *Discourse on Metaphysics* Leibniz argues that by virtue of their cognitive and causal self-sufficiency minds are the most perfect of substances. And since

God aims at the greatest perfection in general, he will take the greatest care of minds; he does this by endowing them with the greatest possible happiness that the universal harmony allows (DM 36, WF 88).

Leibniz's commitment to God's concern to promote the happiness of minds is beyond dispute, but it raises an obvious problem. For if there are both moral and physical criteria of value for possible worlds, it is natural to ask how they are related; are these criteria in conflict with one another or does the best of all possible worlds satisfy them both maximally? (As we shall see, a structurally similar problem of interpretation arises in connection with the criteria of physical perfection.)[3] Just how Leibniz's views in this area should be understood is one of the most controversial issues in the literature, and it is possible that no one interpretation is supported by all the relevant texts. The thesis that will be defended here is that Leibniz's dominant view is that the actual world achieves the best balance between the conflicting goods of moral and physical perfection. Other possible worlds contain more overall happiness than ours, but they do so at such a cost in terms of physical perfection that they are less than optimal; conversely, other possible worlds contain more physical perfection than ours, but they do so at such a cost in terms of happiness that they too are less than optimal.

One strong argument in favour of the view that Leibniz subscribes to the thesis that God chooses the optimal balance between moral and physical perfection is that it preserves the basic consistency of Leibniz's position between the *Discourse on Metaphysics* (1686) and the *Theodicy* (1710). It has sometimes been suggested that in the *Discourse* Leibniz accords much greater weight to the happiness of minds than in the *Theodicy*. On the face of it, this claim has some plausibility. In the *Discourse on Metaphysics* Leibniz writes:

> Only minds are made in [God's] image, and are of his race, as it
> were, or as children of his house, for only they can serve him freely,
> and act with knowledge in imitation of the divine nature. A single

mind is worth a whole world, since it not only expresses the world, but also knows it, and governs itself there after the fashion of God.

(DM 36, WF 88)

In the Theodicy, by contrast, Leibniz writes in a passage which verges on the comic:

It is certain that God sets greater store by (*fait plus de cas de*) a man than a lion; nevertheless, it can hardly be said with certainty that God prefers a single man to the whole species of lions in all respects. Even if that were the case it would by no means follow that the interest of a certain number of men would prevail over the consideration of a general disorder diffused through an infinite number of creatures. This opinion would be a relic of the old and sufficiently discredited maxim that everything is made solely for man.

(H 188)

It may seem, then, that in the Discourse on Metaphysics Leibniz asserts that in the actual world the happiness of spirits is at a maximum whereas in the Theodicy he denies it.

In fact, there need be no basic inconsistency between the positions in the two works. The key to resolving the problem of consistency lies in seeing that in neither work does Leibniz mean to assert in unqualified terms that the happiness of minds is at a maximum in the actual world; he maintains rather that happiness is maximized only so far as is consistent with achieving an optimal balance between moral and physical perfection. It is true that there are differences of emphasis between the two works; indeed, in the Discourse on Metaphysics, in particular, Leibniz may be guilty of a degree of exaggeration. In the Theodicy Leibniz is concerned to stress that God's goals in creation are not confined to moral perfection but include physical perfection as well; he also clearly suggests how these goals may come into conflict: 'And thus there is no reason to suppose that God, for the sake of some lessening of moral evil, would overthrow the whole order of nature' (H 188). In the *Discourse on Metaphysics*, by contrast, Leibniz is concerned to stress that God cares for the happiness of minds. But even in the *Theodicy* Leibniz is prepared to concede that, while it is not his only goal, the happiness of intelligent creatures makes the principal part of God's designs; perhaps in the optimal balance the happiness of minds is weighted somewhat more heavily than the physical perfection of nature. And even in the *Discourse on Metaphysics* Leibniz is prepared to say that God maximizes the happiness of minds only as far as the universal harmony permits. Implicitly, then, Leibniz acknowledges in this work that it is maximizing universal harmony, or as we might say, achieving the optimal balance, which is God's basic goal. Even the God of the *Discourse* would not overturn the whole course of nature for the sake of achieving a modest gain in the happiness of minds, for this would not be consistent with universal harmony.

We can thus defend at least the basic consistency of Leibniz's position in the two works by supposing that he is committed to the 'optimal balance' model. But it must be admitted that in at least one work Leibniz seems to take up a position that is inconsistent with this thesis. In a paper entitled 'On the Ultimate Origination of Things' (1697) Leibniz may seem to say, not that the physical and moral criteria come into conflict, but rather that the world which satisfies the first criterion necessarily satisfies the second criterion:

> In case someone may think that moral perfection or goodness is here being confused with metaphysical perfection or greatness, and may admit the latter while denying the former, it should be pointed out that it follows from what has been said not only that the world is the most perfect physically, or if you prefer it metaphysically, or in other words, that that series of things will be forthcoming which in actual fact affords the greatest quantity of reality, but also that the world should be the most perfect morally, because true moral perfection is physical perfection in minds

themselves. Hence the world is not only the most wonderful
machine but also in regard to minds it is the best commonwealth,
by whose means there is bestowed on minds the greatest possible
amount of felicity or joyfulness; and it is in this that their physical
perfection consists.

(P 141)

It may seem tempting to defend the consistency of this passage
with the 'optimal balance' model by noting that even here Leibniz
does not say that it follows from the fact that the world is physically
the most perfect that it is also morally the most perfect; rather, he
says that the physical and moral perfection of the world both follow
from claims which have been previously established. But Leibniz
goes on to try to build a bridge between the two when he says
that the world is morally the best because true moral perfection is
physical perfection in minds themselves. Whether this move on
Leibniz's part can be defended is moot. The idea seems to be that
moral perfection or happiness of minds is a physical perfection
because the physical is identical with the natural, and it is natural to
minds to be happy; that is, minds fulfil their true nature by achieving happiness.

Leibniz's dominant view thus seems to be that the best possible
world is the one that achieves the optimal balance between moral
and physical perfection. It is natural to adopt the same approach to
a structurally similar problem of interpretation that arises in
connection with the criteria of physical perfection. According to
Leibniz, the best possible world is the one which (judged by the
physical criteria) is simultaneously simplest in theories (hypo-
theses) and richest in phenomena: once again the problem is whether
these criteria are in conflict. And, once again, the correct answer
seems to be that the best possible world is the one that achieves the
optimal balance between these conflicting criteria. Other possible
worlds are richer in phenomena than ours – for instance, there are
worlds which contain an even greater number of species of insects

– but they pay a steep price for such richness in terms of the simplicity of their laws: the laws in such a world are extremely complicated and inelegant. Conversely, there are other possible worlds which are governed by simpler laws than ours – laws that are comprehensible to even the meanest of intelligences – but they pay a steep price for such simplicity in terms of variety of phenomena: such worlds are, as it were, much more boring and monotonous than our own (cf. Rescher 1967: 14).

That this is Leibniz's view is confirmed by the relevant section heading (5) of the *Discourse on Metaphysics*: 'the simplicity of means is balanced against the richness of ends' (WF 57). But there is further evidence of a less direct kind from the *Theodicy* written near the end of Leibniz's philosophical career. In the *Theodicy*, as we have seen, Leibniz seeks to show that, properly interpreted, Malebranche's theodicy is really the same as his own in this area: simplicity and fecundity of laws, which are for Malebranche side-constraints on God's choice of the best world, should be taken to constitute the very criteria of physical value for possible worlds: 'One may, indeed, reduce these two conditions, simplicity and productivity, to a single advantage, which is to produce as much perfection as is possible; and thus Father Malebranche's system in this point amounts to the same as my own' (H 257). Now fecund laws are laws which are in a sense productive of variety; to say that one law is more fecund than another is to say that it explains a wider range of phenomena (Rutherford 1995a: 27). But there is surely no suggestion in Malebranche that even the most fecund laws produce the maximal possible variety. (Perhaps the maximum possible variety of phenomena might be incapable of explanation in terms of laws altogether.) Thus Leibniz's claim that Malebranche's theodicy reduces to his own in this area seems to support the optimal trade-off reading.

THE KINDS OF EVILS

At the beginning of this chapter we noted that Leibniz's theodicy comes in several stages. The first stage consists in defending God's character by showing that he has done the best job open to him: he has created the best of all possible worlds. As we have seen, this stage of the defence requires an extended clarification of the criteria in terms of which possible worlds are to be evaluated. The second main stage consists in defending the thesis that God has created the best of all possible worlds against obvious objections; it is natural to protest, as Voltaire does, that, in view of all the evils it contains, this world surely cannot be the best of all possible worlds.

As God's defence attorney, as it were, Leibniz is prepared to make an initial concession: the world does contain three kinds of evil: metaphysical, physical, and moral. The first kind of evil – metaphysical – presents no problem for Leibniz at this stage of his theodicy, for metaphysical evil is simply the absence of absolute perfection which is incident to any world that God might create. Indeed, the presence of this kind of evil has been conceded at the first stage of Leibniz's theodicy. But the other two kinds of evil – physical (suffering) and moral (sin) – are in a different position, for they do not simply follow, as does metaphysical evil, from the very nature of creation. As Broad points out, there are possible worlds which are wholly devoid of both physical and moral evil: consider, for instance, a possible world which is constituted by bare monads, none of whose perceptions crosses the threshold of consciousness (Broad 1975: 160). And of course it is the presence of these evils – sin and suffering – which is most troubling to Voltaire in *Candide*; it is the experience of 'man's inhumanity to man' and of the pain inflicted by diseases and natural disasters such as earthquakes which comes to undermine Candide's confidence in his master's teaching that this is the best of all possible worlds.

The presence of physical and moral evils in our world thus demands a separate treatment, but in one way such evils are less problematic than they appear. We can see this by returning to the criteria in terms of which possible worlds are evaluated. On the interpretation proposed here Leibniz's God chooses the world in which there is the optimal balance between moral and physical perfection (as measured by happiness on the one hand and the variety/simplicity criterion on the other). Thus Leibniz is not committed to saying that the happiness of minds is strictly at a maximum in our world; he can concede to Voltaire that there are possible worlds that contain less sin and suffering than does our world.

Voltaire's objections, then, are not exactly irrelevant, as some scholars have supposed, but they do lose some of their sting. Moreover, Leibniz has further strategies available to him for showing how the presence of physical and moral evil in our world is consistent with its status as the best of all possible worlds. As we have seen, unlike Epicurus Leibniz is not troubled by the suspicion that such evils are incompatible with divine benevolence and omnipotence, taken together. But it is still fair to say that the first of Leibniz's strategies tends to play down the reality of evil, whereas the third (in contrast to Malebranche) tends to play down divine omnipotence.

The tendency to play down the reality of evil is most evident in the first strategy: evil is something purely negative, or, in technical terms, it is a privation (DM 30, WF 82). This Augustinian doctrine arises naturally from reflection on the theme from the Book of Genesis: according to Genesis, God beheld his creation and saw that it was good. The philosophical moral, then, is that whatever God creates is good, and this is equivalent (by contraposition) to saying that whatever is not good is not created by God. If we add the further plausible premise that whatever is not created by God has no positive reality, the doctrine of the negativity of evil straightforwardly follows.

The doctrine of the negativity of evil fits certain facts rather well. Blindness is an evil, and it is an evil which is constituted by the lack of a certain property – namely vision – which certain creatures ought to have. On the other hand, in the light of modern medical science it may seem that there are other diseases which are more difficult to bring into line with the doctrine. We now know, for instance, that Down's syndrome is associated with the presence of an extra chromosome. Perhaps the defender of the doctrine is not without resources for replying to such objections. For it may be said that what constitutes the evil of Down's syndrome is not the presence of the extra chromosome but the absence of certain skills, and that this absence either supervenes on or is caused by the presence of the extra chromosome. Indeed, it could be said that in this respect Down's syndrome is on a par with blindness which may be caused by the presence of cataracts or by the pressure of fluid on the retina.[4]

Leibniz's second strategy involves no such tendency to play down the reality of evil: it consists rather in the familiar ploy of saying that the presence of local evil is a necessary condition of, and indeed contributes to, the overall goodness of the world. As we might say, local imperfection is in the service of global perfection. This doctrine is typically illustrated by the analogy with 'shadows in a picture'. Taken by itself, in isolation, an area of shadow in a painting is less than optimally attractive, but in a work such as Rembrandt's *Night Watch* even large areas of shadow contribute in an essential way to the excellence of the whole painting. Leibniz is perhaps even more fond of a musical analogy:

> The great composers frequently mingle discords with harmonious chords so that the listener may be stimulated and pricked as it were, and become, in a way, anxious about the outcome; presently when all is restored to order he feels so much the more content.
>
> (P 142)

The dissonant chords thus give spice to many a musical composition, and thereby contribute to their excellence.

Leibniz sometimes employs the picture analogy to make a rather different point, which he does not carefully distinguish from the first: we do not know enough to make informed judgements about the whole universe. According to Leibniz, we are in the position of someone looking at a picture most of which is covered up. Now it would be rash for such a person to make a judgement about the quality of the whole composition on the evidence of the small part of the painting which is exposed. Similarly, it would be rash for us to judge the quality of the universe as a whole on the basis of our experience of a very small part of it. Leibniz seems to blur the distinction between this point and the previous one by saying that the spectator in this position will see only 'a kind of confused medley of colours, without selection, without art' (P 142). Now this of course may be true, but it is also conceivable that the exposed part of the painting might be extremely pleasing to the eye. Even if this were the case, however, it would still be true to say that the spectator would not be in a position to make an informed judgement about the quality of the whole or even to appreciate properly the small part of the painting which was exposed. Thus Leibniz's second point here does not depend in an essential way on a claim about local imperfection.

The first two strategies for reconciling physical and moral evil with the thesis that this is the best of all possible worlds are wholly conventional and traditional. The third strategy, by contrast, employs the distinctive resources of Leibniz's metaphysics: it draws on the theory of complete concepts and on the very conception of a possible world. We may set up this third strategy by considering a very natural line of objection in the spirit of Voltaire. Looking around the world, we are inclined to think that certain obvious improvements could be made. We notice, for example, that our world contains Adolf Hitler. We wonder, then, why an omnipotent and benevolent God did not edit Hitler out of our world and replace him, say, by Adolf Schmitler, a counterpart of Hitler's who is an admirable ruler of Germany between 1933 and 1945.

The distinctive resources of Leibniz's metaphysics allow him to offer two related arguments against objections of this sort. In the first place, Leibniz can exploit his thesis that individuals have complete concepts to mount a *reductio ad absurdum* argument to show why Adolf Hitler could not be edited out of our world while leaving intact, say, its more attractive individuals such as Mother

Theresa. For it is part of the complete concept of Mother Theresa that she died fifty-two years after Hitler's death in the Berlin bunker; any individual to whom that predicate does not apply is not Mother Theresa but someone else. But if *per impossibile* Hitler were edited out of our world, then this predicate would no longer be true of her, for there would be no Hitler to whom she could be related. Thus a contradiction results: it is both true and not true of Mother Theresa that she died fifty-two years after the death of Hitler. It follows, then, that Hitler cannot be edited out of our world while leaving Mother Theresa or indeed any other individual intact. To say this is not to deny that all reference to Hitler can be deleted from the complete concept of Mother Theresa: for no contradiction results from doing so (Hacking 1982: 190). But in that case to conceive of such an individual is no longer to conceive of her or of this world, but rather of another possible individual in another possible world.

Leibniz can thus exploit the theory of complete concepts which express the whole world to show why Hitler could not be edited out of our world while leaving its good individuals intact. Leibniz can also invoke a further distinction which he sometimes draws to show specifically that the notion of replacing Hitler by Schmitler is incoherent. In places Leibniz stresses that not all individuals who are possible in themselves are compossible – that is, logically capable of co-existing in the same world (e.g. L 661–2). The point of Leibniz's distinction is easily explained. Suppose that Smith is 7 feet tall and that Jones is an even more towering 7 feet 6 inches tall; as described so far, these individuals are not merely possible in themselves but compossible as well. But if we suppose that each of these two possible individuals has the further, relational predicate 'is taller than any other human being', then they are no longer compossible. Now by virtue of his theory of complete concepts Leibniz holds that all possible individuals are partitioned off into possible worlds, each of which is incompossible with every other possible world. (A possible world, indeed, might be defined as a maximum set of compossible individuals.) Thus each possible individual is, as we might say, 'world-bound'; it is confined to its particular possible world. It follows, then, that whereas I am compossible with Adolf Hitler, I am not compossible with Adolf Schmitler in, say, possible world #747.

We are now in a position to see how Leibniz can defend God, his client, as it were, against the charges of Voltaire. Recall that Voltaire objects that the actual world cannot be the best of all possible worlds because it contains such monsters as Hitler. Surely, then, God could have created a better world by replacing Hitler; thus God has not done the best job of which he is capable. Leibniz can reply on behalf of his client that he would indeed like to replace Hitler by Schmitler but that his hands are tied by the laws of logic; and it is a fundamental feature of Leibniz's philosophy that divine omnipotence does not extend over logical laws. A possible world is a package deal, or to vary the metaphor, a *table d'hôte*; it is not an *à la carte* menu from which God can pick and choose the dishes that take his fancy.

This third strategy thus draws ingeniously on distinctive features of Leibniz's philosophy, and it is natural to ask how this final strategy is related to the more familiar second strategy. It may seem that the third strategy serves simply as a fall-back position; that is, according to the 'shadows in a picture' approach Leibniz argues that Hitler is like a dark patch in the *Night Watch* which contributes to the greater beauty of the whole; however offensive it may sound to say so, there is a sense in which this world is better for the presence of Hitler. According to the third strategy, by contrast, Leibniz concedes that the world is not better for the presence of Hitler: Hitler is simply the price to be paid for the moral and physical goods of our world. But this is perhaps a superficial view of the relationship between the second and third strategies. For in Leibniz's philosophy to say that this world would be better without Hitler is not coherent, for then we are no longer thinking about this world, but about another presumptively possible world. Thus it may be more correct to say that Leibniz's third strategy is a deep version of his second strategy.

Despite its affinities with Malebranche's teaching in the same area Leibniz's theodicy is much richer in resources for replying to objections. Unlike Malebranche, Leibniz can draw on his theory of complete concepts for individuals and the very nature of a possible world as a maximal set of compossible individuals. A study of Leibniz's theodicy thus reveals how systematic his philosophy can be. Leibniz's theory of truth entails that individuals are world-bound in the sense explained above; it thus does important work in Leibniz's theodicy. Yet ironically, the commitment to the world-boundness of individuals is less helpful to Leibniz's theory of human freedom, for it deprives him of the ability to explain Adam's freedom by saying that there is a possible world which contains Adam in which he does not eat the apple. Leibniz's basic commitments serve his theodicy better than they serve his theory of freedom.

SUMMARY

Leibniz's one published book, the *Essays in Theodicy*, is the culmination of his lifelong interest in the problem of evil – that is, the problem of reconciling the presence of evils in the world with the existence of a just, benevolent, and omnipotent God. So interpreted, the problem of evil is an old one in the history of philosophy: it goes as far back as Epicurus. But it was given a new lease of life in the early modern period not only by the rise of mechanistic science which exhibited the order of the physical world but by the challenge of Spinoza whose pantheistic metaphysics simply dissolves the problem. Leibniz's solution to the problem of evil comes in at least two distinct stages. First, Leibniz argues that God has done the best job open to him: the actual world cannot be absolutely perfect without collapsing back into God himself, but it is the best of all possible worlds. Moreover, Leibniz holds, against Malebranche, that the actual world is the best in an absolute, and not merely relative, sense. Second, Leibniz defends the thesis of optimism against those who object, as Voltaire was later to do, that the actual world cannot be the best in view of all the evils it contains. The first stage of Leibniz's project is clarified through a discussion of the criteria by which possible worlds are evaluated. Some of Leibniz's readers have assumed that the criteria are exclusively physical, and though some passages may seem to support it, this assumption is shown to be mistaken. In contrast to Malebranche, whom in many respects he resembles, Leibniz holds that the happiness of minds is a primary goal of God's in creation: Leibniz grounds this claim in an anti-Malebranchean conception of the excellence of minds. But if Leibniz's God seeks to promote the happiness of minds, it is natural to ask how are the moral and physical criteria of value related to one another. The issue is controversial, but the position defended in this chapter is that Leibniz's God seeks the optimal balance between the competing goods of moral and physical perfection. Such a reading has the merit of preserving basic consistency between Leibniz's views in the *Discourse on Metaphysics* and the *Essays in Theodicy*. A similar approach is adopted to the problem of interpreting the physical criteria of value: Leibniz's God seeks the optimal balance between the competing goods of variety of phenomena and simplicity of laws. The second main stage of Leibniz's project is introduced by noting his distinction between three kinds of evils: according to Leibniz, the world contains metaphysical, physical, and moral evils. Metaphysical evil poses no problem for Leibniz since it is simply inherent in the fact of creation. The other two kinds of evils raise real difficulties. It is argued that Leibniz adopts several strategies for showing how such evils are consistent with divine justice and omnipotence. One strategy turns on the Augustinian thesis that evil is purely negative. A second maintains that evil is like shadows in a picture: local imperfection is in the service of greater global perfection. The third strategy maintains that a possible world is a 'package deal': the evil features cannot be edited out. The first two strategies are entirely traditional; by contrast, the third strategy is distinctively Leibnizian inasmuch as it turns on his thesis that individuals have complete concepts which express their world.

FURTHER READING

D. Blumenfeld (1995) 'Perfection and Happiness in the Best Possible World,' Jolley (ed.), *The Cambridge Companion to Leibniz*. (A careful analytic treatment which is sometimes controversial.)

C.D. Broad (1975) *Leibniz: An Introduction*, Ch. 7. (A clear exposition of the main issues.)

G. Brown (1988) 'Leibniz's Theodicy and the Confluence of Worldly Goods'. (An important scholarly study which defends the overall coherence of Leibniz's position.)

S. Nadler (1994) 'Choosing a Theodicy: The Leibniz–Malebranche–Arnauld Connection'. (An illuminating account of Leibniz's theodicy in relation to Malebranche and Arnauld.)

N. Rescher (1967) *The Philosophy of Leibniz*, Ch 12. (A useful introductory account of the main themes of Leibniz's theodicy.)

D. Rutherford (1995a) *Leibniz and the Rational Order of Nature*, Chs. 1–3. (A scholarly discussion which critcizes the 'optimal balance' interpretation of Leibniz's theodicy).

C. Wilson (1983) 'Leibnizian Optimism'. (Examines Leibniz's views in the light of Voltaire's critique.)

C. Wilson (1989) *Leibniz's Metaphysics*, Ch. 8. (A valuable account of Leibniz's theodicy in its historical setting.)

Seven

Ethics and Politics

Traditionally, Leibniz has not been regarded as a major moral philosopher; indeed, he has not even been regarded as a philosopher who was greatly occupied with ethical questions. Yet it is a striking fact that the famous synoptic expositions of his philosophy, such as the *Monadology* and the *Principles of Nature and Grace*, all culminate in ethics. Even more strikingly such works tend to follow the same plan, at least in broad outline, as the greatest masterpiece of moral philosophy in the period, namely Spinoza's *Ethics*; that is, they begin with metaphysical considerations concerning the nature of substance, and they end with a vision of human happiness, even blessedness.

Whether the parallel is deliberate cannot be established with certainty, but in one way, despite Leibniz's well-known hostility to Spinoza's philosophy, it would not be surprising if it were. For in his moral philosophy, as in some other parts of his system, it is both possible and fruitful to see Leibniz as engaged in transposing Spinozistic themes into a different key; indeed, in some respects Spinoza's ethics lent itself remarkably well to an adaptation along Christian–Platonist lines of the Leibnizian kind. For instance, it is one of the leading themes of Spinoza's ethics that the more virtuous people are, the more they come to imitate God, and conversely. Now Leibniz is committed to the metaphysical thesis that all minds are mirrors or images of God. But he can also hold that this mirroring or imitation admits of degrees. The truly virtuous person is one who imitates God as perfectly as is consistent with his or her status as a creature. As we shall see, the imitation of God is a theme not only in Leibniz's ethics but in his theory of the state; it helps to explain why Leibniz stands aside from some of the dominant trends in seventeenth-century political philosophy.

MORAL PSYCHOLOGY

In company with the leading moral philosophers of the period, Leibniz grounds his ethical theory in moral psychology, that is, in a set of theses concerning the nature of human choice and motivation. None of the doctrines in question is strictly original with Leibniz: some have parallels in Spinoza and Hobbes; others find precedents in the teachings of Plato and Aristotle. But they all receive a distinctive colouring from Leibniz's metaphysical commitments.

The doctrine that the human mind is made in the image of God is clearly visible in one of Leibniz's central theses about the nature of choice; for Leibniz, an agent chooses a course of action if and only if he or she judges it to be best of the available alternatives.[1] To say this is not of course to say that there are no differences between human and divine choice; indeed, in places it is the differences, resulting from God's superior knowledge, which Leibniz seems to want to emphasize: 'When God chooses, it is through his knowledge of the best; when man does so, it will be the alternative which has struck him the most' (G III 402). Leibniz thus wants to say that whereas God always chooses the real good, human beings always choose the apparent good. But to draw the contrast between divine and human choice in this way is potentially misleading, for unlike some philosophers Leibniz does not regard these goods as mutually exclusive. For Leibniz, the real good is simply a species of the seeming or apparent good: one and the same object (such as a charitable donation) can be both a real good and an apparent good.[2] Thus it is equally true of God and of human beings that they always choose the apparent good. Of course there will be many cases where the apparent good chosen by human beings diverges from the real good, but there will also be many cases where they coincide.

Leibniz's doctrine of the nature of choice may seem unexceptionable in the case of God, but its application to human beings is more controversial. For it has consequences for an age-old debate in moral psychology; it implies that, strictly speaking, there is no such thing as weakness or perversity of will. That is, there are no cases where an agent fails to choose what he judges to be best, and there are no cases where an agent chooses what he judges to be worse. That there is a distinction worth drawing here is suggested by various cases. Consider, for example, the case of John, who, in view of his weight, judges that it is best to join a gym, but does nothing about it. In this case John is clearly weak of will, for he fails to choose what he judges to be best. But it might seem odd to say that his will was perverse. For one thing, one might wish to deny that he made any choice at all.

Leibniz is not only prepared to accept the consequences of his theory of choice for human beings; he also sketches strategies for finessing some of the many apparent counterexamples. In the passage contrasting human and divine choice, Leibniz immediately continues:

> If nevertheless [a man] chooses what appears to him less useful or pleasant, it will perhaps have come to seem the most pleasant because of a whim, by a spirit of contradiction, and by similar reasons of a corrupt taste that are still determining reasons even though they would not be conclusive reasons.
>
> (G III 402)

Thus, in a case where, for example, a man stakes his entire fortune on the throw of a die, Leibniz is certainly prepared to say that there is something about him that is corrupt or perverse. But it is the judgement, not the choice, which has become corrupt or perverse. As in the case of God, his will lines up with his judgement about the good.

Leibniz's most extended discussion of the phenomenon is found in his reply to Locke in the *New Essays*. There Leibniz is forced to confront Locke's example of a drunkard who deliberately chooses to return to the tavern in full knowledge that his drinking is a threat to his health, wealth, and reputation. Such a person, says Locke, is in the position of that 'unhappy complainer' described by Ovid: '*Video meliora proboque, deteriora sequor*' (I see and approve the better, I follow the worse) (*Essay* II.xxi.35). Locke's drunkard is not only weak of will (he fails to choose what he judges to be best); he is also perverse of will (for he chooses what he judges to be worse).

In reply Leibniz seems to signal his determination to maintain his theory; he says, for instance, that he would not wish to give up the old axioms that the will pursues the greatest good, and flees the greatest evil, of which it is sensible (NE II.xxi.35, RB 185). Leibniz's chosen strategy of defence in the *New Essays* turns on an appeal to the notion of what he calls 'blind thoughts':

> The neglect of things that are truly good arises largely from the fact that, on topics and in circumstances where our senses are not much engaged, our thoughts are for the most part what might be called blind . . . I mean that they are empty of perception and sensibility.
>
> (NE II.xxi.35 RB 185)

But as a strategy for denying weakness of will, this seems unsatisfactory; it seems in danger of conflating the question of whether an agent has a belief, with the separate issue of how the agent holds the belief. If Leibniz is to maintain that the will always follows the judgement, then he needs to establish that, at the time of his choice, the drunkard does not really believe that health, wealth, and reputation are greater goods than the pleasure of drinking. But what Leibniz shows is that the drunkard does not have the belief in a way that is sufficiently vivid to influence or determine his choice. To say this is not to show that the drunkard does not really have the belief in question. Thus it seems that Leibniz may have abandoned the principle that if an agent judges x to be better than y, he will choose x rather than y; he has retreated to the weaker principle that if the agent judges x to be better than y, and this judgement or belief is sufficiently vivid, then he will choose x rather than y (Vailati 1990: 213–28).

The image of God doctrine leads Leibniz to the denial of weakness and perversity of will in the case of human beings. The doctrine is less obviously visible in Leibniz's commitment to the thesis of psychological egoism; here it is rather the affinities with, and possible influence of, the moral psychology of Hobbes and Spinoza, which are most striking. Leibniz is as uncompromising as they are in maintaining that no one deliberately does anything except for the sake of his or her own welfare, for one seeks the good even of those whom we love for the sake of the pleasure we derive from their happiness (A VI.1.41).

The doctrine of psychological egoism is no less controversial in moral psychology than the denial of weakness and perversity of will, but again there are familiar strategies for defending the doctrine. To a large extent it seems that Leibniz is prepared to endorse such strategies. Perhaps the most famous line of defence emerges best from the anecdote that is told about Hobbes by his biographer, John Aubrey:

> One time, I remember, goeing in the Strand, a poore and infirme old man craved his Almes. He beholding him with eies of pitty and compassion, putt his hand in his pocket and gave him 6d. Sayd a Divine that stood by, Would you have donne this, if it had not been Christ's command? Yea, sayd he. Why? Quoth the other. Because, sayd he, I was in paine to consider the miserable condition of the old man; and now my almes, giving him some reliefe, doth also ease me.
>
> (Aubrey 1972: 236)

If Leibniz is in a position to add to this defence, it is by deploying the resources of his theory of minute perceptions and appetites. Thus Leibniz need not be moved by the objection that introspection often fails to turn up or disclose selfish motives; he can reply that such motives are always present in the mind, but frequently in an unconscious form. Indeed, the mind has been so programmed by God that it is always striving consciously or unconsciously to attain its own good.

Psychological egoism occupies a central place in Leibniz's moral psychology, and it is clearly consistent with his central commitments, such as the theory of unconscious perception. But is it consistent with Leibniz's doctrine that the human mind is made in the image of God? At first sight the answer to this question seems obviously 'no'; indeed, it may seem that a yawning chasm is in danger of opening up between divine and human motivation. Surely Leibniz would not want to say that there is any sense in which God is driven by selfish motives. But further reflection suggests that there is no real problem of consistency here. For one thing, as we shall see, in his moral theory proper Leibniz is at pains to show that psychological egoism is consistent with our having a moral duty to promote the happiness of others. Further, there need be nothing heretical involved in the claim that God's motivation is in a sense selfish. Even the pious Malebranche maintains (perhaps more strongly and with fewer qualifications than Leibniz) that God can act only for the sake of his glory (*Dialogues on Metaphysics* IX; cf. G VII 74).

THE CITY OF GOD

Perhaps the central theme of Leibniz's moral philosophy is that all minds or spirits are members of what, following Augustine, he calls the City of God; the City of God is proclaimed to be the most perfect possible state ruled by the most perfect of monarchs or sovereigns (*Monadology* 85, WF 280). According to Leibniz, membership of this community is based on the fact that all minds are images of the divinity (83, WF 280). It is clear that, for Leibniz, this moral community is more like a constitutional monarchy or even a republic than an absolute and arbitrary state in which the will of the sovereign stands for law, for Leibniz insists that all members of the community are bound by common standards of goodness and justice which are independent of the divine will.

Leibniz's insistence that all members of the moral community are bound by such common standards reflects one of the most obviously Platonic themes in his moral philosophy. In Plato's early dialogue, the *Euthyphro*, Socrates debates the nature of virtue in general in terms of the specific case of holiness or piety: is piety a virtue because it is pleasing to the gods or is it pleasing to the gods because it is a virtue? That is to say, the issue is whether virtues are constituted as virtues by their being willed by God or whether they are virtues independently of a divine will which simply underwrites them. Throughout his philosophical career Leibniz comes down firmly on the latter side of the debate; that is, he is at one with Socrates and Plato in rejecting the voluntarist option. Thus to say that God wills what is good does not reduce to an empty tautology:

> It is agreed that whatever God wills is good and just. But there remains the question whether it is good and just because God wills it or whether God wills it because it is good and just; in other words, whether justice and goodness are arbitrary or whether they belong to the necessary and eternal truths about the nature of things, as do numbers and proportions. The former opinion has been followed by some philosophers and by some Roman and Reformed theologians; but present-day Reformed theologians usually reject the doctrine, as do all of our theologians and most of those of the Roman Church.
>
> Indeed, it would destroy the justice of God. For why praise him because he acts according to justice, if the notion of justice in this case adds nothing to that of action? And to say *stat pro ratione voluntas*, my will takes the place of reason, is properly the motto of a tyrant.
>
> (R 45–6)

Elsewhere, in the *Discourse on Metaphysics*, Leibniz insists that no real sense can be given to the Genesis text that God saw that his creation was good if we adopt the voluntarist option (DM 2, WF 45). For if this view were correct, God would not, as it were, have had to look at his creation to see that it was good; it would have been made good by the mere fact that it was the product of his will.

Leibniz's stand on the *Euthyphro* problem helps us to see how we should understand his further claim that, while all created spirits imitate God to some degree, they should strive to imitate him as much as possible (*Monadology* 90, WF 281). To say this is not to say that such imitation of God actually constitutes the basis of morality, for that would come perilously close to the voluntarist option that Leibniz rejects. But there is still a sense in which Leibniz can claim that a person should seek to imitate God. Consider a sporting analogy. We might advise a young golfer to model his swing as far as possible on Tiger Woods, and even say that he will be a good golfer to the extent that he succeeds in doing so. But to give this advice does not commit us to saying that such imitation is what actually constitutes the goodness of the golf swing. What makes the golf swing good is independent of its being an imitation of Tiger Woods and of the fact that Woods himself embodies this kind of swing.

There is a sense, then, in which created minds should strive to imitate God as far as possible. Now God manifests his goodness in creation by seeking to maximize the happiness of minds, at least as far as universal order permits. Thus – with a similar caveat – we should likewise strive to maximize the happiness or welfare of minds. Leibniz is thus close to the modern doctrine of utilitarianism which holds that the maximization of happiness is the fundamental rule of morality (cf. Rescher 1967: 143). But the fact that Leibniz seems to impose a qualification on the maximization of happiness prevents us from saying that he is utilitarian in the strict sense.

One problem posed by Leibniz's ethics is the difficulty of understanding its key terms. For while 'happiness' is defined straightforwardly as a lasting pleasure, pleasure and pain themselves are defined more obscurely: pleasure is said to be a sense of perfection and pain a sense of imperfection (NE II. xxi.41, RB 194). Since these formulations do not wear their meanings on their faces, it is tempting to seek outside assistance, and here Spinoza seems to offer help; for Spinoza had given somewhat similar definitions: 'pleasure' is defined in terms of a (passive) transition to a state of greater perfection and 'pain' in terms of a (passive) transition to a state of lesser perfection (Ethics III P10S). Now in Spinoza's philosophy it is at least reasonably clear that such definitions are to be unpacked in terms of his doctrine of mind–body parallelism. To say that pleasure is a transition to a greater state of perfection is to say that it is an expression in mental terms of an increase in the vitality of the body. The jogger's 'high', for example, is simply the psychological aspect or counterpart of the toning up of the organism as a result of the exercise.

Although Leibniz's definitions of 'pleasure' and 'pain' make no reference to a change of state, the fact that he, like Spinoza, is in possession of a doctrine of mind–body parallelism makes it tempting for us to try to interpret him along the same lines. But it is not clear that the Spinozistic model is really the right one here. To bring the problem of interpretation into sharp focus consider the case of someone who experiences pleasure while contemplating a painting. We might say, along Spinozistic lines, that the pleasure is the psychological equivalent of the increase in vitality or perfection that the body undergoes as a result of being affected by the painting. But we might also say that the pleasure consists in a sense of the perfections or positive qualities of the painting itself. It is clear that Spinoza wishes his definition of 'pleasure' to be understood in the first sense, but there are indications that Leibniz wishes his definition to be understood in the second sense.[3]

The problem of interpreting his definition of 'pleasure' is one that Leibniz leaves to his readers to disentangle. But there is also a problem arising from his moral psychology to which Leibniz is acutely sensitive; it is the problem of reconciling psychological egoism and ethical altruism. The difficulty which faces Leibniz here is indeed a familiar one. On the one hand, as Hostler points out, Leibniz is committed to saying that our motives are always selfish; we always desire our own good (Hostler 1975: 49–52). On the other hand, he wants to maintain that we have a moral duty to promote the happiness or welfare of other minds. But how can we have such a duty if we are necessarily selfish in our motivation?

Leibniz most typically formulates the problem as one about love; alluding to contemporary debates on the issue in France and England, he asks in effect how pure or disinterested love is possible.[4] Leibniz insists that the solution to the problem depends on finding the proper definition of 'love':

> You will find my definition of love in the preface of my Diplomatic Code, where I say: to love is to delight in the happiness of another. . . . And through this definition we can resolve that great question how genuine love can be disinterested, although it is true that we do nothing except for our own good. The fact is that all things we desire in themselves and without any view to our interest are of such a nature as to give us pleasure by their excellent qualities, with the result that the happiness of the beloved object enters into our own. Thus you see, Sir, that the definition ends the debate in a few words, and that is what I love.
>
> (G III 207)

Elsewhere Leibniz elaborates his conception of disinterested love by contrasting two ways in which one can desire the welfare of another (A VI.i 464). The scheming man seeks the welfare of another as a means to his own welfare; consider, for example, the case of a wealthy businessman who donates a million pounds to charity in order to get a knighthood. The disinterested lover, by contrast, seeks another's good as if it is his own welfare. Here we might consider the case of someone who restores a lost article, such as a wallet, to another and finds his or her own pleasure in the happiness of the person to whom the article is restored.

One problem posed by Leibniz's proposed solution is whether he can really do justice to the claim that the lover is seeking the welfare of others for its own sake. For it seems on Leibniz's psychological theory that if counterfactually the action taken for the welfare of others did not bring pleasure to the agent, then he would have no reason to perform it, and thus to the extent that he is enlightened he will not perform it. (Imagine, for example, that in order to restore the lost wallet to its owner, the agent had to go on a long, difficult, and dangerous journey in terrible weather.) But if the agent would not perform the action, we would not wish to say that he desires the other's welfare for its own sake, for this phrase normally carries the implication that even if acting to promote the other's welfare did not bring pleasure to the agent, he or she would still perform the action. Thus Leibniz may seem to solve his problem only at the cost of operating with a very weak notion of what it is to seek another's welfare for its own sake.

The problem of reconciling psychological egoism and moral altruism naturally raises the issue of whether virtue, for Leibniz, is its own reward, and in what sense. In Leibniz's time the issue had come into prominence in ethics as a result of the resounding proposition with which Spinoza concludes his *Ethics*: 'Blessedness is not the reward of virtue but virtue itself' (V P42). Spinoza's target of attack was the orthodox Christian theologians who hold, as he supposed, that we would have no reason to pursue virtue and shun vice unless virtue were crowned with rewards in an afterlife: such theologians, on Spinoza's view, tended to regard virtue as a bitter pill which needed the jam of heavenly rewards to make it palatable to a rational person. If there were no such rewards in an afterlife, at least in many cases vicious action would be rational. But although Spinoza treats this crude conception of virtue with unqualified contempt, he is himself committed to a fundamentally egoistic view of the reasons for living a life of virtue. For Spinoza, virtue is its own reward in the sense that the practice of the virtues – the list of which overlaps with but is by no means identical with the traditional Christian list – is itself pleasant, and it is this anticipated pleasure which gives us reason to be virtuous. Thus even Spinoza does not hold that virtue is its own reward independently of the psychological satisfaction it brings.

Where does Leibniz stand on this issue? From what we have seen so far, it seems that Leibniz is close to Spinoza: virtue is its own reward in the sense that the life of virtue is more pleasant than the life of vice. But the issue is complicated by a key difference in their metaphysical commitments, for Leibniz, unlike Spinoza, believes that there is an afterlife in which virtue will be rewarded with eternal happiness and vice will be punished with eternal pain. Leibniz could of course maintain that even without such external rewards and punishments, it would still be rational for enlightened egoists to prefer a life of virtue over a life of vice. Now although Leibniz does make claims to this effect, he does not consistently stick to this position; in places he seems to help himself to the idea of external rewards and punishments in just the way that Spinoza excoriates (M 21). It is the prospect of heavenly bliss which makes it rational for the virtuous person to endure torture on the rack. In such contexts Leibniz seems to concede that it is at least not generally true that virtue is its own reward.

JUSTICE

We have seen that the concept of love figures prominently in Leibniz's attempt to reconcile psychological egoism with moral altruism. Somewhat surprisingly the concept of love also figures prominently in Leibniz's thinking about justice; for Leibniz's preferred definition of 'justice' is that it is the love (or charity) of the wise [*caritas sapientis*]. It is natural to object that justice cannot be properly defined in terms of love, for it is part of the 'common concept of justice' that it is something owed or due to a person. To say that justice demands, for instance, that I be tried by impartial judges or jurors is to say that such a trial is owed to me; it is something that I can claim as of right. It may be unfair to object that charity, by definition, is not something that is owed, for there may be a danger here of equivocating on the expression 'charity'. Still, Leibniz's preferred definition of 'justice' does not seem to capture the heart of the notion.

There are two possible ways of responding to this objection on Leibniz's behalf. In the first place, one might try to explain what Leibniz is about by saying that the definition forms part of his project of 'universal jurisprudence'. That is, Leibniz is in search of a definition that can apply to both God and human beings, and for this purpose a more traditional definition of 'justice' in terms of giving people what is their due is of no avail, for God can owe no duties (Riley 1988: 4). Now it is certainly true that Leibniz's preferred definition of 'justice' as the love or charity of the wise does fit the bill; it can apply univocally to God and to human beings. But it is less clear that it is correct to say that the traditional definition would not apply to God. For in view of Leibniz's stance on the Euthyphro dilemma, there is surely a perfectly good sense, for Leibniz, in which God does owe duties, even to finite spirits. He is, for example, under a duty not to damn the innocent for all eternity. Leibniz is clear that if God were to damn the innocent, he would do something paradigmatically unjust. It may of course be true that because of the Christian doctrine of original sin, there are no human beings who are strictly innocent, but that is a different matter.

Fortunately, a more satisfactory response to the objection is available: it consists in emphasizing Leibniz's links to the philosophical tradition. Leibniz is following in the footsteps of Plato and Aristotle in thinking of justice as comprehending all virtuous conduct towards others; he is thus seeking to define 'justice' understood in a broad sense which has become unfamiliar today. Leibniz then puts a distinctively Christian interpretation on justice so construed by equating it with a form of love or charity. Such an approach allows Leibniz to recognize that his definition of 'justice' does not capture the narrower concept. Indeed, Leibniz himself seeks to capture the narrower sense of the term 'justice' when he says that the precept of what he calls 'social justice' is to give each man his own (M 13, 95).

THE POLITICAL COMMUNITY

Human beings are not only all members of the City of God; they are of course also members of political communities which in Leibniz's time were typically ruled by monarchs or princes. Now Leibniz is fond of saying that such sovereigns are images of divine authority, especially in his encomiastic writings (R 88), and such claims were not unusual among political writers of the period; they are indeed part of the stock in trade of conservative political writers. But because of his underlying metaphysical and ethical commitments Leibniz arguably takes such claims more seriously than do most of his contemporaries; indeed, such commitments help to explain why Leibniz stands curiously apart from the main currents of seventeenth-century political theory.

The age of Leibniz was not only a period of political turmoil; it was also a period that witnessed an explosion of new ideas about the fundamental questions of politics. The most radical political theories – such as egalitarian democracy and even communism – competed in the marketplace of ideas with the most reactionary.[5] But between these extremes it is possible to identify two main currents of thought about the grounds and limits of political obligation. Intellectually conservative thinkers tended to embrace some version of 'divine right' theory; taking their stand on St Paul's Epistle to the Romans (Chapter 13), they argued that political authority was underwritten by God, and was to be obeyed conscientiously by Christians accordingly. Intellectually progressive thinkers, by contrast, tended to favour some version of 'social contract' theory; they argued that our duty to obey the state derives from an implicit or even hypothetical contract which was (typically at least) regarded as setting limits to such obligation. 'Social contract' theory could take many different forms and could be put to a variety of ideological uses: Hobbes erected a case for absolutism on contractarian assumptions, whereas Locke argued for limited, constitutional government on a not wholly dissimilar basis. But what such versions all have in common is an insistence that political obligation is anchored in the voluntary actions of individuals. It is clear, then, that despite some rather disingenuous remarks of Hobbes to the contrary, 'divine right' theory and 'social contract' theory are essentially in competition with one another. In modern jargon, 'divine right' theory offers a top-down account of the basis of political obligation; it derives our obligation to obey the state from the higher authority of God. 'Social contract' theory, by contrast, offers a bottom-up account: it derives such obligation from the people themselves who enter a contract to set up a state with authority over them.

Leibniz is unusual among political philosophers of the period in that he cannot be classified straightforwardly in either camp. On the one hand, he is not a contractarian theorist, for he rejects the doctrine of the equality of human beings in the pre-political state of nature which was shared by proponents of the theory. Leibniz is explicit that such a doctrine is to be rejected in favour of the traditional Aristotelian assumption of the natural inequality of human beings (R 192). On the other hand, though he can help himself to its language on occasion, he is not a classic 'divine right' theorist either. Indeed, this doctrine is alien to Leibniz in two respects; it takes its stand on revelation rather than reason, and it derives authority from the divine will rather than the intellect.

Leibniz's major pronouncements in political theory are somewhat scattered, but they seem to reveal the presence of two main strands in his political thinking. One such strand is the Platonic thesis that 'government belongs to the wisest'; the best in terms of political talent and expertise have a right to rule precisely because they are the best: Leibniz expresses this idea uncompromisingly in the context of criticizing Locke's contractarian approach and his doctrine of equal natural rights:

> If several men found themselves in a single ship on the open sea, it would not be in the least in agreement with either reason or nature, that those who understand nothing of seamanship should claim to be pilots; thus, following natural reason, government belongs to the wisest.
>
> (R 192; translation modified)

It is not difficult to see why the Platonic doctrine should have appealed to Leibniz. It is clear that, for Leibniz, the sovereignty of God derives from his being the most perfect being in terms of wisdom. Since human political institutions should strive to imitate God as far as possible, their authority will be genuine to the extent that it derives from the same source. Once again it is important to note the role played by the imitation of God doctrine here: strictly speaking, the imitation of God doctrine does not ground the justice of rule by the best. Rather, Leibniz would say that there is a principle of justice which states quite generally that sovereignty is founded in wisdom, and that this principle is to be numbered among the eternal truths in the divine understanding. As we have seen, these same principles of justice hold independently of the divine will, and are equally binding on God and human beings alike.

The case for the rule of the best can be made to seem persuasive independently of Leibniz's philosophical commitments. As the letter to Burnett shows, Leibniz, like Plato himself, is prepared to argue for the thesis from the all-too seductive analogy with seamanship or navigation; in the *Republic*, for instance, Plato deploys the analogy as part of a rhetorically brilliant and powerful case against democracy (VI.488). But this kind of argument is open to the objection that the analogy, seductive as it is, is in fact a false one.[6] The objection begins by pointing out that government is more a matter of setting policy goals or ends than of deciding on the best means to implement agreed policies: governments must decide, for instance, on whether to give priority to promoting liberty or equality, or to give a more concrete example, on whether to maintain full employment at the expense of inflation. Thus the true analogy is not with the navigator who knows how to plot a course to avoid dangerous reefs; it is rather with the owners of the shipping company or even the passengers who decide on the destination for the ship. The next step in the critique is equally vital: it consists in saying that though there is room for expertise concerning means, there is no such room for expertise concerning ends or goals; economists, for instance, can tell us how best to achieve full employment, but they cannot tell us whether this is the right policy to adopt. Since government is about policy goals, and there cannot even in principle be experts in this area, the Platonic argument by analogy is a failure. How Leibniz would respond to this critique may only be conjectured; it is perhaps worth remarking that, living in a political culture in which the interests of different classes could not be openly articulated in a public forum, he may have found it easier than we do to assume that the ends of politics are simply given.

If it is easy to see why the Platonic thesis appealed to Leibniz, it is no less easy to see why this strand could hardly be found in a pure form in his political theory. For taken seriously it seems to condemn all or most of the states of Leibniz's time to illegitimacy, and Leibniz was at once too conservative and too close to the political establishment to be willing to accept that result. It would be Panglossian in the extreme to try to maintain that the states of Leibniz's time, which were mostly hereditary monarchies and principalities, in fact embodied the principle of the rule of the best. It is true that in some of his encomiastic writings Leibniz claims of some particular prince that he is the person best qualified to rule (R 86). And in a more intellectually serious vein Leibniz seeks to emphasize the role of education in bridging the gap between the hereditary principle and natural aristocracy: princes should be educated so as to display all the virtues required for good government

(R 92). But Leibniz is not generally committed to taking such a Panglossian view of the qualities of seventeenth-century rulers.

The Platonic thesis, then, cannot serve all Leibniz's main purposes in political theory. Not surprisingly, even when stating the thesis Leibniz indicates the presence of another strand in his thinking. Thus in the letter to Burnett where Leibniz claims that according to reason government belongs to the wisest, he immediately goes on to add:

> But the imperfection of human nature causes people not to want to listen to reason, which has forced the most wise to use force and cunning to establish some tolerable order, in which providence itself takes a hand. But when a certain order has been established, one should not overturn it without extreme necessity, and without being sure of succeeding in it *pro salute publica* [for the public safety], in a way which does not cause worse evils.
>
> (R 192)

The Platonic strand is thus here accompanied by what we might call a providentialist strand deriving from Augustine: divine Providence itself plays a role in the establishment of political society. Elsewhere Leibniz develops this second strand by saying that even *de facto* regimes which arise from usurpation or conquest are established by Providence, and are to be obeyed accordingly (R 214–17). Indeed, the very success of such regimes in gaining ascendancy is evidence of divine favour.

It is natural to suppose that the providentialist thesis is simply 'divine right' theory under a different name, but that would be a mistake. There is reason to distinguish Leibniz's providentialist teachings from 'divine right' theory, at least in its classical form. In the first place, as we have seen, 'divine right' theory takes its stand on revelation; it is because of what St Paul says in his Epistle to the Romans that we have grounds for submitting to existing political authorities. By contrast, for Leibniz, the fact that the universe is governed by divine Providence is something that can be known by reason. Further, as we have seen, 'divine right' theory makes an essential appeal to the divine will: St Paul reveals that God has commanded obedience to the 'powers that be'. By contrast, providentialism turns more on an attribute of God that is distinct from his power; what is relevant to our duty to obey the state is the fact that the universe is governed and directed by divine wisdom.

LEIBNIZ'S CRITIQUE OF HOBBES

Much of Leibniz's political thought is a more or less explicit commentary on Hobbes, and it is not difficult to see why. For one thing, as Leibniz recognized, Hobbes stood head and shoulders above his contemporaries in political philosophy; he clearly fascinated Leibniz not only by the brilliance and systematic character of his thinking but also by virtue of the fact that in key respects his political theory was an inverted image of his own.[7] For like Leibniz Hobbes stresses the parallel between divine and human sovereignty – he even describes Leviathan or the state as a 'mortal god' (*Leviathan* II.17) – but from Leibniz's perspective he does so in precisely the wrong way. Hobbes grounds God's authority over his creation in the fact of his irresistible power; crudely, divine might makes right. And Hobbes could be read as grounding human political authority in power as well. For anyone schooled in Hobbes's political thought today this might seem like a gross misinterpretation; it is natural to insist that the true basis of political authority in Hobbes is the covenant or contract made among individuals. But it is easy to forget that Hobbes had said that if there were a human being endowed with irresistible power, he would *ipso facto* have a right to rule over others (*Leviathan* II.31). Moreover, Hobbes's acknowledgement of the duty of submission to conquerors could be taken to imply that in human affairs, as in the case of God, might makes right. Thus it is not difficult to see why Leibniz should have viewed Hobbes as the paradigm example of a philosopher who makes the cardinal error of grounding divine and earthly authority in power rather than wisdom.

Leibniz's obsession with criticizing Hobbes can also be seen as an expression of his adherence to Plato. Leibniz is fond of remarking that the trouble with Hobbes is that he seeks to revive Thrasymachus's opinion that justice is the interest of the strongest (R 207); as Leibniz says, such an opinion is the motto of the tyrant. Now Thrasymachus is the character in Plato's *Republic* whose assertion of this opinion helps to fuel the subsequent investigation into the nature of justice; indeed, the *Republic* might be regarded as an extended refutation of Thrasymachus. Thus, by criticizing Hobbes Leibniz is in effect engaged in the project of defending Platonic theories against their modern detractors.

The conviction that Hobbes is too close to Thrasymachus is also evident in Leibniz's hostility to Hobbes's theory of law. According to Hobbes, the essence of law in general is command; more precisely, it is the command of a sovereign addressed to people formerly obliged to obey him (*Leviathan* II.26). Such a theory is one of the earliest and most influential statements of what has come to be known as 'legal positivism'; in other words, the criterion for deciding whether a rule is a genuine law is entirely formal or procedural. For example, in modern British terms if a bill has passed both Houses of Parliament and received the royal assent, then it is a genuine law and not otherwise. We might summarize the theory by saying that it is form, not content, which determines whether a rule is law. Although such a theory has become highly influential, it is not difficult to see that it would have been anathema to Leibniz, for it abstracts entirely from questions of reasonableness and natural justice: according to legal positivism, such issues are irrelevant to questions of legality. It is not surprising, then, that Leibniz rejects Hobbes's legal positivism in favour of the older 'natural law' theory associated with Thomas Aquinas; on this theory, nothing can be law unless it derives from natural justice.[8] The 'natural law' theory has been revived in recent times during the Nuremberg trials in order to find a basis for prosecuting the leaders of Nazi Germany as war criminals; it was argued that though the

Nazi leaders had acted in compliance with the laws of their state, these so-called laws were not genuine laws since they were so flagrantly unjust and immoral.

In his opposition to legal positivism Leibniz appears to be returning to older, medieval ideas; the same tendency to revive medieval thought is visible in his opposition to the Hobbesian theory of sovereignty. For Hobbes, any properly constituted state must be united in the person of an absolute sovereign. Such a sovereign not only concentrates all the powers of government in a single pair of hands, but he cannot be bound either by a constitution or by allegiance to any external authority such as Pope or Emperor.[9] Hobbes indeed is the supreme apologist of the modern nation state. Leibniz, by contrast, sought to revive a weaker conception of sovereignty which was consistent in particular with recognition of such external allegiances. Here Leibniz's stand must be understood at least in part in terms of his role as an apologist for his electoral patrons. For, as Riley observes, the minor German principalities such as Leibniz's Hanover recognized for some purposes the higher authority of the Holy Roman Emperor in Vienna, but they also sought to be accorded the status of sovereigns in international relations (for example, in concluding peace treaties) (R 26–30). Leibniz was in effect trying to defend the coherence of such a position against the objections of Hobbes that such states were not properly constituted (R 118–20).

Although it is Leibniz's opposition to Hobbes that is most striking, it would be misleading to suggest that his attitude was entirely hostile or that there were was no common ground between them. Consider, for instance, the implications of the providentialist strand in Leibniz's political thinking; as we have seen, Leibniz is committed by this strand to holding that subjects are justified in switching allegiance to a new regime if it supersedes a government which has lost the power to protect them. Hobbes had similarly argued in *Leviathan* that there is a 'mutual relation between protection and allegiance' ('Review and Conclusion') and that 'the obligation of subjects to the sovereign is understood to last as long, and no longer than, the power lasteth by which he is able to protect them' (II.21). Thus Leibniz is at one with Hobbes in holding that the ability to provide protection is both necessary and sufficient to generate political obligation. Indeed, it is not unfair to say that Leibniz's providentialism is essentially the Hobbesian doctrine with a theological top dressing.

The fact that Leibniz's providentialism is a close cousin of Hobbesian doctrine makes it natural to enquire whether it is consistent with his opposition to Hobbes on other issues. One might wonder, in particular, whether providentialism can be reconciled with Leibniz's commitment to the Thomistic theory of law and to his consequent rejection of legal positivism. If Leibniz really holds that protection is both necessary and sufficient to give rise to obligation, then it is difficult to see how he can also hold that edicts are neither legally nor morally binding unless they derive from eternal principles of justice. Consistently with his strict providentialism, Leibniz can say that the edicts of *de facto* regimes which protect their subjects are not properly laws unless they are just; what he cannot say is that they have no claim to be obeyed. Perhaps Leibniz could modify his providentialism by denying that protection is strictly sufficient to give rise to obligation; in addition to protecting its subjects, a regime must enact nothing but genuine laws (that is, rules which conform to eternal principles of justice). But on this interpretation Leibniz's providentialism turns out to be a very weak thesis which would sanction obedience to few *de facto* regimes; it is conceivable, but unlikely, that a regime which owes its origin to conquest or usurpation will satisfy the conditions for obligation. In fact, at least on occasion, Leibniz tends to go in the other direction; he seems to suggest that *de facto* regimes should be obeyed even if their edicts fail to qualify as genuine laws (R 216–17). But to say this is really to abandon the commitment to Thomistic natural law theory.

Perhaps the most fascinating aspect of Leibniz's contributions to

moral and political theory is their continuity with his other philosophical commitments; even if there are not always tight logical
connections, at the least the same themes recur in the normative
and metaphysical parts of his philosophy. The thesis that the human
mind is made in the image of God is no less important in his value
theory than in his metaphysics and philosophy of mind. Few
readers today are likely to come away thinking that Leibniz is a
moral or political philosopher of the front rank; his positive teachings in the area of political philosophy may seem particularly dated
and unfruitful. Yet such a judgement would be unfair. In one
respect at least there is almost an uncanny resemblance between
Leibniz's concerns and those which we have today. As we have
seen, Leibniz devoted considerable energy to the problem of reconciling the sovereignty of the German states with their allegiance to
the Holy Roman Empire. Such a concern has a number of parallels
in the modern world. In the United States of America it anticipates
long-standing debates about states' rights within a federal system;
on the other side of the Atlantic, it anticipates more recent debates
about the place of traditional nation states such as France and Britain
within the framework of the European Union.

SUMMARY

Traditionally, Leibniz has not been regarded as a moral or political
philosopher of the front rank. Yet, like Spinoza's *Ethics*, the famous
summaries of his philosophy, such as the *Monadology*, all culminate
in ethics – that is, a vision of human happiness or blessedness.
Leibniz's ethics is in some degree an adaptation of Spinozistic
themes along Christian lines; for instance, like Spinoza he holds that
the more virtuous people become, the more they imitate God. The
'mirror of God' theme is also prominent in Leibniz's political philosophy where he stands apart from the main trends of the period.
The first main section of the chapter shows that Leibniz's ethics
is grounded in a moral psychology, that is, a theory of human
motivation. Here Leibniz defends two controversial main theses:

First, human beings always choose what seems to them to be best; there is no weakness or perversity of will. Second, human beings always necessarily choose their own good; that is, Leibniz is a psychological egoist. Leibniz makes a distinctive contribution to the defence of psychological egoism by invoking his theory of unconscious motivation. Surprisingly perhaps, not only the first but also the second of these two theses is consistent with Leibniz's doctrine that human minds are mirrors of God. The next section examines Leibniz's moral philosophy itself. Here it is shown that the central theme of Leibniz's ethics is that all minds are members of the City of God; that is, they are all bound by standards of goodness and justice which are independent of the divine will and apply to God himself. Leibniz thus takes a firm anti-voluntarist stand on the problem debated in Plato's *Euthyphro*. Leibniz argues that, like God himself, human beings have a duty to promote overall happiness; however Leibniz introduces some qualifications which distinguish his position from strict utilitarianism. In his moral philosophy Leibniz further addresses the problem of reconciling psychological egoism with moral altruism. His solution to the problem turns on the concept of disinterested love which involves finding one's own happiness in the happiness of another person. Surprisingly, the concept of love is also central to Leibniz's definition of justice: according to Leibniz, justice is the love (or charity) of the wise. Leibniz's definition of justice in these terms is clarified by setting it in the context of Greek ethics where justice is often identified with virtuous conduct in general: Leibniz also recognizes a narrower sense of 'justice' which is closer to the modern sense. The final two sections of the chapter examine Leibniz's political philosophy. Here it is shown that Leibniz's position cannot straightforwardly be classified as a version either of 'divine right' theory or 'social contract' theory, the two leading options in the early modern period. Instead, Leibniz's political philosophy combines Platonic and Augustinian elements: Leibniz adopts Plato's view that, according to reason, the wisest have a right to rule, and

Augustine's view that Providence plays a role in establishing political societies. According to Leibniz, even de facto regimes are established by Providence. Leibniz's revival of Platonic themes is conspicuous in his critique of Hobbes, the greatest political philosopher of the age. Despite his admiration for the brilliant and systematic character of his thought, Leibniz is hostile to Hobbes for holding, as he believes, that might makes right. Leibniz further criticizes Hobbes's commitment to legal positivism in the philosophy of law: in opposition Leibniz maintains a version of natural law theory deriving from Aquinas. However, such a theory is seen to be in some tension with Leibniz's thesis that even de facto regimes are to be obeyed.

FURTHER READING

G. Brown (1995) 'Leibniz's Moral Philosophy,' N. Jolley (ed.), The Cambridge Companion to Leibniz. (A valuable survey of Leibniz's moral philosophy.)

J. Hostler (1975) Leibniz's Moral Philosophy. (A valuable study; the only book in English on the subject.)

P. Riley (1996) Leibniz's Universal Jurisprudence: Justice as the Charity of the Wise. (An important scholarly study.)

P. Riley (ed.) (1988) Introduction, Leibniz's Political Writings. (A helpful survey of Leibniz's political philosophy which emphasizes Platonic themes.)

E. Vailati (1990) 'Leibniz on Locke on Weakness of Will'. (A penetrating and sympathetic account of Leibniz's views.)

Eight

Legacy and Influence

In the three hundred years or so since his death Leibniz's reputation has been subject to wild fluctuations. To a large extent these fluctuations coincide with changes in philosophical fashion. When metaphysics itself has enjoyed high esteem Leibniz has tended to be an object of fascinated admiration; when metaphysics has been in disrepute he has tended to go into eclipse accordingly. The uncompromising nature of his commitment to metaphysics of the most revisionist kind undoubtedly left him more than usually exposed to such changes in philosophical climate.

But the history of Leibniz's legacy and influence cannot be written simply in these terms; it needs to take account of the peculiar circumstances of his career and compositions. The fact (to which Catherine Wilson has recently drawn attention) that Leibniz's reputation as a major philosopher was slow to develop can be understood in part – but only in part – in terms of the reaction against metaphysical system-building which set in after his death (C. Wilson 1995: 442–74);[1] it must also be understood in terms of the fragmentary character of his published legacy which made it difficult for his readers to obtain a clear view of his overall philosophical achievement. With the exception of the *Theodicy*, Leibniz's philosophical publications during his lifetime consisted of short essays scattered throughout the learned journals of his age. Much of his philosophical work which we hold in highest esteem today did not appear in print until long after his death. The *Discourse on Metaphysics*, for instance, which has since achieved the status of a classic, was not published until the middle of the nineteenth century. Not surprisingly, periods which have seen a flurry of publications from the vast archive have tended to be followed by an upsurge of interest and attention as unsuspected facets of Leibniz's thought have been disclosed to readers. The publication of the *New Essays on Human Understanding* in 1765 introduced Kant and others to Leibniz the epistemologist; the publication of Leibniz's logical papers around the turn of the twentieth century encouraged a generation of readers to look for the foundations of his metaphysics in a theory of truth.

THE REACTIONS OF LEIBNIZ'S CONTEMPORARIES: FRANCE AND ENGLAND

Although Leibniz had admirers on either side of the Channel, he also fell victim to chauvinistic attitudes in both France and England, the two most intellectually advanced European countries of the time. Leibniz had set himself in opposition to the leading philosophers and scientists of both countries, and to some extent he excited resentment on these grounds. In France and England there was no shortage of intellectuals ready to rally round the national heroes, even icons, whose reputations Leibniz had attacked.

In France Leibniz was seen above all perhaps as the scourge of Descartes and Cartesianism. This view of Leibniz is captured in a famous remark by one of Descartes's most loyal disciples; the physicist Pierre-Sylvain Regis complained with some bitterness that Leibniz was seeking to build his own reputation on the ruins of Descartes's (G IV 333). There was some justification for such a charge; in fact Leibniz had attacked the Cartesian legacy on a number of fronts. In physics Leibniz never lost an opportunity to expose Descartes's errors, especially concerning the laws of impact. And in philosophy Leibniz in effect launched his own system on the world through an attack on Descartes's inability to solve the problem of mind–body interaction. It is fair to say that in France Leibniz was found more persuasive for his technical criticisms of Descartes's physics than for his own positive metaphysical doctrines. Leibniz's seemingly perverse insistence on reviving the discredited Scholastic doctrine of substantial forms did little to recommend his metaphysical theories with sophisticated French readers who prided themselves on their emancipation from medieval barbarism.

Although allowance must be made for the occasion, the eulogy which Bernard le Bovier de Fontenelle delivered to the French Academy of Sciences conveys some idea of how Leibniz's reputation stood in France at the time of his death. Fontenelle is generous in his tributes to Leibniz's accomplishments as a mathematician and physicist, and to the polymathic genius which found expression in his contributions to law, history, geology, and even diplomacy. Nonetheless, Fontenelle displays a certain coolness when he comes to treat of Leibniz's metaphysical system. Fontenelle complains that when Leibniz was no longer constrained by strict necessity, as in logic and mathematics, he had a tendency to make arbitrary assumptions (Barber 1955: 93). Such a charge was to be echoed by subsequent critics down the centuries. In the Preface to his pioneering study of Leibniz Bertrand Russell tells how the system of monadology initially struck him as wholly arbitrary until he discovered, as he believed, how Leibniz's metaphysics followed from a small set of premises.

If, in France, Leibniz was valued most for his achievements in science and mathematics, in England even those achievements (at least in mathematics) were viewed with some suspicion. Here the 'priority dispute' with Newton over the discovery of the differential calculus played a major role. The dispute dragged on for years from the time of Newton's initial suspicions to the eventual unfavourable verdict handed down by the tribunal of the Royal Society charged with investigating the matter. The existence of this ugly dispute is arguably relevant to an understanding of Leibniz's relations with all English intellectuals during the latter part of his life.

The battle between the two giants is certainly part of the background to Leibniz's relations with Locke. Although it was sometimes put to the test, Locke enjoyed a close friendship with Newton during this period, and he was surely privy to Newton's antagonism to his great rival. As we have seen, Locke refused to be drawn into correspondence with Leibniz about the philosophy of his great *Essay Concerning Human Understanding*. Locke professed himself disappointed by the quality of the mildly critical comments contained in an otherwise admiring paper which Leibniz sent him; writing to his friend William Molyneux, Locke gave a very dismissive verdict:

> I must confess to you that Mr. Leibnitz's great name had raised in me an expectation which the sight of his paper did not answer, nor that discourse of his in the *acta eruditorum*, which he quotes, and I have since read, and had just the same thoughts of it, when I read it, as I find you have. From whence I only draw this inference, That even great parts will not master any subject without great thinking, and even the largest minds have but narrow swallows.
>
> (10 April 1697, Locke 1981: 86–7)

Locke was never a generous opponent in controversy, and he was always sensitive to the least criticism of his *Essay Concerning Human Understanding*. Perhaps also his mind had been poisoned against Leibniz by Newton's hostility. However that may be, it is not difficult to sympathize with the disappointment which Locke felt on reading Leibniz's paper. Leibniz's criticisms of Locke, mild as they were, made little sense when detached from the rest of his philosophy. Moreover, in this paper as in the *New Essays* itself, Leibniz made no real attempt to enter into the spirit of Locke's philosophy or to understand his way of thinking (cf. RB xi). In particular, Leibniz had no sympathy whatever with Locke's proto-Kantian insistence on the need for a critique of the human understanding and of the very possibility of speculative metaphysics.

Locke of course, unlike Leibniz, was not a dogmatic metaphysician; as Leibniz himself noted when he read Locke's comments in print, he and Locke were a little too different in principles for a fruitful exchange of views between them to be possible (L 656). But it is a mistake to suppose that hostility to Leibniz's philosophy in England was always based on a radical contrast of philosophical assumptions and presuppositions. Samuel Clarke was a disciple of Newton's and an able and sometimes penetrating critic of Leibniz's philosophy, but he was just as much a rationalist metaphysician as Leibniz himself; he was committed to a priori principles and he is famous for his version of the cosmological argument for the existence of God. Clarke's objection to Leibniz is not that he is a rationalist or a dogmatic metaphysician but that his metaphysics is simply wrong on important substantive issues such as the nature of space and time, and the proper interpretation of the Principle of Sufficient Reason. In general, there is a danger of a premature dating of the English rejection of metaphysics in favour of the more cautious philosophy, which is also more respectful of experience, that is associated with Locke and to some extent with Newton. Recent research has shown that versions of Platonism, for instance, continued to flourish in England long after the publication of Locke's *Essay Concerning Human Understanding*.[2]

THE REACTION AGAINST SYSTEMS

The eighteenth century was indeed to witness a reaction against metaphysical systems such as Leibniz's doctrine of monads. In many ways the reaction was the philosophical counterpart of the change in architectural fashion from the Baroque to the Palladian style. When the reaction came, it hit France as heavily as England. It is true that the reaction was fuelled by admiration for English achievements in physics (Newton) and in philosophy (Locke). But in fact (before Kant at least) the case against metaphysical system-building was most powerfully articulated not in England but by French writers such as Condillac and Voltaire.

We have seen that a certain coolness towards Leibniz's metaphysics could already be detected in the eulogy which Fontenelle delivered on the occasion of Leibniz's death. Such reservations about the whole enterprise of speculative metaphysics come to the fore in the writings of Etienne Bonnot de Condillac (1714–80). Already in his first work, the *Essay on the Origin of Knowledge* (1746), Condillac had contrasted two kinds of metaphysics. The first kind is grandiose in its ambitions: it seeks to solve all the mysteries of nature and to discover the essences and hidden causes of things. The second kind is more modest in its goals: 'unconcerned about what lies beyond its grasp, it seeks to seize what lies within it' (Condillac 2001: 3). Locke's *Essay Concerning Human Understanding* is praised as an example of the latter kind of metaphysics: drawing its inspiration from Bacon, it seeks to observe how ideas and knowledge arise in the mind, and in this relatively unexciting enterprise it is successful. The philosophy of Leibniz and his disciples is singled out as a conspicuous example of the former kind of metaphysics: the Leibnizians practise no such intellectual self-discipline as Locke: they flatter themselves without justification that they can explain the nature, essence, and all the properties of the mind. Like the Cartesians they allow themselves to be seduced by their own system (Condillac 2001: 3–8). Condillac might have said of Leibniz what Voltaire said of Descartes: he composed a novel of the mind.

Condillac's critique finds its fullest expression in his *Traité des Systèmes*, a work which has been aptly described as the 'severest attack upon speculative metaphysics which the century produced in France' (Barber 1955: 199–200). As the title suggests, Condillac is concerned with systems in general, but he reserves a chapter for a critical examination of Leibniz's doctrine of monads as it is articulated in the *Monadology*. Condillac finds the system of monads guilty of several related failings. In the first place, the system is guilty of seeking to explain the obscure through the more obscure: such a failing is visible in Leibniz's attempt to explain the phenomenal world of bodies in terms of monads which underlie them. Now Condillac is not so insensitive to the metaphysical impulse as to deny the difficulty of the issues to which the monadology is proposed as a solution; unconsciously echoing Leibniz's own remarks about the composition of the continuum Condillac notes: 'the composite – that is, the infinitely divisible – is a thing in which the mind loses itself: the more one analyzes the idea, the more it seems to involve contradictions' (Condillac 1991: 111). But Condillac denies that the nature of matter is made any more intelligible by postulating the existence of monads or simple substances. To characterize these simple substances negatively by denying them the properties of matter is not to give a clear idea of their nature. However, when Leibniz does attempt to offer a positive characterization of monads by saying that they all have the capacity for perception, he invokes a faculty which we understand only dimly in ourselves.

When Condillac turns his attention to the other main property of monads, appetition, he has a rather different criticism to make. Condillac does not deny that we have a grasp on the concept of force. But we understand force only in physical contexts; we understand it in terms of the effort involved in seeking to overcome felt obstacles. For Leibniz, however, there can be no effort in monads or simple substances, for there are no obstacles to overcome; it is thus meaningless to ascribe force or appetition to such substances (Condillac 1991: 113). Condillac is led in this way to voice the distinctly proto-Kantian complaint that Leibnizian metaphysics seeks to extend respectable concepts beyond their legitimate sphere of application.

Condillac's final complaint against Leibniz is that he resorts to figurative language instead of offering precise explanations.[3] We are told, for instance, that monads are living mirrors of the universe but no clear sense can be given to such expressions when they are used in this metaphorical way:

> In fact, these terms, moving from the literal [*propre*] to the figurative, have only a vague relationship with the first sense that they have had. They signify that there are representations in simple beings, but representations very different from those with which we

are acquainted, that is, representations of which we have no idea. To say that the perceptions are representative states is thus to say nothing. . . . The mistake [*méprise*] of this philosopher is in not having paid attention to the fact that these terms which in the literal sense have a precise meaning arouse no more than vague notions when he employs them figuratively. He believed that he was explaining phenomena when he employs only the unphilosophical language of metaphors; and he has not seen that when one is obliged to use these sorts of expressions, it is a proof that one has no idea of the thing one is talking about.

(Condillac 1991: 116)

Leibniz may well seem to be an easy target here, for there is no doubt that his metaphysics does abound in metaphors: monads, for example, are not only mirrors but windowless. Yet it may be questioned whether Condillac is entirely fair to Leibniz here: at least in some contexts Leibniz does provide us with precise ways of unpacking his metaphors. To say that monads are mirrors of the universe is to be understood, in part at least, in terms of Leibniz's technical notion of expression. To say that they are windowless is simply to deny that they causally interact with one another (where interaction is understood in terms of the transmission of properties).

Condillac was not alone among the French philosophers of the eighteenth century in attacking the doctrine of monads; he was joined by the most famous voice of the Enlightenment, namely Voltaire. Philosophically, Condillac and Voltaire were indeed kindred spirits; they scorned alike the baroque metaphysics of the previous age and sympathized entirely with Locke and Newton. Voltaire, like Condillac, could make serious, even if sometimes misguided, criticisms of the doctrine of monads; it is incoherent, he emphasizes, to hold that infinitely divisible matter is composed of indivisible monads. But, as we would expect, Voltaire's most distinctive contribution lay in the ridicule which he heaped on the system of monads. 'Can you really claim [bien avancer] that a drop of urine is an infinity of monads, and that each one of these has ideas, however obscure, of the whole universe?' (Barber 1955: 189).

VOLTAIRE, OPTIMISM, AND THEODICY

Although they display his characteristic wit and intelligence, Voltaire's criticisms of the system of monads are largely forgotten today. By contrast, his critique of the other main side of Leibniz's thought, his theodicy, is anything but forgotten. As a satire of Leibnizian optimism Voltaire's short novel *Candide* was an immediate and lasting success. Indeed, at least in the popular mind, this classic did more to damage Leibniz's reputation than any other critique before or since.

The story of Voltaire's engagement with the doctrine of optimism is marked by a certain irony. At one time in his life Voltaire himself flirted with the doctrine; he was drawn to it in part perhaps because of its seeming incompatibility with the Christian doctrine of original sin which Voltaire himself detested. Certainly Voltaire was an admirer of Pope's *Essay on Man* (1732–4) which gave polished and popular expression to the philosophy of optimism. But in 1755 Lisbon was devastated by an earthquake which shocked Voltaire profoundly; in correspondence he wrote of this event: 'there's a terrible argument against optimism' (Barber 1955: 224). In a poem on the Lisbon earthquake Voltaire expressed his view that philosophical systems like Leibniz's theodicy offer no help to human beings in their attempt to make sense of such terrible events:

> Leibniz ne m'apprend par quels noeuds invisibles,
> Dans le mieux ordonné des univers possibles,
> Un désordre éternel, un chaos de malheurs,
> Mêle à nos vains plaisirs de réelles douleurs,
> Ni pourquoi l'innocent, ainsi que le coupable,
> Subit également ce mal inévitable,
> Je ne conçois pas plus comment tout serait bien:
> Je suis comme un docteur; hélas, je ne sais rien.

(Leibniz does not teach me by what invisible knots,/in the best ordered of possible worlds,/a chaos of misfortunes mingles real sufferings with our empty pleasures,/nor why the innocent, as well as the guilty,/suffers equally this unavoidable evil./I do not understand any more how everything should be well; I am like a learned man; alas! I understand nothing.)

(Barber 1955: 225; translation mine)

Other events in the period likewise conspired to deepen Voltaire's disenchantment with optimism. In Voltaire's eyes the outbreak of the Seven Years War showed that the two supposedly most advanced countries of the time, France and England, were prepared to sacrifice thousands of lives in their competition to gain control of the icy wastes of Canada.

In *Candide* Leibnizian optimism is satirized in the ridiculous figure of Doctor Pangloss (that is, one who glosses or explains everything). Pangloss is a German academic and pedant who teaches 'metaphysico-cosmo-theolo-nigology'; Voltaire's description of his teachings is full of comic allusions to Leibnizian themes such as the Principle of Sufficient Reason. Pangloss is tutor to the ingenuous youth Candide at a country mansion in the German province of Westphalia. When Candide is expelled from the house following a sexual indiscretion, he is forced to seek his fortunes in the wider world. In the course of his travels Candide is witness to all sorts of moral and physical evils, in Leibnizian terminology. He arrives in Lisbon just in time for the notorious earthquake, and in addition to such natural disasters, he encounters manifold instances of human atrocities, and flagrant acts of injustice such as the execution of Admiral Byng. ('In that country [i.e., England] it is a good idea to kill an admiral from time to time to encourage the others' [Ch. 23].) In the face of such disasters Pangloss — from whom he is separated for a time — continues to maintain stoutly that all is for the best in the best of all possible worlds. Finally Candide loses patience with his former tutor and sardonically asks the memorable question: 'If this is the best of all possible worlds, what can the rest be like?' (Ch. 6). The moral of the fable is expressed in the final exchange between Pangloss and Candide. In spite of the many chastening experiences that he himself has endured, Pangloss is still not cured of his optimism and makes a speech to the effect that everything in the saga has turned out for the best. Candide replies: 'That's well said, but we must cultivate our garden' (Ch. 30). In other words, the sensible response to the horrors of the world is not fatalism or despair, but a life of honest toil dedicated to making modest improvements in our limited sphere of action.

Brilliant and memorable satire that it is, *Candide* is obviously not a philosophical refutation of Leibniz's optimistic stance in theodicy. Indeed, as we have seen, even its relevance to the Leibnizian thesis that this is the best of all possible worlds has been (perhaps unfairly) disputed. Voltaire may have made no close study of Leibniz's somewhat indigestible book, the *Essays in Theodicy*, and though Leibniz is clearly the intended target, the characterization of Pangloss's views is sometimes more reminiscent of Pope than Leibniz. But, as Catherine Wilson has argued, if Voltaire did not exactly refute Leibnizian optimism, he overwhelmed it (C. Wilson 1983: 766). In the eyes of the educated public the Leibnizian thesis that this is the best of all possible worlds came to seem wickedly callous and insensitive in the face of so much human suffering and evil; it is made to appear as a position which no thoughtful or civilized person could possibly adopt. And despite the difference in fortune of the two critiques Voltaire's ridicule of optimism is informed by the same attitude as his attack on the system of monads: contempt for abstract theorizing which takes no account of facts and experience.

LEIBNIZ, KANT, AND GERMAN IDEALISM

Leibniz's reputation in his native Germany never sank as low as it did in France and England. His metaphysics had been perpetuated and hardened into dogmatism in the writings of his junior contemporary, Christian Wolff, who was precisely one of those German pedants so despised by Voltaire. But although it may never have suffered a total eclipse in his native country, his philosophical reputation received a definite and unexpected boost from the post-humous publication of the *New Essays on Human Understanding* in 1765; this was his point-by-point reply to Locke's *Essay Concerning Human Understanding*. As various scholars have shown, the reception of the *New Essays* was not wholly uncritical (Tonelli 1974: 437–54; C. Wilson 1995); nonetheless, the work made a positive impression on publication by disclosing a side of Leibniz's philosophy which was previously unsuspected; it revealed Leibniz as an epistemologist concerned with such questions as the nature and sources of a priori knowledge. The degree of attention which Leibniz pays to epistemological issues in the *New Essays* can hardly be disputed, but whether questions in the theory of knowledge are really the chief focus of the work is more controversial; Leibniz himself said that his main aim in the work was to defend an immaterialist theory of mind against Locke's 'thinking matter' hypothesis. Thus even in this work Leibniz is arguably motivated by a metaphysical impulse (Jolley 1984).

The appearance of the *New Essays on Human Understanding* coincided with a formative period in Kant's development. Kant's attitude to Leibniz's philosophy was complex and ambivalent, but there is little doubt that the anti-empiricist doctrine of innate ideas and knowledge which Leibniz defends in the *New Essays* was powerfully attractive to Kant; echoes of the Leibnizian doctrine can be heard in the opening sentence of the *Crtique of Pure Reason*. For Kant, as for Leibniz, the mind is not a blank slate on which the finger of experience subsequently writes; it is so constituted as to interpret the empirical data in terms of pure concepts, such as the concepts of substance and causality, which are derived not from experience but from the understanding itself. Indeed, Leibniz's doctrine of innate ideas is a significant precursor of the mature Kantian doctrine of categories or pure concepts which help to constitute our experience of an objective, spatio-temporal world. Real as they undoubtedly are, the similarities between Kant and Leibniz should not be exaggerated. Leibniz's innate ideas apply to supersensible objects such as God; the Kantian categories, by contrast, have no legitimate application beyond the limits of possible experience. Indeed, Kant's thesis that a priori knowledge is limited to objects of possible experience is the core thesis of his own distinctive doctrine of transcendental idealism.

Kant, then, was undoubtedly attracted and stimulated by Leibniz's theory of innate ideas and knowledge. Yet on fundamental issues Kant's attitude to Leibniz's philosophy was hostile. One of the most famous themes of Kant's theory of knowledge is its attempt to portray Leibniz and Locke, for all their differences, as guilty of a common error: Leibniz and Locke are alike in supposing that the intellectual and the sensory, thinking and sensing, are on a continuum with one another. Kant argues that in reality the faculties of understanding and sensibility are two different stems of human cognition, even if he concedes that they may arise from a common, but to us unknown, root (*Critique of Pure Reason* A 15/B 29). Kant can echo Leibnizian criticisms of Locke when he charges that Locke 'sensualizes the pure concepts of the understanding' (A 271/B 327); that is, Locke treats what are in fact purely intellectual ideas as if they were mental images derived from sensory experience and the imagination. But though he proves a serviceable ally, Leibniz himself fares no better in Kant's eyes, for he is guilty of the complementary error of treating sensory experience as if it were constituted of ideas of the intellect which have become obscure and confused. Kant makes a deep and powerful, related criticism of Leibniz when he observes that the Leibnizian principle of the Identity of Indiscernibles is true only at the level of concepts: if concepts A and B have all their properties in common, they are one and the same concept. Leibniz's mistake is to suppose that the principle is true at the level of particulars given in sensory experience.

As a critic of Leibniz Kant is important in other respects as well.

In the first place, the Critique of Pure Reason represents the culmination of the distrustful attitude towards speculative metaphysics which is characteristic of so much of eighteenth-century thought. As we have seen, Condillac's objections in the Traité des Systèmes are by no means negligible, and even anticipate Kantian insights in places. But it is fair to say that Kant raised the art of criticizing the enterprise of speculative metaphysics to a new level; in the section of the Critique of Pure Reason entitled Transcendental Dialectic Kant offers an incomparably more penetrating and profound diagnosis of the illusions to which the metaphysicians fall victim. The discussion of the Antinomies, for instance, mounts a decisive challenge to the enterprise of rational cosmology by seeking to show that reason becomes divided against itself and falls into contradictions when it seeks to go beyond the limits of possible experience.

Kant's critical engagement with Leibniz is important in a very different way. In his opposition of Leibniz and Locke we find the germs of the canonical division of early modern philosophers into the camps of Rationalists and Empiricists, which was later to become standard and entrenched; indeed, it was this division which was to form the basis for many a university curriculum. It is well to recognize that Kant's own habit of treating Leibniz and Locke as opposed to one another is philosophically somewhat self-serving; Kant wishes to portray his great predecessors as mired in a series of distortions and half-truths which are to be superseded by his own Critical philosophy. Whatever we may think of its merits as philosophical historiography, Kant's critique of his predecessors played a major role in shaping later attitudes to the philosophy of Leibniz.

THE REDISCOVERY OF LEIBNIZ

In 1900 Bertrand Russell published a book entitled *A Critical Exposition of the Philosophy of Leibniz*. The date of publication is apt. The pioneering interpretation which Russell advanced in this work was to exert a huge influence on Leibniz studies, especially in the English-speaking world, for much of the twentieth century.

In the Preface to his study of Leibniz Russell offers an illuminating account of the book's genesis. He tells the reader how, when he was preparing a set of lectures on Leibniz at Cambridge, the philosophy of the monadology initially appeared to him, as it did to Fontenelle, as a kind of fantastic fairy tale, 'coherent perhaps but wholly arbitrary'. But when he turned to the study of the *Discourse on Metaphysics* and the correspondence with Arnauld, a light began to dawn; he saw, as he thought, how Leibniz derived his metaphysics from a small set of premises which included his concept-containment theory of truth:

> Suddenly a flood of light was thrown on all the inmost recesses of Leibniz's philosophical edifice. I saw how its foundations were laid, and how its superstructure rose out of them. It appeared that this seemingly fantastic system could be deduced from a few simple premises which, but for the conclusions which Leibniz had drawn from them, many if not most philosophers would have been willing to admit.
>
> (Russell 1937: xiii–xiv)

Russell thus came to believe that Leibniz's philosophy begins, as in his view all sound philosophy should begin, with an analysis of the nature of propositions. For this reason Russell decided that Leibniz's stature as a philosopher was much greater than he had formerly supposed.

Russell drew heavily for his interpretation on texts such as the *Discourse on Metaphysics* and the letters to Arnauld, which had become known only within living memory. To that extent, then, the story of Russell's dealings with Leibniz illustrates once again how original approaches to his philosophy are driven by new publications from the archives. But in this case the interplay between new editions and new interpretations is rather more complex. Russell's 'logicist' interpretation received perhaps its most powerful support from texts which were published actually after the appearance of his study. Couturat's edition of Leibniz's papers three years later revealed a Leibniz who not only made pioneering contributions to philosophical logic but also, in such works as 'Primary Truths', did indeed seek to derive metaphysical doctrines from premises concerning the nature of truth.[4]

The 'logicist' interpretation, as it has come to be called, is not the only original thesis that Russell advanced; particularly in the Preface to the second edition of his book and in his History of Western Philosophy (1945), Russell popularized the idea that Leibniz really had two distinct philosophies, an official and an unofficial one. The official one was popular, shallow, incoherent, and orthodox; it was represented by such works as the Theodicy, which Leibniz allegedly wrote to win the applause of princes and, even more, princesses. The unofficial philosophy, by contrast, was coherent, deep, and profoundly unorthodox; it tended in the direction of Spinozistic necessitarianism and monism; that is, it led to the denial of contingent truths and to the doctrine that there is only one substance. This unofficial philosophy was clearly not for public consumption; accordingly, Leibniz buried it in private manuscripts, which were kept under lock and key until they were discovered and published by editors long after his death.

Russell's two main interpretative theses about Leibniz have had very different fortunes. The first – the so-called 'logicist' thesis – opened up a fruitful new approach to Leibniz's metaphysics which, as we have seen, dominated Leibniz scholarship for much of the last century. By contrast, the thesis that Leibniz had two distinct philosophies has been greeted with scepticism by most historians of philosophy, at least in the Anglo-American world. If the second thesis had any sort of success, it was of a rather indirect kind; it lay in the close attention that came to be paid to Leibniz's theories of modality and in a new appreciation of the difficulties that Leibniz encountered in accommodating contingency within a theoretical framework which maintains that all true propositions are analytic. But few philosophers have seriously doubted that, whatever his degree of success, even in his private papers Leibniz strove hard to find a place for contingent truths.

Although it stimulated a renaissance of interest in his philosophy, even Russell's logicist thesis is viewed today with scepticism for two main reasons. In the first place, as we have seen, the project of deriving metaphysical doctrines from the theory of truth is confined to a certain stage of Leibniz's philosophical career; it is prominent in writings around the time of the *Discourse on Metaphysics*, but as even Russell half-acknowledges, it tends to disappear from view in later writings such as the *Monadology*. The logicist project thus seems today less like a key which unlocks all the secrets of Leibniz's metaphysics than an argumentative strategy which found favour with Leibniz at one stage, but was later discarded. Moreover, even in those texts where it is prominent, the logicist project has less power to illuminate the metaphysics than Russell suggests. Russell tended to write as if the metaphysics was validly derived from the logic; other readers, by contrast, have been struck by difficulties in the derivation. Many scholars today would thus tend to agree with Ayers's remark that Leibniz did not so much derive his metaphysics from his logic as tailor his logic (i.e., his theory of truth) to a metaphysics to which he was independently attracted (Ayers 1978: 45).

In this chapter we have seen how Leibniz's reputation has tended to rise and fall with the tide of the larger fortunes of metaphysics, though we have also seen that the discovery of new Leibnizian texts is a cross-current in the story. In our own age, interest in Leibniz's philosophy is perhaps greater than at any previous time. To say this is not necessarily to say that speculative or revisionist metaphysics of the Leibnizian variety has returned to favour with philosophers; on the whole, this is far from being the case. It is true that doctrinaire opposition to metaphysics of the kind that was standard in the days of logical positivism and linguistic philosophy is no longer the norm; with some exceptions, however, philosophers who practise metaphysics today tend to view their enterprise as a descriptive one; that is, they seek to explore the implications of our basic conceptual scheme rather than to challenge it in the fundamental way characteristic of revisionist metaphysicians such as Leibniz.[5] But even metaphysicians of the descriptive kind may find much to admire in Leibniz; he can be praised, for instance, for his penetrating contributions to the theory of identity and individuation. Moreover, although advanced in the context of largely alien theological concerns, Leibniz's theory of possible worlds has at least been an inspiration to modern philosophers who seek to understand the nature of modality.

A further reason why Leibniz is of such interest today is his conviction that philosophy, if it is to be worth anything, must be responsive to, and even continuous with, the science of the time. For much of the last century such an assumption was deeply out of favour. Philosophy was regarded generally as a 'second-order activity'; its task was supposed to be to provide knowledge about knowledge rather than to make the kind of direct contributions to the advancement of knowledge characteristic of the natural sciences. Many philosophers today, however, would reject this picture of the relationship between philosophy and science in favour of the view that places them on a continuum rather than on different levels. Leibniz himself was not only a mathematician of genius and a physicist of distinction; he was also a philosopher who sought a metaphysical picture of the world which at once accommodated and grounded the scientific discoveries of his time. Prominent among such discoveries was the new science of dynamics to which Leibniz himself was a leading contributor.

But there is another dimension to the current obsession with Leibniz which is perhaps not always openly acknowledged by those who study him. Since Plato the idea that, at least in terms of its basic structure, the universe lies open to reason has exerted a powerful hold on the Western intellect and imagination. Although it has been attacked as misguided from time to time (for example, by Kant), the idea continues to exert a fascination even on the minds of those who recognize the force of Kantian objections and scruples.

Leibniz's metaphysics represents one of the most impressive attempts ever made to articulate this fundamental idea. Indeed, in the modern period perhaps Leibniz is rivalled only by Spinoza. In resourcefulness in argument Leibniz is clearly Spinoza's superior; in breadth of vision arguably he is his equal. But the philosophical visions which Leibniz and Spinoza articulate are different, if undoubtedly related. For Spinoza, the universe itself is God; for Leibniz, by contrast, the universe is not itself God, but rather a collection of substances which mirror the deity.

SUMMARY

Fluctuations in Leibniz's reputation over the centuries have tended to coincide with changes in philosophical fashion. Leibniz's reputation has stood high when metaphysics itself has been held in high regard. However, other factors have been at work. The fragmentary character of Leibniz's published legacy has often made it difficult for readers to appreciate his full achievement. During his lifetime Leibniz was to some extent the victim of chauvinistic attitudes in France and England, the two most intellectually advanced European countries. In France Leibniz was viewed as above all the scourge of Descartes, a national hero; he was more influential through his technical criticisms of Descartes's physics than for his positive anti-Cartesian contributions to metaphysics, which struck some readers as arbitrary. In England even Leibniz's achievements in mathematics and science fell under suspicion; Leibniz was accused by Newton and his disciples of plagiarizing the differential calculus. The so-called 'priority dispute' forms part of the background to the unhappy relationship between Leibniz and Locke. Locke's low opinion of Leibniz's philosophical abilities was shared by Newton's disciple Samuel Clarke who, as a rationalist metaphysician, was philosophically more akin to Leibniz than Locke was. The debate between Leibniz and Clarke shows that rationalist metaphysics survived even in England well into the eighteenth century. In the next section, however, it is shown that the century following

Leibniz's death witnessed a reaction against grand metaphysical systems such as the doctrine of monads. This reaction is evident in the writings of French thinkers such as Condillac and Voltaire. Condillac contrasts the grandiose metaphysical ambitions of Leibniz with the more modest ones of Locke, to the advantage of the latter. Leibniz's theory of monads is criticized for explaining the obscure through the more obscure and for its reliance on figurative language. The next section examines Voltaire's devastating satire on Leibniz's optimism in his novel *Candide*. Although not strictly a philosophical refutation of such optimism, Voltaire's satire made it seem both callous and incredible. Like his own critique of the doctrine of monads, Voltaire's satire on optimism exhibits a contempt for abstract theorizing which takes no account of experience. In Germany Leibniz's reputation never sank as low as it did in France or England, but it received an unexpected boost from the publication of the *New Essays* in 1765. A section on Kant shows how this work introduced readers to Leibniz's theory of knowledge, a previously unknown side of his philosophy. The discovery of the *New Essays* played an important role in Kant's philosophical development. Leibniz's doctrine of innate ideas attracted Kant, and it has some affinities with his own doctrine of categories. However, on fundamental issues concerning knowledge Kant was hostile to Leibniz: he was critical of Leibniz's tendency to regard the sensory and the intellectual as on a continuum. Further, the Transcendental Dialectic in the *Critique of Pure Reason* represents the culmination of the distrust of speculative metaphysics seen earlier in the century in Condillac. In connection with Leibniz Kant is also important for sowing the seeds of the canonical division of early modern philosophers into Rationalists and Empiricists. In the final section of the chapter it is shown that Bertrand Russell's book on Leibniz is a milestone in the modern rediscovery of the philosopher. Drawing on Leibnizian texts which had been published in living memory Russell claimed to see how Leibniz's metaphysical doctrines followed from a small set of premises. Together with a French scholar, Russell pioneered the so-called 'logicist' interpretation of Leibniz according to which his metaphysics is derived from a theory of truth. Russell advanced another interpretative thesis that Leibniz had two philosophies – one official, the other unofficial. This second thesis, however, was much less influential than the first. Among contemporary philosophers Leibniz's reputation stands remarkably high. This fact does not mean that speculative or revisionist metaphysics has returned to philosophical fashion; nonetheless, even descriptive metaphysicians admire Leibniz's penetrating contributions to the discussion of such issues as identity, individuation, and modality. Leibniz is also admired today for his insistence that philosophy should be responsive to, and even continuous with, the best science of the time. A less openly acknowledged reason perhaps is that the idea of the universe as lying open to reason continues to fascinate philosophers. Leibniz's philosophy, like Spinoza's, represents one of the most ambitious attempts ever made to articulate this idea.

FURTHER READING

W.H. Barber (1955) *Leibniz in France from Arnauld to Voltaire: A Study in French Reactions to Leibnizianism 1670–1760*. (An informative scholarly study.)

L.W. Beck (1969) *Early German Philosophy: Kant and his Predecessors*. (A scholarly survey by a leading Kant specialist.)

G. Tonelli (1974) 'Leibniz on Innate Ideas and the Early Reactions to the Publication of the *Nouveaux Essais* (1765)'. (A detailed scholarly study.)

C. Wilson (1995) 'The Reception of Leibniz in the Eighteenth Century,' Jolley (ed.), *The Cambridge Companion to Leibniz*. (A valuable scholarly survey which focuses on German reactions to Leibniz's philosophy.)

absolutism in political theory the thesis that the authority of the state should be unlimited (by, for example, a constitution or bill of rights).

analytic truth a proposition whose truth is guaranteed by the meaning of the terms and the laws of logic (for example, 'All bachelors are unmarried'); contrasted with 'synthetic truth'. The terms 'analytic truth' and 'synthetic truth' were introduced into philosophy by Kant.

antinomies in Kant's philosophy pairs of contradictory propositions in metaphysics: for each member of the pair there are equally compelling proofs. Invoked by Kant to expose the limits of pure reason and the illusions of speculative metaphysics.

apperception mental state involving self-consciousness, or at least consciousness. The term was introduced into philosophy by Leibniz.

appetition the endeavour or striving in a monad by virtue of which it passes from one perceptual state to its successor.

a priori capable of being known independently of experience (literally, 'from the former'); contrasted with 'a posteriori'. The terms were first used in this sense in philosophy by Kant.

Cartesianism philosophical sect whose members were disciples of René Descartes (1596–1650). Although Cartesians departed from Descartes's teachings on some issues, they generally accepted his thesis that mind and body are really distinct substances.

compatibilism   the doctrine that determinism is consistent or compatible with free will and moral responsibility.

compossible   logically capable of coexisting; belonging to the same possible world.

conatus   endeavour or striving.

contingent truths   truths whose opposite does not imply a contradiction (for example, 'Julius Caesar crossed the Rubicon').

cosmological argument   proof of the existence of God which seeks to infer his existence as first or ultimate cause of the series of events in the world.

determinism   the theory that every event (including human actions and choices) is caused by prior events in accordance with laws.

eclecticism   an approach to philosophy which seeks to combine and even synthesize the views of different philosophical schools.

ecumenism   in religion the commitment to finding common ground and even reunion with other churches and sects.

empiricism   the theory that all knowledge is grounded in experience. Concept-empiricism holds that all ideas or concepts are derived from experience: there are no innate ideas. Knowledge-empiricism holds that all legitimate claims to knowledge are to be justified by an appeal to experience.

ens rationis   literally, 'being of reason'; a construction of the human mind.

expression   according to Leibniz, 'one thing *expresses* another (in my language) when there is a constant and ordered relation between what can be asserted of the one and what can be asserted of the other' (P 71). The idea seems to be that if A expresses B, then one can in principle read off the properties of B from the properties of A alone.

extension   in logic, the class of entities to which a term, such as 'human being', applies.

extrinsic denomination a relational property of an individual (for example, that of being a father) as opposed to an intrinsic property.

fallacy of composition the fallacy of inferring from what is true of the parts to what is true of the whole, or from what is true of the members of a series to what is true of the series itself.

fideism the thesis that religious beliefs cannot be rationally justified and must be accepted on faith alone.

final causes causes which appeal to a goal or purpose. (The term 'final' here does not mean 'last' or 'ultimate'.) See also **teleological explanation**.

hypothetical necessity necessary on the assumption or hypothesis of something else. (For example, if John is a bachelor, then it is hypothetically necessary that he is unmarried.) Contrasted with 'absolute necessity'.

idealism any theory which holds that reality is ultimately mental or spiritual in nature, or at least non-material.

Identity of Indiscernibles the thesis that if A and B share all their properties, then A is identical with B.

individuation that which numerically distinguishes two individuals of the same kind.

influx in Scholastic philosophy a causal process whereby a property passes over or flows from the cause to the effect.

intension in logic the sense of a term or the concept which it expresses; contrasted with 'extension'.

Jansenism theological movement whose members were disciples of Cornelius Jansen (1585–1638). Jansenism was an austere form of Roman Catholic theology whose teachings on grace and

original sin were heavily influenced by Augustine and seemed to
its opponents to be virtually indistinguishable from Protestant
doctrines.

law of continuity   the thesis that nature makes no leaps:
employed by Leibniz in a variety of contexts, both technical and
non-technical.

legal positivism   in legal philosophy the theory that the criterion
of the validity of a law is wholly formal or procedural and has
nothing to do with its justice.

Leibniz's law   in logic, if A is identical with B, then A and B share
all their properties; converse of the Identity of Indiscernibles.

liberty of indifference   the power to act without being causally
determined by prior motives.

Lutheranism   Protestant religious sect whose members were
disciples of the theologian Martin Luther (1483–1546).

materialism   the thesis that reality is ultimately material or
physical in nature.

monad   a simple, immaterial, soul-like substance endowed with
perception and appetition. The term derives from the Greek
word for 'unity'.

monism   either the thesis that there is only one thing in the
universe or the thesis that there is just one kind of thing in the
universe.

nativism   the doctrine that the human mind contains innate ideas
and knowledge.

necessitarianism   the thesis, associated with Spinoza, that every
truth is a necessary truth.

Neoplatonism   philosophical school or movement, originating
in the post-classical world, which is inspired by the teachings of
Plato and seeks to extend them in a more dogmatic and mystical
direction. Founded by Plotinus (205–70), the movement

was revived in the Renaissance by such figures as Pico Della Mirandola (1463–94) and Marsiglio Ficino (1433–99).

occasionalism   the doctrine that God alone is a true cause and that particular events, such as the collision of two billiard balls, are simply the occasions on which God's causal power is exercised.

ontological argument   proof of the existence of God which seeks to show that his existence is logically implied by his essence as the most perfect being. The first version of this proof was advanced by St Anselm (1033–1109).

optimism   in philosophy the thesis that the actual world is the best of all possible worlds.

pantheism   the doctrine that God is identical with Nature.

phenomenalism   the theory that bodies or physical objects are simply the contents of perceptions and have no existence outside human minds. In the twentieth century, phenomenalism has chiefly been a theory about the meaning of propositions about bodies or physical objects.

predicate   that which is ascribed to the subject of a proposition.

pre-established harmony   the doctrine that all created substances have been programmed with all their states by God in such a way that they appear to interact.

prime matter   in Aristotle's philosophy matter considered in abstraction from form. The concept is reinterpreted in Leibniz's theory of monads.

providentialism   in political theory, the doctrine that governments have a right to be obeyed because they are established by divine Providence.

psychological egoism   the doctrine that human beings always necessarily desire their own good.

rationalism   the theory that the human mind is capable of knowing substantive truths about the world by reason or independently of experience.

reductionism   any philosophical theory which seeks to collapse a commonly accepted dichotomy (for example, between the mental and the material) and thereby reduce the number of entities in the world.

Scholasticism   medieval philosophical movement, originating in the universities or 'Schools', inspired by the teachings of Aristotle and characteristically seeking to integrate them with the doctrines of the Catholic Church. The leading Scholastic philosopher was St Thomas Aquinas (1225–74).

Socinianism   Protestant religious sect, founded by Faustus Socinus (Fausto Sozzini) (1539–1604), which denies the doctrines of the Trinity and the divinity of Jesus Christ; the precursor of modern Unitarianism.

stipulative definition   a definition which announces that a term will be used in a certain way; contrasted with a lexical definition which reports how a term is actually used.

subjunctive conditional   conditional proposition whose antecedent (the proposition in the 'if-clause') is, typically at least, contrary to fact (for example, 'If this glass were dropped on the kitchen floor, it would break').

substantial form   in medieval philosophy that by virtue of which an individual belongs to a certain natural kind and is a genuine unity. The substantial form is the source of all changes in a thing which arise from its nature.

supervenience   a relation of dependence of one property on another property, called the base, which is both non-causal and non-logical. (For example, the goodness of an apple may be said to supervene on its ripeness.)

teleological explanation   explanation in terms of goals or causes. See also **final causes**.

theism   the doctrine that there exists a personal God who is creator of the universe.

theodicy   the project of defending the justice of God against objections drawn from the presence of evils in the world such as sin and suffering. The term was introduced into philosophy by Leibniz.

Thomism   philosophical sect whose members were disciples of the Scholastic philosopher and theologian St Thomas Aquinas (1225–74).

transcendental idealism   in Kant's philosophy the doctrine that we know only appearances, which depend on the constitution of the human mind, and not things as they are in themselves.

transubstantiation   in theology, the Roman Catholic dogma that in the Mass the substance of the consecrated bread and wine is miraculously converted into the substance of the body and blood of Christ, while leaving the accidents or appearances intact.

tropes   instances of properties which are unique to individuals. (For example, while redness is a property common to many fire engines, the trope or redness-instance is peculiar to a particular fire engine.) Sometimes called 'individual accidents'.

utilitarianism   in ethics, the doctrine that the right action is the one which produces the greatest overall pleasure or happiness.

verificationism   the thesis, associated with the Logical Positivists, that the meaning of a statement is its method of verification. Verificationism holds that metaphysical statements are strictly meaningless since they cannot in principle be verified.

Notes

INTRODUCTION

1 For a valuable account of Aristotle's conception of metaphysics, see Barnes 1995: 66–108.
2 See also Mercer 2000. This magisterial study emphasizes the Neoplatonic influences on Leibniz's early philosophy. Cf. also Craig 1987 for a suggestive discussion of the role played in early modern philosophy by the thesis that the human mind is made in the image of God.
3 For an influential version of this accusation see Russell 1937.
4 For some discussion of the meaning of the term 'system' in Leibniz, see Ross 1984: 73.

ONE LEIBNIZ: LIFE AND WORKS

1 I am indebted to Ian Hacking for this phrase.
2 For an illuminating discussion of Arnauld's polemic, see Moreau 2000: 87–111. Moreau convincingly explains why Arnauld felt that he needed to preface an attack on Malebranche's doctrine of grace by a critique of his theory of ideas.
3 The Jansenists, named after the Dutch theologian Cornelius Jansen (1585–1638), were an austere religious order within the Roman Catholic Church who adopted strictly Augustinian views on grace and predestination. They incurred the disfavour of the Catholic authorities because their views on these issues seemed too close to those of the Protestants.

TWO THE METAPHYSICS OF SUBSTANCES: UNITY AND ACTIVITY

1 For a helpful survey of the principal arguments for occasionalism, see Nadler 2000: 112–38.
2 I have developed this approach at greater length in Jolley 1998.

3 According to Sleigh, Leibniz also toys with an early version of the doctrine of monads in the writings of his middle period. See Sleigh 1990: 110–11.

THREE THE THEORY OF MONADS

1 The issue of the status of organisms in Leibniz's theory of monads is controversial. See 'Corporeal substance and the *vinculum substantiale*' below.
2 For a discussion with a somewhat different emphasis see Hartz and Cover 1988: 493–519. Hartz and Cover deny that space and time are phenomenal for the mature Leibniz. However, it seems accurate to say that space and time are phenomenal in the minimal sense that they apply only to appearances and not to monads.

FOUR MIND, KNOWLEDGE, AND IDEAS

1 Leibniz to Bierling, undated draft of the letter of 24 October 1709 (G VII 485), manuscript; quoted in Jolley 1984: 164.
2 A classic illustration of the invalidity of arguments which invoke Leibniz's Law in such contexts is the following: (1) Adolf Hitler is well known as a mass murderer. (2) Adolf Schicklgruber is not well known as a mass murderer. Therefore (3) Adolf Hitler is not identical with Adolf Schicklgruber.
3 There is some controversy as to whether by 'apperception' Leibniz means self-consciousness or simply consciousness. For a discussion of the issues and the relevant texts, see McRae 1976: 30–5 and Kulstad 1991.
4 For a suggestive modern exploration of the same issues see, for instance, Williams 1973: 46–63.
5 I owe this graphic formulation of the problem to Jonathan Bennett.

FIVE HUMAN AND DIVINE FREEDOM

1 The theme is explored in an interesting way in Davidson 1998: 387–412.
2 The other labyrinth is the so-called 'labyrinth of the continuum'. This is the problem of how a space can consist of points which do not fill space. For a helpful discussion of the issues see Rescher 1967: 105–13.
3 There is some controversy as to whether Spinoza is a strict necessitarian. If Spinoza is not a necessitarian, then there is an ironic contrast between Spinoza and Leibniz. Spinoza may have sought to be a necessitarian, but is forced to recognize the fact of contingency; Leibniz seeks to find room for contingency in his philosophy, but is pulled towards strict necessitarianism.
4 Mates argues that the distinction between absolute and hypothetical necessity is based on a fallacy; see Mates 1986: 117–21.

5   See Mates 1986: Chapter 6. For criticism of an earlier expression of this view see Fried 1981: 77–88.

6   For an illuminating discussion of the 'possible in its own nature' defence and of Leibniz's doctrine of contingency in general, see Adams 1982.

7   Leibniz often says that motives 'incline without necessitating' (see, for example, NE II.xxi.8; RB 175). Surprisingly perhaps, the phrase is borrowed from the astrological dictum that the stars incline without necessitating (*Astra inclinant, non necessitant*). However, despite appearances this claim is not intended to exclude the strict causal determination of human choices in accordance with laws of psychology; it is intended only to exclude the thesis that such choices are logically or metaphysically necessitated by motives. Cf. Editors' Introduction, RB, xxiii.

8   Leibniz's denial in this paper that the mind always chooses what seems best is non-standard. For a discussion of his more usual position, see Chapter 7 below.

SIX   THE PROBLEM OF EVIL

1   The sentences 'Then is he impotent' and 'Then is he malevolent' are statements, not questions.

2   For a helpful study of Malebranche's contribution to theodicy, see Rutherford 2000: 165–89. See also Nadler 1994: 573–89.

3   For positions in varying degrees opposed to the one defended here, see Blumenfeld 1995: 382–410; G. Brown 1998: 571–91; Rutherford 1995a: Chs. 1–3.

4   Broad (1975: 159) points out an ambiguity in the doctrine of the negativity of evil. 'The doctrine of the negativity of evil might mean that the characteristic "evilness" is purely negative, like blindness, i.e. that it is just non-goodness. Or it might mean that, whilst "evilness" is a positive characteristic, it attaches to things only in virtue of what they lack and not in virtue of anything positive in them.'

SEVEN   ETHICS AND POLITICS

1   Although this is Leibniz's usual position, there are some anomalous passages which point in the other direction. See the passage cited in Ch. 5 above.

2   Hostler's fine study draws on many of the most important texts for an understanding of Leibniz's ethics.

3   For a helpful discussion of Leibniz's definition of pleasure, see Rutherford 1995a: 49–52.

4   The possibility of disinterested love was debated in France by François Fénelon

and Jacques-Bénigne Bossuet and in England by William Sherlock and John Norris. See Hostler 1975: 50–1.

5 The astonishing variety of seventeenth-century political thought, at least in England, is well illustrated in the anthology edited by David Wootton (1986).

6 For this line of objection, see the classic article by Bambrough 1956: 98–115.

7 As a young man Leibniz wrote an admiring letter to Hobbes in which he said that he had 'profited from [Hobbes's writings] as much as from few others in our century' (L 105); however, Hobbes did not respond.

8 For a more detailed discussion of the contrast between legal positivism and Thomistic natural law theory, see Hampton 1986: 107–10.

9 Strictly speaking, for Hobbes, the sovereign need not be a single person; it can also be an assembly.

EIGHT LEGACY AND INFLUENCE

1 Wilson also points out that, unlike Descartes, Leibniz did not found a philosophical sect.

2 For an account of the persistence of Platonism in England, especially in a form influenced by Malebranche, see McCracken 1983: 156–204.

3 That this is a different criticism from the previous one is shown by the fact that Leibniz would not concede that talk of force in monads is merely metaphorical.

4 Although the 'logicist' thesis is often attributed to both Russell and Couturat, the claim that Leibniz derived his metaphysics from his logic is due more to Couturat than to Russell. See Couturat 1972: 19–46.

5 See Strawson 1959: 9–12 for a classic statement of the distinction between descriptive and revisionist or speculative metaphysics.

Bibliography

Note: Works cited in the Abbreviations list are not included

Adams, R.M. (1972) 'Must God Create the Best?', Philosophical Review 81, 317–32.
—— (1982) 'Leibniz's Theories of Contingency,' M. Hooker (ed.), Leibniz: Critical and Interpretive Essays, Minneapolis: University of Minnesota Press, 243–83.
—— (1994) Leibniz: Determinist, Theist, Idealist, New York and Oxford: Oxford University Press.
Aiton, E. (1985) Leibniz: A Biography, Bristol: Adam Hilger.
Ariew, R. (1995) 'Leibniz, Life and Times', N. Jolley (ed.), The Cambridge Companion to Leibniz, Cambridge: Cambridge University Press, 18–42.
Aristotle (1984) Categories, in The Complete Works of Aristotle: The Revised Oxford Translation, J. Barnes (ed.), Princeton: Princeton University Press.
—— (1984) Metaphysics, in The Complete Works of Aristotle: The Revised Oxford Translation, J. Barnes (ed.), Princeton: Princeton University Press.
Aubrey, J. (1972) Brief Lives, O.L. Dick (ed.), Penguin: Harmondsworth.
Ayers, M.R. (1978) 'Analytical Philosophy and the History of Philosophy,' J. Ree, M.R. Ayers, and A. Westoby (eds.), Philosophy and its Past, Brighton: Harvester.
Bambrough, R. (1956) 'Plato's Political Analogies,' P. Laslett (ed.), Philosophy, Politics, and Society, First Series, Oxford: Blackwell, 98–115.
Barber, W.H. (1955) Leibniz in France From Arnauld to Voltaire: A Study in French Reactions to Leibnizianism 1670–1760, Oxford: Oxford University Press.
Barnes, J. (1995) 'Metaphysics,' J. Barnes (ed.), The Cambridge Companion to Aristotle, Cambridge: Cambridge University Press, 66–108.
Beck, L.W. (1969) Early German Philosophy: Kant and his Predecessors, Cambridge, Mass.: Harvard University Press.
Bennett, J. (1984), A Study of Spinoza's Ethics, Indianapolis: Hackett.
Berlin, I. (1953) The Hedgehog and the Fox, New York: Simon and Schuster.
Blumenfeld, D. (1982) 'Superessentialism, Counterparts, and Freedom,' M. Hooker

(ed.), Leibniz: Critical and Interpretive Essays, Minneapolis: University of Minnesota Press, 103–23.

—— (1995) 'Perfection and Happiness in the Best Possible World,' N. Jolley (ed.), The Cambridge Companion to Leibniz, Cambridge: Cambridge University Press, 382–410.

Broad, C.D. (1975) Leibniz: An Introduction, Cambridge: Cambridge University Press.

—— (1981) 'Leibniz's Last Controversy with the Newtonians,' R.S. Woolhouse (ed.), Leibniz: Metaphysics and Philosophy of Science, Oxford: Oxford University Press, 157–74.

Brown, G. (1988) 'Leibniz's Theodicy and the Confluence of Worldly Goods,' Journal of the History of Philosophy 26, 571–91.

—— (1995) 'Leibniz's Moral Philosophy,' N. Jolley (ed.), The Cambridge Companion to Leibniz, Cambridge: Cambridge University Press, 411–41.

Brown, S. (1984) Leibniz, Brighton: Harvester.

—— (1999) 'The Proto-Monadology of the De Summa Rerum,' S. Brown (ed.), The Young Leibniz and His Philosophy (1646–76), Dordrecht: Kluwer, 263–87.

Condillac, E. Bonnot de (1991) Traité des Systèmes, Paris: Fayard.

—— (2001) Essay on the Origin of Knowledge, H. Aarsleff (trans. and ed.), Cambridge: Cambridge University Press.

Cottingham, J. (1988) The Rationalists, Oxford: Oxford University Press.

Couturat, L. (1901) La logique de Leibniz, Paris: Alcan.

—— (1972) 'On Leibniz's Metaphysics,' H.G. Frankfurt (ed.), Leibniz: A Collection of Critical Essays, New York: Doubleday, 19–45.

Craig, E. (1987) The Mind of God and the Works of Man, Oxford: Clarendon Press.

Davidson, J. (1998) 'Imitators of God: Leibniz on Human Freedom,' Journal of the History of Philosophy 36, 387–412.

Frankfurt, H. (ed.) (1972) Leibniz: A Collection of Critical Essays, New York: Doubleday.

Fried, D. (1981) 'Necessity and Contingency in Leibniz,' R.S. Woolhouse (ed.), Leibniz: Metaphysics and Philosophy of Science, Oxford: Oxford University Press, 55–63.

Friedmann, G. (1946) Leibniz et Spinoza, Paris: Gallimard.

Furth, M. (1972) 'Monadology,' H.G. Frankfurt (ed.), Leibniz: A Collection of Critical Essays, New York: Doubleday, 99–135.

Garber, D. (1985) 'Leibniz and the Foundations of Physics: The Middle Years,' K. Okruhlik and J.R. Brown (eds), The Natural Philosophy of Leibniz, Dordrecht: Reidel, 27–130.

Hacking, I. (1982) 'A Leibnizian Theory of Truth,' M. Hooker (ed.), Leibniz: Critical and Interpretive Essays, Minneapolis: University of Minnesota Press, 185–95.

Hall, A.R. (1980) *Philosophers at War: The Quarrel Between Leibniz and Newton*, Cambridge: Cambridge University Press.

Hampton, J. (1986) *Hobbes and the Social Contract Tradition*, Cambridge: Cambridge University Press.

Hartz, G. (1998) 'Why Corporeal Substances Keep Popping Up in Leibniz's Later Philosophy,' *British Journal of the History of Philosophy* 6, 193–207.

Hartz, G., and Cover, J. (1988) 'Space and Time in the Leibnizian Metaphysic,' *Nous* 22, 493–519.

Hobbes, T. (1994) *Leviathan*, E.M. Curley (ed.), Indianapolis: Hackett.

Hostler, J. (1975) *Leibniz's Moral Philosophy*, London: Duckworth.

Hume, D. (1980) *Dialogues Concerning Natural Religion*, R.H. Popkin (ed.), Indianapolis: Hackett.

Jolley, N. (1984) *Leibniz and Locke: A Study of the New* Essays on Human Understanding, Oxford: Clarendon Press.

—— (1986) 'Leibniz and Phenomenalism,' *Studia Leibnitiana* 18, 38–51.

—— (1990) *The Light of the Soul: Theories of Ideas in Leibniz, Malebranche, and Descartes*, Oxford: Clarendon Press.

—— (1998) 'Causality and Creation in Leibniz,' *The Monist* 81, 591–611.

—— (ed.), (1995) *The Cambridge Companion to Leibniz*, Cambridge: Cambridge University Press.

Kant, I. (1929) *Critique of Pure Reason*, N. Kemp Smith (trans.), London: Macmillan.

Kulstad, M. (1991) *Leibniz on Apperception, Consciousness, and Reflection*, Munich: Philosophia Verlag.

Leibniz, G.W. (1903) *Opuscules et fragments inédits de Leibniz*, L. Couturat (ed.), Paris: Alcan.

—— (1953) *Discourse on Metaphysics*, trans. P.G. Lucas and L. Grint, Manchester: Manchester University Press.

—— (1956) *The Leibniz–Clarke Correspondence*, H.G. Alexander (ed.), Manchester: Manchester University Press.

—— (1966) *G.W. Leibniz: Logical Papers: A Selection*, trans. G.H.R. Parkinson, Oxford: Clarendon Press.

—— (1967) *The Leibniz–Arnauld Correspondence*, trans. H.T. Mason with an Introduction by G.H.R. Parkinson, Manchester: Manchester University Press.

—— (1988) *G.W. Leibniz: Discourse on Metaphysics and Related Writings*, R.N.D. Martin and S. Brown (trans. and eds), Manchester: Manchester University Press.

—— (1991) *G.W. Leibniz's Monadology: An Edition for Students*, N. Rescher (ed.), Pittsburgh: University of Pittsburgh Press.

—— (1997) *Leibniz's 'New System' and Associated Texts*, R.S. Woolhouse and R. Francks (trans. and eds), Oxford: Oxford University Press.

Locke, J. (1975) *An Essay Concerning Human Understanding*, P.H. Nidditch (ed.), Oxford: Clarendon Press.
—— (1981) *Correspondence of John Locke*, Vol. 6, E.S. De Beer (ed.), Oxford: Clarendon Press.
Lodge, P., and Bobro, M. (1998) 'Stepping Back Inside Leibniz's Mill,' *The Monist* 81, 553–72.
Loeb, L. (1981) 'Leibniz's Denial of Causal Interaction Between Monads,' in Loeb, *From Descartes to Hume: Continental Metaphysics and the Development of Modern Philosophy*, Ithaca, New York: Cornell University Press.
Malebranche, N. (1992) *Treatise on Nature and Grace*, P. Riley (trans.), Oxford: Oxford University Press.
Mates, B. (1986) *The Philosophy of Leibniz: Metaphysics and Language*, New York and Oxford: Oxford University Press.
McCracken, C.J. (1983) *Malebranche and British Philosophy*, Oxford: Clarendon Press.
McRae, R. (1976) *Leibniz: Perception, Apperception, and Thought*, Toronto: University of Toronto Press.
Mercer, C. (2000) *Leibniz's Metaphysics: Its Origins and Development*, New York and Cambridge: Cambridge University Press.
Moreau, D. (2000) 'The Malebranche–Arnauld Debate,' S. Nadler (ed.), *The Cambridge Companion to Malebranche*, Cambridge: Cambridge University Press, 87–111.
Müller, K., and Krönert, G. (1969) *Leben und Werk von G.W. Leibniz: eine Chronik*, Frankfurt am Main: Klostermann.
Murray, M. (1995) 'Leibniz on Divine Foreknowledge of Future Contingents,' *Philosophy and Phenomenological Research* 55, 75–108.
Nadler, S. (1994) 'Choosing a Theodicy: The Leibniz–Malebranche–Arnauld Connection,' *Journal of the History of Ideas* 55, 573–89.
—— (2000) 'Malebranche on Causation,' S. Nadler (ed.), *The Cambridge Companion to Malebranche*, Cambridge: Cambridge University Press, 112–38.
Okruhlik, K., and Brown, J.R. (eds), (1985) *The Natural Philosophy of Leibniz*, Dordrecht: Reidel.
Parkinson, G.H.R. (1965) *Logic and Reality in Leibniz's Metaphysics*, Oxford: Clarendon Press.
—— (1970) *Leibniz on Human Freedom*, Studia Leibnitiana Sonderheft 2, Wiesbaden: Franz Steiner.
Plato (1941) *Republic*, F.M. Cornford (trans.), Oxford: Clarendon Press.
Rescher, N. (1967) *The Philosophy of Leibniz*, Englewood Cliffs, NJ: Prentice Hall.
—— (1981) *Leibniz's Metaphysics of Nature*, Dordrecht: Reidel.
Riley, P. (1996) *Leibniz's Universal Jurisprudence: Justice as the Charity of the Wise*, Cambridge, Mass.: Harvard University Press.

Ross, G. MacDonald (1984) *Leibniz*, Oxford: Oxford University Press.

Russell, B. (1937) *A Critical Exposition of the Philosophy of Leibniz*, 2nd edn, London: Allen and Unwin.

Rutherford, D. (1995a) *Leibniz and the Rational Order of Nature*, Cambridge: Cambridge University Press.

—— (1995b) 'Metaphysics: The Late Period,' N. Jolley (ed.), *The Cambridge Companion to Leibniz*, Cambridge: Cambridge University Press, 124–75.

—— (2000) 'Malebranche's Theodicy,' S. Nadler (ed.), *The Cambridge Companion to Malebranche*, Cambridge: Cambridge University Press, 165–89.

Simmons, A. (2001) 'Changing the Cartesian Mind: Leibniz on Sensation, Representation and Consciousness,' *Philosophical Review* 110, 31–75.

Sleigh, R.C., Jr (1990) *Leibniz and Arnauld: A Commentary on their Correspondence*, New Haven and London: Yale University Press.

Spinoza, B. (1982) *The Ethics and Selected Letters*, S. Shirley (trans.), S. Feldman (ed.), Indianapolis: Hackett.

Strawson, P.F. (1959) *Individuals*, London: Methuen.

Tonelli, G. (1974) 'Leibniz on Innate Ideas and the Early Reactions to the Publication of the *Nouveaux Essais* (1765),' *Journal of the History of Philosophy* 12, 437–54.

Vailati, E. (1990) 'Leibniz on Locke on Weakness of the Will,' *Journal of the History of Philosophy* 28, 213–28.

—— (1997) *Leibniz and Clarke: A Study of Their Correspondence*, New York and Oxford: Oxford University Press.

Voltaire (François-Marie Arouet) (1947) *Candide, or Optimism*, J. Butt (trans.), Harmondsworth: Penguin.

Williams, B. (1973) 'The Self and the Future,' in Williams, *Problems of the Self*, Cambridge: Cambridge University Press, 46–63.

Wilson, C. (1983) 'Leibnizian Optimism,' *Journal of Philosophy* 80, 765–83.

—— (1989) *Leibniz's Metaphysics: A Historical and Comparative Study*, Princeton: Princeton University Press.

—— (1995) 'The Reception of Leibniz in the Eighteenth Century,' N. Jolley (ed.), *The Cambridge Companion to Leibniz*, Cambridge: Cambridge University Press, 442–74.

—— (1999) 'The Illusory Nature of Leibniz's System,' R.J. Gennaro and C. Huenemann (eds), *New Essays on the Rationalists*, New York and Oxford: Oxford University Press, 372–88.

Wilson, M. (1999) *Ideas and Mechanism: Essays on Early Modern Philosophy*, Princeton: Princeton University Press.

Woolhouse, R.S. (ed.) (1981) *Leibniz: Metaphysics and Philosophy of Science*, Oxford: Oxford University Press.

—— (1988) 'Leibniz and Occasionalism,' R.S. Woolhouse (ed.), *Metaphysics and Philosophy of Science in the Seventeenth and Eighteenth Centuries: Essays in Honour of Gerd Buchdahl*, Dordrecht: Kluwer, 165–83.

—— (1994) *G.W. Leibniz: Critical Assessments*, 4 vols, London: Routledge.

Wootton, D. (ed.) (1986) *Divine Right and Democracy*, Harmondsworth: Penguin.

Index